Urdu Ghazals
An Anthology
From 16th to 20th Centu

This book is a companion volume to K.C. Kanda's earlier book, *Masterpieces of Urdu Ghazal* which contained English translations of 108 *ghazals* selected from nine major poets: Wali, Dard, Mir, Ghalib, Momin, Hasrat, Iqbal, Firaq and Faiz. The present volume contains 129 *ghazals*, representing 20 outstanding urdu poets: Mohd. Quli Qutab Shah, Siraj, Sauda, Zafar, Insha, Aatish, Zauq, Ameer Meenai, Dagh, Hali, Akbar, Shad Azimabadi, Fani, Chakbast, Asghar, Jigar, Josh, Sahir Ludhianvi, Nasir Kaazmi, and Bani. Thus this anthology, taken together with *The Masterpieces*, may rightly claim to be a fully representative collection of Urdu *ghazals* in English translation.

The *ghazals* included in this volume are carefully selected, keeping in view their intrinsic, artistic quality, the universality of their content, and their accessibility for the average reader. Each *ghazal* is first presented in Urdu calligraphics; this is followed, on the opposite page, by its English translation which, in turn, is followed by the Romanized version of the Urdu text. Further, the selection of each poet is preceded by a brief biographical-cum-critical note, and an authentic portrait of the poet. Another important feature of the book is the introductory essay on Urdu *ghazal*, which discusses in detail the origin, development, and peculiar characteristics of this art form.

K.C. Kanda has taught English literature to under-graduate and post-graduate students for over 30 years in Delhi University. He holds a Doctorate in English from the University of Delhi, and M.A. degrees from Panjab and Nottingham University (U.K.). He is also a first class M.A. in Urdu from Delhi University. While English poetry has been his speciality professionally, Urdu poetry has been his love since his school days. His publications include: An Anthology of English Poetry *(Arnold Heinemann, 1976);* The Two Worlds of Tennyson *(Doaba House, 1985);* Masterpieces of Urdu Ghazal *(Sterling Publishers, 1990);* Masterpieces of Urdu Rubaiyat *(Sterling Publishers, 1994). The earlier volume,* Masterpieces of Urdu Ghazal, *is now counted among the bestsellers. Dr. Kanda is currently working on the* Master Poems of Urdu, *which would contain English translations of famous Urau nazms in verse form.*

Excerpts from the reviews

Masterpieces of Urdu Ghazal

"It is a miracle that despite the strait-jacket in which it was enclothed, the ghazal not only survived but flourished through the centuries.... I recommend this anthology to lovers of Urdu poetry."

—*Khushwant Singh, Sunday*

"All in all, it is a book for the shelves of both who know and love Urdu and would like to be conversant with its best form of poetry."

—*The Pioneer*

"Mr. Kanda in his well-researched volume has painstakingly brought out the best of Urdu Ghazal, and this concise volume could well be considered a boon for research scholars in Urdu poetry."

—*The Hindu*

Urdu Ghazals: An Anthology

"Mr. K.C. Kanda has painstakingly included in the Anthology an excellent selection of Urdu ghazals, not only in Urdu (Persian) script, the English translation of a high quality, but, more importantly, the transcription in Roman as well. The volume would rank high among other works of a similar nature."

—*The Hindu*

Masterpieces of Urdu Rubaiyat

This book contains English translations of 269 rubaies, chosen from the works of 25 famous poets, chronologically arranged. It covers a wide spectrum of Urdu poetry, from Mir and Sauda in the 18th century to Josh and Firaq in the 20th century.

—*Globe*

Masterpieces of Urdu Nazm

This book is intended to introduce the reader to the best specimens of the Urdu *nazm*, as distinguished from the *ghazal*. It contains English translations of 42 *nazms*, chosen from the works of 19 famous poets, such as Mir Taqi Mir, Nazir Akbarabadi, Shauq Lucknavi, Iqbal, Josh, Hafeez, Akhtar Sheerani, Majaaz, Faiz, and Sahir. The poets are presented in chronological order, and each is introduced with an authentic portrait, and a brief biographical-cum-critical note. The "Introduction" attempts in lucid prose a definition of the *nazm*, and describes its characteristic features as an art form.

Published by
Sterling Publishers Private Limited

URDU GHAZALS

An Anthology

From 16th to 20th Century

K.C. KANDA

A Sterling Paperback

STERLING PAPERBACKS
An imprint of
Sterling Publishers (P) Ltd.
A-59 Okhla Industrial Area, Phase-II,
New Delhi-110020.
Tel: 6386165, 6386209, 6387070, Fax: 6383788
E-mail: ghai@nde.vsnl.net.in
Website: www.sterlingpublishers.com

Urdu Ghazals: An Anthology (From 16th to 20th Century)

ISBN 81 207 1826 7
Reprint 1996, 1999
Reprint 2003

Published by **Sterling Publishers Pvt. Ltd., New Delhi-110016.**
Printed at Saras Graphics, Mayapuri, New Delhi.
Cover design by **Biplab**

To
My Grandsons

GAURAV & KUNAL
SAHIL & AABHAS

PREFACE

This book is a companion to my earlier volume, *Masterpieces of Urdu Ghazal,* which was published in 1990, and contained English translations of 108 selected *ghazals* from nine major poets: Wali, Dard, Mir, Ghalib, Momin, Hasrat, Iqbal, Firaq, and Faiz. *The Masterpieces* received some good, commendatory reviews in various journals and newspapers, and is now classed, according to the *Indian Review of Books* (March-April, 1993) among the top ten best-selling books of non-fiction. Some reviewers of the said volume had opined that my selection, rich and representative within its limits, had left out certain famous Urdu poets, whose contribution to the *ghazal* is by no means inconsiderable. In fact, I was myself aware of this deficiency, and had expressed the hope, in the Preface, that I would, in due course, produce the second volume, which would fill the gap and introduce the readers to another set of outstanding poets whose *ghazals* now form a valuable part of our literary heritage. Accordingly, I present in the following pages a collection of 129 *ghazals,* representing 20 poets, arranged in a chronological order: Mohammed Quli Qutab Shah, Siraj, Sauda, Zafar, Insha, Aatish, Zauq, Amir Meenai, Dagh, Hali, Akbar, Shad, Fani, Chakbast, Asghar Gondvi, Jigar, Josh, Sahir, Nasir Kaazmi and Bani.

Anyone interested in Urdu poetry would agree that these are the most well-known poets whose *ghazals* are much sought after at literary and cultural gatherings. It was the want of space, and not the want of deserts on the part of these poets, which compelled me to exclude them from *The Masterpieces.* Mohammed Quli Qutab Shah, the first poet of the series, has a unique historical importance, for he is the founding father of

Urdu poetry and has left behind him a voluminous collection of rich and varied verse. Insha, Aatish, Amir Meenai, Shad, and Chakbast are representatives of the Lucknow School, without whom the story of the Urdu *ghazal* would remain incomplete. Nasir Kaazmi and Bani represent the new trends in modern Urdu *ghazal*, which is eager to break with the traditional poetry of love and romance, and explore new recesses of the human mind. This anthology, taken together with its companion volume, may thus rightly claim to be a fully representative collection of Urdu *ghazals* in English translation. The present-day living Urdu poets are, however, outside the plan of this book.

The *ghazals* included in this volume are carefully selected, keeping in view their intrinsic artistic quality, the universality of their content, and their accessibility for an average reader. These poems are then rendered into simple, lucid, and rhythmical English, taking care to preserve their sense and spirit, and to reflect, as far as it is possible in translation, the cadence and metrical effect of the original. Feeling that an essential part of the appeal of the *ghazal* lies in the music of its rhymes, I have attempted rhymed verse in my translations. However, when a suitable rhyming word eluded my grasp, I have taken recourse to assonance instead of rhyme.

I am aware of the inadequacy of translation as a substitute for the original. The inadequacy becomes all the more pronounced when the language of translation is as far removed from the language of the original, as is English from Urdu. But I am assisted in my task by my innate love of Urdu poetry, and an intimate understanding of English poetic idiom, acquired over a long period of studying and teaching English as a student and university teacher. Moreover, I am prompted to undertake this task not by any external pressure, or by considerations of material gain, but by spontaneous impulse, and a desire to propagate the pleasures of Urdu poetry. There is no gainsaying the fact that poets are great benefactors of society. They give us intellectual and emotional delight, uphold us in times of distress and depression, humanise our feelings and enrich our mind. This translation is my humble return for the rich fund of joy which these poets have offered me at all hours of rain or sunshine.

The pattern followed in this book is similar to the one adopted in *The Masterpieces of Urdu Ghazal*. Each *ghazal* is first presented in Urdu calligraphics; this is followed, on the opposite page, by its English translation, which, in turn is followed by the Romanised version of the Urdu text. The Romanised version should enable even the non-Urdu knowing readers to have a feel and flavour of the Urdu language. Further, the selection of each poet is preceded by a brief biographical-cum-critical note which should help the reader in relating the poet to his milieu, and in understanding the features of his mind and art. The biographical note is also accompanied by an authentic picture of the poet.

Another important feature of the book is the introductory essay on the *ghazal*, which discusses in a clear, lucid manner, the origin, development, and characteristics of this art form, and explains, with suitable illustrations, the kind and quality of its salient themes, imagery and idiom. The introductory essay is, in fact, a revised version of the one prefixed to the *Masterpieces*. It is hoped that the book will succeed in kindling and satisfying the intellectual and aesthetic tastes of the lovers of poetry.

I am beholden to all my friends who provided me with necessary assistance and encouragement in the writing of this book. I am specially grateful to Professor J.S. Neki, my friend and counsellor, from whose valuable advice I have always benefited. I am also thankful to Professor Gopi Chand Narang, the renowned scholar and National Professor of Urdu, who gave me the initial stimulus to undertake this work, helped me in choosing the poets and getting useful background information about them. For my source material I have drawn entirely upon Delhi University Library (North Campus), and this would not have been possible without the help and cooperation of my valued friends in the library: Mr. M.L. Saini, Mr. N.A. Abbasi and Mr. R.C. Chibber, to all of whom I offer my sincere thanks. I am no less indebted to Mr. Ali Siddiqui, Founder and Organising Secretary of the Aalmi Urdu Conference, who, as before, furnished me with the portraits of some of the poets, which now adorn these pages. Affectionate thanks are also due to my son, Dr. Arun Kanda, who painstakingly scrutinised the manuscript and proofs, and pointed out many typographical errors. Finally, I am obliged to Shri S.K. Ghai, Managing Director, Sterling Publishers, who took sustained interest in the preparation of this book, and gave it its present beautiful shape.

CONTENTS

INTRODUCTION : URDU GHAZAL

In the introductory essay on the *Ghazal* pre-fixed to *The Masterpieces of Urdu Ghazal,* I have discussed in detail the salient features of this form, and examined its characteristic themes, imagery and technique. For the benefit of those who haven't had an occasion to read this essay, I reproduce below the main points of my argument, with suitable illustrations, chosen, generally, from the poets included in this volume.

The form of the *ghazal* originated in Iran in 10th century A.D. It grew from the Persian *qasida,* which verse form had come to Iran from Arabia. The *qasida* was a panegyric written in praise of the emperor or his noblemen. The part of the *qasida,* called *tashbib,* got detached and developed, in course of time, into the *ghazal.* Whereas the *qasida* sometime ran into as many as 100 couplets or more in monorhyme, the *ghazal* seldom exceeded twelve and settled down to an average of seven or nine couplets. Because of its comparative brevity and concentration and its lyrical potential, the *ghazal* soon eclipsed the *qasida* and became the most popular form of poetry in Iran. It was nurtured, among others, by Rodki, Saadi, Hafiz, Naziri, Iraqi, Maulana Romi and Urfi.

In its form, the *ghazal* is a short poem rarely of more than a dozen couplets in the same metre. It always opens with a rhyming couplet called *matla.* The rhyme of the opening couplet is repeated at the end of the second line in each succeeding verse, so that the rhyming pattern may be represented as AA, BA, CA, DA and so on. It is not just the rhyme at the end of the line, returning in every alternate line which produces the special musical effect of the ghazal. This effect derives itself from the combined action of what are technically called *qafia* and *radif.* *Qafia* is a rhyme-word which generally occurs towards the end of the line, but before the *radif* which marks the end of the line, and is repeated, often unchanged, throughout the *ghazal* in the second line of each couplet. In the following line of Ghalib: "Dil-e-nadaan tujhe hua kya hai", "hua" is the *qafia,* and "kya hai" is the *radif.* "Kya hai" occurs throughout the poem at the end of each line, whereas "hua" is replaced by different words on the same rhyme, such as "dawa", "muddaa", "majra", "ada", "hawa", "duaa", etc. Although there are *ghazals* which do not adhere to the system of *qafia* and *radif,* the overall proportion of such *ghazals* is small, and their popularity has never equalled that of the traditional *ghazal,* supporting *qafia* and *radif.*

To the readers of English poetry, accustomed to the natural flow of blank verse or free verse, the observance of *qafia* and *radif,* in addition to that of metre, may seem an unnecessary encumbrance, but not so to the Urdu poets and their readers who have learnt to enjoy the added pleasure of the extended rhyme. If *radif* and *qafia* tend to curb the flight of imagination, they also enforce artistic discipline and enhance the magic and musicality of verse. In fact, an audience used to the style and content of Urdu poetry, always gets a special delight by anticipating the rhyme word or phrase, and by chanting it along with the poet like a member of the chorus. The opening couplet of the *ghazal* is always a representative couplet; it sets the mood and tone of the poem and prepares us for its proper appreciation. The last couplet of the *ghazal,* called *maqta,* often includes the pen-name of the poet, and is more personal than general in its tone and intent. Here the poet may express his own state of mind, or describe his religious faith, or pray for his beloved, or indulge in poetic self-praise. The different couplets of the *ghazal* are not bound by the unity and consistency of thought. Each couplet is a self-sufficient unit, detachable and quotable, generally containing the complete expression of an idea. Those who look for the logical evolution of thought in a poem may be disappointed by the fragmentary thought-structure of the *ghazal.* In fact, some important critics have pointed out this flaw and pleaded for reform. Taking this advice, some poets, including Hasrat, Iqbal, Akbar and Josh have written *ghazals* in the style of a *nazm*, based on a single theme, properly developed and concluded. But such *ghazals* are an exception rather than a rule, and the traditional *ghazal* still holds the sway. However, we do come across, off and on, even in the works of classical poets, a set of verses connected in theme and thought. Such a thematic group is called a *qita*, and is presumably resorted to when the poet is confronted with an elaborate thought difficult to be condensed in a single couplet.

The *ghazal* came to India with the advent and extension of the Muslim influence from 12th century onwards. The Moghuls brought along with them Iranian culture and civilisation, including Iranian poetry and literature. When Persian gave way to Urdu as the language of poetry and culture in India, the *ghazal*, the fruit of Indo-Iranian culture, found its opportunity to grow and develop. Although the *ghazal* is said to have begun with Amir Khusro Dehlvi (1253-1325), Deccan in the South was its real home in the early stages. It was nursed and trained in the courts of Golconda and Bijapur under the patronage of Muslim rulers. Sultan Mohammed Quli Qutab Shah (1565-1611) whose *ghazals* mark the beginning of this anthology, was the founding father of the *ghazal*. He has left behind him a collection of 50,000 verses, including, not only *ghazals*, but also *marsias, masnavis, rubaies*, and *qitas*. Among the other poets of Deccan, Wajhi, Hashmi, Nusrati and Wali may be counted among the pioneers. It was Wali Deccany (1667-1707) who was instrumental in synthesizing the poetic streams of the South and the North. Wali's visit to Delhi made in 1700 was an event of historic significance. His poetry introduced the Persian-loving North to the beauty and richness of Urdu language, and acquainted them with the true flavour of the *ghazal*, thus encouraging its rapid growth and popularity. In course of time the *ghazal* attained wide acceptance and currency. It became the darling of the poets, the ornament of the courts, and a source of aesthetic and emotional delight for the whole lot of sensitive commonfolk.

Eighteenth and nineteenth centuries may be regarded as the golden period of the Urdu *ghazal*, for it was during this time that the *ghazal* developed and attained its high stature. The main centres of Urdu poetry where the *ghazal* was specially nursed and refined were Delhi and Lucknow. The illustrious *ghazal* writers, Mir, Sauda, Dard, Ghalib, Momin, Zauq and Zafar, all belong to the Delhi School, whereas Mushafi, Insha, Jurrat, Shad and Aatish are among the better known poets of the Lucknow School. Of the two, Delhi School is adjudged superior. The poetry of this school is remarkable for its imaginative insight, truth of observation, and appropriateness of style. The *ghazal* of the Lucknow School, comparatively speaking, is wanting in the depth and genuineness of feeling, which it tries to make up by surface elegance and alacrity of style.

In fact, the difference in the poetry produced by these two schools has much to do with the different social and cultural environments which nurtured the two varieties. Delhi of the times of Mir, Momin and Ghalib was a place of social and political unrest. The Moghul empire was speedily disintegrating. One after the other, Nadir Shah, Ahmed Shah, Marhattas and Jats carried on their savage raids on the lives and properties of the populace, and left behind them a trail of destruction and deprivation. Compelled by poverty and a feeling of insecurity, all kinds of people — traders, professionals, soldiers, artists and poets — were quitting Delhi in search of more peaceful pastures, which they found in Lucknow and its neighbourhood. For Lucknow was a haven of peace, and the nawabs and noblemen of the court had both the time and taste for the finer pleasures of poetry, music and dancing. Even Mir and Sauda, we may recall, went to Lucknow to try their luck, though their sensitive, self-respecting temperaments could not for long withstand the sycophantic air of the royal resorts. But for more pragmatic natures like Insha or Mushafi, it was a change from penury to luxury, from the chaos of Delhi to the pleasure palaces of Lucknow, albeit this change for a better material environment was not conducive to the Muse. The *ghazal* of the Lucknow School acquires a new sprightliness and sparkle, but it is a surface glitter, derived from cunning artistry and linguistic jugglery rather than from deeply felt emotion or thought. The poetry of the Delhi School, when handled by masters like Mir, Sauda, or Ghalib, rings true, and sounds the depths of the human heart. The poetry of the Lucknow School, on the other hand, is a thing of diversion and amusement, meant for public consumption and poetic competitions. This poetry tries to look tall by walking on tiptoe, by making a lavish display of wit, conceit and verbal skills, which are no substitutes for emotional intensity and sincerity. But this criticism does not apply, let me hasten to add, to all the poets of the Lucknow School, and surely not to the poets included in this volume, for Insha, Shad, Amir Meenai, Aatish and Chakbast are generally free from the faults of their lesser comperes, and their best *ghazals* — allowing for the individual difference of taste and temperament — are comparable to the best of the Delhi School. However, it should not be forgotten that the poets of the Lucknow School made a valuable contribution towards refining the Urdu language and making it a fit instrument of polite, cultured speech. Moreover, the Lucknow School deserves credit for preserving and continuing the tradition of the *ghazal* at a time when the literary life of Delhi stood paralysed due to political turbulence.

Although the *ghazal* deals with the whole spectrum of human experience, its central concern is love. *Ghazal* is an Arabic word which literally means talking to women. As the favourite topic of conversation with women is love, love, with its resultant complex of emotional and psychological situations, became the dominant theme of the *ghazal.* In the medieval Islamic society where purdah system prevailed and a rigid moral code denied to the young the freedom to mix and converse, love could only be indulged in secret, and expressed with indirection, in hushed tones, often with the aid of allusion and innuendo. This accounts for the peculiar suggestiveness and ambiguity of address adopted by the *ghazal* writers. This also explains the convention of using the equivocal pronoun *woh,* often in the masculine sense ("he" rather than "she"), even when the person addressed is clearly the poet's mistress. Furthermore, as love outside marriage was deemed immoral, inimical to the conventional code of conduct, the lover quite often became the target of public anger and hatred. And his beloved, likewise, fretting under the strain of social and parental taboo, could hardly be expected to alleviate his miseries or respond boldly to his overtures. Under these conditions love could hardly result in a happy ending. The sad, plaintive note insistently heard in the *ghazal* proceeds from frustrated desire that often forms its subject matter. Which reminds us of the other etymological meaning of the word *ghazal*: "the painful wail of a wounded deer", called *ghazaal* in Arabic. The lover is a "wounded deer", pierced by the arrows of love, and hounded by a hostile society. He is conventionally presented in the *ghazal* as a persecuted being, "haggard and woebegone", palely loitering, like Keats's "knight-at-arms", in the lonely wilds of love. His mistress, on the other hand, emerges as "La Belle Dame Sans Merci", a woman exceedingly beautiful and exceedingly cruel, shooting from behind her veil the arrows of her glances at the tender heart of her lover. The following verse of Mir contains the conventional image of a man in love:

یہ زرد زرد چہرہ، یہ لاغری بدن میں
کیا عشق میں ہوا ہے اے میرؔ حال تیرا

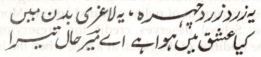

Your face so pale, your frame so lean,
O Mir, what love has made of you!

And here is how Ghalib describes the conventional heroine of the *ghazal*

دشنۂ غمزہ جانستاں ناوکِ ناز بے پناہ
تیرا ہی عکسِ رخ سہی سامنے تیرے آئے کیوں

Deadly the daggers of your glance, relentless your beauty's darts,
Granted, 'tis your image true, how dare it stare you in the face?

However, these are not the only pictures obtainable in the *ghazal,* for we do come across more realistic, flesh-and-blood portraits of the lovers and their mistresses. Read, for instance, the *ghazals* of Hasrat, Firaq, or Faiz, who bring to love a balanced, unidealised approach. Or, read the following couplet of Jigar Moradabadi, where the lover, instead of blaming his beloved for her cruelty, sympathises with her helpless state:

ادھر سے بھی سوا ہے کچھ اُدھر کی مجبوری
ہم نے آہ تو کی ، ان سے آہ بھی نہ ہوئی

Stronger perhaps are the constraints on the other side,
I, at least, could heave a sigh, to her was even this denied.

We may further note that the term love as used in Urdu poetry has wide connotations. It does not necessarily refer to the poet's attachment with a real-life woman; it could also imply his devotion to an ideal — be it spiritual, moral, social or political. Any ideal, like earthly love, is both desirable and unattainable, and hence entails passionate quest and yearning. Next to earthly love, it is the ideal of mystical or divine love that provides an important theme of Urdu *ghazal.* Though every poet is not a mystic (like Siraj, Dard or Asghar, for instance), nearly every poet has written mystical verse. Wali, one of the early masters of the *ghazal,* has neatly summed up the two essential concerns of the *ghazal* writer:

شغل بہتر ہے عشق بازی کا
کیا حقیقی و کیا مجازی کا

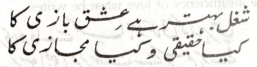

Of all pursuits love is best,
Be it sensuous or sublime.

Quite often the mystical and mundane elements of love co-exist in the same *ghazal,* nay, in the same verse. This is rendered possible by the linguistic and thematic ambiguity which is a common feature of this verse form. Moreover, the ideal of divine love is generally expressed in the *ghazal* through the idiom of romantic love, as in the following couplet of Mir which is a fine blend of loving artistry and imaginative skill:

چشم انجم سپہر جھمکے ہے
واہ رے تیرے انکھڑیاں لڑانے کے

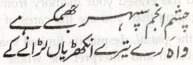

Its starry eyes, the welkin winks,
How wondrous, ah! Thy amorous blinks!

Or, read this couplet of Quli Qutab Shah which works on both the spiritual and secular plains:

مرے جیو آرسی میں خیال تج مکھ کا سو دِستا ہے
کرے او خیال منج دِل میں نشانی زرفشانی کا

In the mirror of my heart resides your image, dazzling bright,
Dispelling all its inner gloom, spreading like the golden light.

Although love is the dominant theme of the *ghazal,* it is not its only theme. Urdu poets know too well that life cannot be lived with love alone. It needs for its subsistence several mundane supports, such as food, shelter and clothing, and a measure of security and social acceptability. Urdu poets' consciousness of the limitations of love, of its inconsistency and involuntariness, has found repeated expression in the *ghazal.* Ghalib is pointing to the insufficiency of love when he writes:

تیری وفا سے کیا ہو تلافی کہ دہر میں
تیرے سوا بھی ہم پر بہت سے ستم ہوئے

How can your fidelity offer recompense?
I've suffered many blows besides those of love.

And, Faiz, in our own times, finds the concerns of life more captivating than love:

دنیا نے تیری یاد سے بیگانہ کر دیا
تجھ سے بھی دلفریب ہیں غم روزگار کے

The world has erased your memory from my mind,
More engaging than you are the cares of life.

Happily, the *ghazal,* despite its limited space, has sufficient capacity to absorb and interpret the whole range of human experience. It has been used for the sundry tasks of ethical reflection and philosophical contemplation, for intellectual probing into the mysteries of life and death, for patriotic exhortation or for the portrayal of nature. Examples can be multiplied, but I'll content myself with just two quotations, one from Siraj Aurangabadi, who describes the beauty of spring in sensuous, bacchanalian terms, and one from Zafar who strikes, in the couplet here cited, a moral and didactic note:

بہار ساقی ہے، بزمِ گلشن، ہیں مطربانِ چمن شرابی
پیالہ گل، سروِ سبز شیشہ، شراب بُو اور کلی گلابی

Spring is the server, garden the gathering, songsters quaff the bowl,
Flower the cup, cypress the flask, bud, the bottle holds.

SIRAJ

ظفر آدمی اسکو نہ جانیے گا، وہ ہو کتنا ہی صاحبِ فہم و ذکا
جسے عیش میں یادِ خدا نہ رہی، جسے طیش میں خوفِ خدا نہ رہا

Call him not a man, Zafar, however wise he be,
Who, in joy, forgets his God, in rage respects no qualms.

ZAFAR

The *ghazal* has also served the ends of social and political satire, generally directed against priests and public censors, the self-righteous custodians of morality. Here is Sauda making a dig at the puritanical priests:

گر ہو شراب و خلوت و محبوبِ خوب رُو
زاہد قسم ہے تجھ کو جو تُو ہو تو کیا کرے

If wine, seclusion, and a darling sweet together lie in wait,
Confess, O priest, what would you do, if you were in my place?

As if to counterbalance the excessive denigration of the priests at the hands of the poets, here is Jigar Moradabadi counselling restraint, and calling for a respectful attitude towards the clerics:

رندوں نے جو چھیڑا زاہد کو، ساقی نے کہا کس طنز سے آج
اوروں کی وہ عظمت کیا جانیں، کم ظرف جو انساں ہوتے ہیں

When the revellers teased the priest, the saqi archly quipped:
"How can the petty minds the soul of goodness spot?"

But a great master of social satire is Akbar Allahabadi, who, with his inimitable wit and humour, exposes the hypocrisy of the priestly class and castigates the contemporary craze for the Western ways of life. Here is a specimen:

ہوئے اس قدر مہذب کبھی گھر کا منہ نہ دیکھا
کٹی عمر ہوٹلوں میں مرے اسپتال جا کر

So civilized have we grown, never do we see our home,
In hotels we spend our lives, in hospitals we die.

It is difficult to exhaust the endless variety of themes treated in the *ghazal*. It may be safely said that the *ghazal* is an all-embracing form, fully responsive to the emotional and intellectual needs of the poet. There is another point to note. Though the reflections contained in a *ghazal* are derived from the poet's personal experience, and are presented from his subjective point of view, they are charged with universal significance, so that the *ghazal,* basically a subjective poem, acquires a popular and public appeal. That is why it is greeted with applause and cries of "encore" at *mushairas* and cultural meets. It would appear that the poet, while interpreting his own experience, enters into the mind not only of his own age, but of all ages. A good *ghazal* contains deeply felt universal truths, expressed in the best of words, arranged in the best order. Ghalib was pointing to these very qualities when he wrote:

دیکھنا تقریر کی لذّت کہ جو اُس نے کہا
میں نے یہ جانا کہ گویا یہ بھی میرے دل میں ہے

Mark ye, the beauty of speech, whatever he said,
I felt as if it were a depiction of my thoughts.

To achieve this "beauty of speech" and a universal appeal the poet needs a highly perceptive mind, and a mastery of his craft. Though there exists in Urdu the tradition of extempore poetic competitions, a really good *ghazal*, destined to live down the ages, needs for its making the combined contribution of inspiration and industry. A high-quality *ghazal* is not the "spontaneous overflow of powerful emotion", but "emotion recollected in tranquillity", and disciplined by the laws of poetic composition. The teacher-pupil tradition in Urdu poetry, and the practice of getting one's verses scanned and corrected by the veterans of the art, are a recognition of the fact that the *ghazal* is a serious art form, not an idler's vocation. A famous critic and poet, Firaq Gorakhpuri, has aptly compared the state of a poet who has come out of the travails of poetic composition to a burnt-out lamp, flickering and dying in the small hours of the night.

کبھی پچھلی پہر کو دیکھ لے کسی سانس لیتے چراغ کو
جو غزل ہوئی تو شعور میں وہی خستگی ہے وہی تھکن

Watch sometimes at the end of night a fading lamp, breathing hard.
The poet is left as weak and worn, after a *ghazal* is done.

And yet, as the adage goes, art lies in concealing art. A good *ghazal*, however diligently conceived, must give the impression of spontaneity and naturalness. The words of W.B. Yeats occurring in "Adam's Curse" can fitly apply to the art of the *ghazal*.

A line will take us hours, maybe;
Yet if it does not seem a moment's thought
Our stitching and unstitching has been naught.

However, mere "stitching and unstitching" cannot produce a good *ghazal*. Like all art, the *ghazal* draws its strength from life, which, in turn, it tends to nurture and refine. The vital link between life and poetry is beautifully underscored by Asghar Gondvi in the typical idiom of the *ghazal*:

اصغر غزل میں چاہیے وہ موجِ زندگی
جو حسن ہے بتوں میں جو مستی شراب میں

The *ghazal,* Asghar, should pulsate with life,
As belles with beauty, with rapture, wine.

We may now turn to consider the nature and form of the imagery used in Urdu *ghazal.* A bulk of this imagery, it must be conceded, is imported from Iran, or from Arabia via Iran. There is a frequent mention of the proverbial pairs : rose and nightingale, moth and candle, wine and saqi, boat and tempest, sea and shore, cage and nest, Moses and the Mount, Khizar and Sikander, or of the legendary lovers: Laila-Majnu, Shirin-Farhad, Yousaf-Zuleikha. Urdu poets have, in fact, been criticised for their obstinate adherence to imagery which, it is alleged, is both effete and alien. But this criticism is not wholly valid. True, this imagery is basically foreign, but it has been so assiduously cultivated by several generations of Urdu poets that it has by now become an integral part of Urdu poetry. It has been accepted by poets and lauded by readers who have become fully conversant with the multiple connotations ambushed in these images. The mention of the moth and the candle, or of the rose and the nightingale, immediately touches a responsive chord in their hearts and makes them a sharer of the poet's thoughts and dreams. Further, this imagery, though traditional, is not worn out. Every great poet has invested these images with new meanings in order to express his individual perspectives. Handled with sensitivity and discreetness, the seemingly commonplace imagery of the *ghazal* is capable of expressing profound truths of life, or compressing, within a few words, stories long enough to fill pages in prose. In one of his often quoted couplets Ghalib upholds the use of traditional imagery in the interest of economy and effect:

ہر چند ہو مشاہدۂ حق کی گفتگو
بنتی نہیں ہے بادہ و ساغر کہے بغیر

Be our subject Truth sublime,
We needs must mention draughts of wine.

Like its imagery, the diction of the *ghazal* too bears a deep imprint of the Persian influence. It needs no reminding that Urdu language itself is the product of Indo-Persian interaction, consequent upon the advent of Muslims in India in the 13th century. In the poems of Amir Khusro (1253-1325), the earliest exponent of the *ghazal,* we can find the two streams of Persian and Hindi flowing hand in hand, waiting to be merged, as, for instance, in the following couplet:

شبانِ ہجراں دراز چوں زُلف و روزِ وصلت چوں عمر کوتاہ
سکھی پیا کو جو میں نہ دیکھوں تو کیسے کاٹوں اندھیری رتیاں

Long like locks, the separation night, the day of union short as life,
How hard to pass the gloomy nights without seeing my love!

In verses like this, the two languages seem to stand face to face, with their arms stretched, poised, as if, for a handshake. In the poetry of Quli Qutab Shah (1565-1611), Hindi and Persian no longer stand shyly apart, but have already merged, resulting in the formation of a new poetic language to be christened as *Rekhta,* or Urdu. His language is a rich blend of Persian, Hindi, Sanskrit, Arabic, Deccany, and even Punjabi dialects and marks a considerable improvement on the language of Amir Khusro. With the shifting of the centre of cultural and poetic activity, in the 18th century, from Deccan to Delhi, the seat of the Moghul power, the Persian influence on Urdu becomes still more assertive. Under this influence, the local Hindi diction sheds its rusticity and gets spruced up so as to become a worthy mate to its Persian counterpart with which it will henceforth be interlaced. Nearly all Urdu poets take pride in adopting Persian modes and motifs, borrowing Persian figures of speech and Persian vocabulary, and incorporating, at times, complete lines and couplets of Persian verse for added effect and weight. From the Persian grammar they learn the use of *Izafat,* (-e-), to join a noun either with its adjective, or with its possessive. This single device of *Izafat* accounts, in a large measure, for the economy and compression of Urdu verse.

The practice of writing Persianised Urdu, begun under Muslim influence, continued unabated even after the disintegration of the Moghul empire, and right through the time of the British rule in India, when Urdu had nearly attained the status of the lingua franca, specially in the Northern region. But with the partition of the country in 1947, Urdu language suffered a serious setback. While in Pakistan Urdu consolidated its position still further, and rose to the rank of the National language, in India it yielded its place of pride to Hindi. Although Urdu continues to be one of the 14 officially recognised languages of India, there is a sudden drop in its popularity and currency. The number of schools and colleges offering Urdu as a subject of study has come down fast. Consequently, the younger generation of readers are getting alienated from the language, so that a couplet of the *ghazal* which could win instantaneous applause from the listeners some 30 or 40 years ago, now seems to fall on deaf ears. This does not auger well for the future of the *ghazal,* written in chaste, Persianised language. Realising the need for simplifying the language, some Urdu poets, notably, Firaq, Nasir Kaazmi or Bani, have attempted to wean Urdu away from the apron-strings of the Persian language, and draw it closer to Hindi and Hindustani. It is a welcome move, though it is not sufficiently widespread and well-orchestrated to redeem the status of Urdu.

Notwithstanding a perceptible decline in the percentage of the Urdu-knowing people in India, there is no decline in the popularity of the *ghazal*. If anything, it has gained in popularity. During the recent years there has been a remarkable revival of interest in the *ghazal,* as is evidenced by the rise, on both sides of the Indo-Pak border, of numerous singers of *ghazals,* whose performances at cultural gatherings, on television screen, and on cassette players, are eagerly sought after. A visit to a *mushaira* or a musical concert will show how some enthusiasts of the *ghazal,* unfamiliar with the Urdu script, eargerly jot down their favourite verses in the language they know, so that they could return to them and decipher their full import at leisure. In fact, the influence of the *ghazal* is spreading, and besides Urdu, many other Indian languages, including Hindi, Punjabi,

Bengali, Gujarati, Sindhi and Kashmiri, have also adopted the convention of the *ghazal*. All this speaks volumes for the inherent strength of this poetic form.

To grasp the secret of this strength, let us remind ourselves, in the end, of the peculiar characteristics of this form. We are struck first of all by the concision and compression of the *ghazal*, which makes a negligible demand on the reader's time, and yet provides a rich fund of aesthetic and intellectual delight, and an insight into the complexities of human thought and mind. For the art of the *ghazal* is the art of condensing in a few words the profound truths of love and life, experienced by the poet at the actual or imaginative level. Secondly, there is the completeness and detachability of each separate couplet of the *ghazal* which allows the reader the freedom to pick and choose, in obedience to his taste and judgement. Thirdly, the *ghazal* impresses us by its amazing capacity to record and interpret all interests of life — secular, spiritual, social, political, and even scientific. It is responsive to all sorts of moods — romantic, pensive, humorous or hilarious, and can serve, with equal ease, the varied purposes of panegyric or satire, elegy or parody. Fourthly, the *ghazal* can successfully exploit the whole range of literary devices for the execution of its design. It expresses the poet's insights in a measured, musical language, which quite often enacts and evokes, and not merely narrates, a particular scene or situation, an idea or a mood. *Qafia, radif,* imagery and allusions are some of the essential components of the *ghazal*, which enhance its beauty and enrich its meaning. Moreover, as the *ghazal* is meant to be read as well as heard it has an inbuilt cadence which enchants the ears and reflects the mood of the poet. The recurring rhyme at the end of every alternate line provides a link of unity to its separate parts, and helps to make its verses easily memorable. Fifthly, the couplets of a *ghazal* have an aphoristic and quotable quality, and are often used as aids to conversation, to stress a point, or clinch an argument. The striking couplets of a good *ghazal* travel imperceptibly, by word of mouth, from person to person, and generation to generation, and become deeply entrenched in the collective consciousness of the cultured classes. And, finally, as the *ghazal* deals primarily with the fundamental passion of love, which knows no barriers of age or clime, caste or class, it stands in no danger of losing its strong appeal, provided, of course, it is handled with artistic care and competence.

Mohammed Quli Qutab Shah
(1565-1611)

MOHAMMED QULI QUTAB SHAH
(1565-1611)

Sultan Mohammed Quli Qutab Shah, son of Ibrahim Qutab Shah, was the ruler of the state of Golconda, and founder of the city of Hyderabad. He was a contemporary of Emperor Jalal-ud-din Akbar, and was, like Akbar, a liberal, kind-hearted ruler, a lover of peace and amity, and a patron and promoter of the fine arts of poetry, music and architecture. More than that, he was a great poet, the author of a rich collection of 50,000 couplets, comprising *ghazals, masnavis, qasidas, rubaies* and *qitas*. It is now generally agreed that Quli Qutab Shah, rather than Wali Deccany, was the founding father of Urdu poetry. He may also be called the architect of Urdu language which he built by blending together Persian and Hindi, with a sprinkling of words and phrases drawn from Punjabi, Arabic, and local Deccany dialects. He, however, saw to it that the new product remained close to the language of common speech. He may truly be called a poet of the people, who has written poems to celebrate the popular Indian festivals like Holi, Diwali, Eid, Basant or the New Year Day. But he was, basically, a lover and a poet of love. A man of romantic temperament, his privileged position as a ruler allowed him easy access to the society of women, and it was this amorous involvement with the fair sex that inspired the poet in him. In a series of poems he has chosen to dwell on the graces and charms of his twelve mistresses, who are remembered by such endearing names as "Gori", "Nanhi", "Piari", "Sanwli", "Chhabeeli", etc. It is interesting to recall that the city of Hyderabad, founded by him was first named "Bhag Nagar", after the name of his beloved, Bhag Mati. But Qutab Shah was also a mystic poet and a devout Muslim. Love of women and love of Mohammed are the two recurring subjects of his poetry. Out of the five *ghazals* selected for this book, the opening one is a pure devotional hymn, whereas the other four are love poems, interspersed here and there with the praise of the Prophet, without whose grace earthly love cannot come to fruition.

Excessive drinking and a sensual way of life told heavily on his health, and he died at the comparatively young age of 47. But he'll be remembered for his service to Urdu language and poetry, and for founding the beautiful city of Hyderabad.

سلطان محمد قلی قطب شاہ

دلا منگ خدا کن کہ خدا کام دِویگا
تمن من کے مراداں کے بھرے جام دِویگا

خوارج کی اگن قہر کے پانی سوں بوجھا گا
براہیم تمن مجکوں سکھ آرام دِویگا

دو عالم کے دوارے کھلے ہیں عیش کے خاطر
جے کوئی نبیؐ نام سوں دل رام دِویگا

جے دل میں محبت علی و آلِ علی ناہ
اسے خونِ جگر دار وئے ناکام دِویگا

نہ کھا غم توں زمانے کا ترا کام خدا سوں
ہر اک پستی منے تجکوں بلند نام دِویگا

اپن بخت حقیرے تھے کدیں دل میں نکر غم
تجے دار دئے صحت سوں شفا جام دِویگا

رقیباں کے دکھوں سیتی قطب شہ نوں نکر غم
خدا سارے رقیباں کے گلے دام دِویگا

Mohammed Quli Qutab Shah

Bank upon God, O heart, He'll fulfil all thy needs,
Thy desires will come to bloom, if thou kiss His holy feet.

He will vanquish all thy foes, scotch their fire with His wrath,
Ibrahim-like, He'll prove a fount of solace deep.

The doors of joy stand ajar in both the worlds for him,
Who, the holy name of Nabi day and night repeats.

The heart which respects not Ali or His holy seed,
Will find its very life-blood deadly venom breed.

Be not afeared of the world, thou art the child of God,
He'll raise thee to the sky, support thy tottering feet.

Let not thy humble fate cause thee much concern,
He'll give thee nectarous drink, all thy ailments heal.

Let not the rivals' thought, Qutab, upset your peace,
God will hang them by the neck, their designs defeat.

Dila mang Khuda kan Keh Khuda kaam divega,
Tuman man ke muradaan ke bhare jaam divega.

Khwaraj ki agan qahr ke paani son bojhaga,
Braahim naman mujkon sukh aaraam divega.

Do aalam ke dawaare khule hain aish ke khaatir,
Je koi Nabi naam son dil raam divega.

Je dil mein muhabbat Ali-o-aal-e-Ali naa,
Use khoon-e-jigar daaroo-a-nakaam divega.

Na kha ghum tun zamaane ka tira kaam Khuda son,
Har ik pasti mane tujkon buland naam divega.

Apan bakht haqire the kadin dil mein na kar ghum,
Tuje daaroo-e-sihat son shifa jaam divega.

Raqibaan ke dukhon saiti Qutab Shah tun na kar ghum,
Khuda saare raqibaan ke gale daam divega.

قلی قطب شاہ

سب اختیار میرا تج ہات ہے پیارا
جس حال سوں رکھیگا ہے او خوشی ہمارا

نیناں انجھوں سوں دھوؤں پگ اپ پلک سوں جھاڑوں
جے کوئی خبر سو لیا وے مکھ پھول کا تمہارا

تج نا نین تیرے ہو رہت نین کیاں پتلیاں
مجھ نین ہیں پوجاری پوجا ادھان ہمارا

اس پتلیاں کی صورت کئی خواب ہیں جو دیکھے
رشک آئے مجھ، کرے مت کوئی سجدہ اس دوارا

تج عاشقاں ہیں ہوتا جنگ و جدل سو سب دن
ہے شرع احمدی تج انصاف کر خدارا

تج خیال کی ہوس تھے ہے جیو ہمن سو زندہ
او خیال کد بجاوے ہم سر تھے ٹک بہارا

جب توں لکھیا قطب شہ مہر محمدؐ اپ دل
ہے شش جہت میں تجھکو حیدر رکہ توا دہارا

Quli Qutab Shah

You control everything in my chequered life,
I rejoice in your will, treat me as you like.

I'll wash his eyes with tears, with my eyelids wipe his feet,
Whosoever brings your tidings, O, my rose of life!

Your eyes are the idol-house, their pupils, idols twain,
I, the priest of your shrine, worship is my creed of life.

If someone sees even in dream, the pupils of your eyes,
Let him not adore these doors, lest I with envy die.

Jealous lovers contend and quarrel, for your beauty's prize,
Judge them by thy code divine, and their fate decide.

Your thought sustains the heart that lies within my breast,
Nothing can defraud me of this deep delight.

Ever since I stamped my heart with Mohammed's seal sublime,
His grace abounding flows on me from every nook and side.

Sab akhtiaar mera tuj haat hai piara,
Jis haal son rakhega hai o khushi hamara.

Nainaan anjhun son dhoun, pag ap palak son jhaarun,
Je koi khabar so liawe mukh phool ka tumhara.

Butkhana nain tere, hor but nain keaan putleaan,
Mujh nain hain pujari, pooja udhaan hamara.

Us putleaan ki surat koi khwab mein jo dekhe,
Rashk aae mujh, kare mat koi sijda is dawara.

Tuj aashiqaan mein hota jang-o-jadal so sab din,
Hai shara-e-Ahmedi tuj insaaf kar Khuda ra.

Tuj khayaal ki hawas the hai jeu haman so zinda,
O khayaal kad na jaawe hum sar the tuk bahara.

Jab ton likhia Qutab Shah muhr Mohammed ap dil,
Hai shash jihat mein tujkon Haider keh tu udhara.

قلی قطب شاہ

باغِ دل میں تج محبت کا اچنبا پھل لگیا
باس سنگ پھولاں عرق کا میں ہوا ہوں ڈگمگیا

یے علم ہور یے کتب ہور کس تھے بوجھیا جائے نا
عالماں بیچارہ دکھ کر اس کی تک میں رہے تھکیا

سانولی قد سرو کوں لاگے ہیں اب میٹھے نبات
چکھنے جا کر میں ڈراں سیتی رہیا ہوں دہک دہکیا

شیشے کی قلقل تھے پیالے میانے باندھے بڑبڑے
بڑبڑا دو یہ کے زوراں سوں جگ میں جگمگیا

توں اندھارے پنتھ میں نا منگ روشنی اغیار تھے
روشنی تج دیوے کوں قدرت اجالے کا لگیا

میں اُمّی کر گنتے ہیں سب امیاں تو علم میں
موزبانی کا قلم تج وصف لکھ نا سک بھگیا

تم معانی کے گناہاں کا رقم کرتے ہیں کے
میں محمد نانوں تھے دو نوں جہاں میانے جگیا

Quli Qutab Shah

A strange flower of your love has blossomed in my heart,
Its intoxicating scent makes me faint and fall.

The lore of love is a different thing, hidden from learned eyes,
In vain they strive to read this book, in vain their brains exhaust.

Delicious fruits are hanging on my cypress, sweet and tall,
But I dare not touch or taste, fear nags my heart.

The gurgling flask creates bubbles in the foaming cup,
Lighted by the fire of love, the bubble spreads its sheen afar.

Why look for borrowed light in the darkened path of life?
Your lamp derives its glow from innate, natural spark.

I'm called a learned man by the learned folk,
Your grace defies my pen, your worth I can't record.

Why do they keep a count of Maani's sins and faults?
Mohammed's name makes me sparkle like a bright star.

Bagh dil mein tuj muhabbat ka achamba phul lagia,
Baas sung phulaan arq ka main hua hun dagmagia.

Yeh ilm hor yeh kutab hor kis the bojhia jaae na,
Aalmaan bechara dukh kar uski tak mein rahe thakia.

Sanwli qad sarw kon laage hain ab meethe nabaat,
Chakhne ja kar main daran saiti rahia hun dahk dahkia.

Sheeshe ki qulqul the piale meaane baandhe burbure,
Burbura wo neh ke zoraan son jag mein jagmagia.

Tun andhare panth mein na mang roshni aghiaar the,
Roshni tuj deewe kon qudrat ujaale ka lagia.

Main ummi kar ginte hain saab ammian to ilm mein,
Mu zabaani ka qalam tuj wasf likh na sak bhagia.

Tum Maani ke gunahaan ka raqm karte hain kya,
Main Mohammed naaun the donon jahan meaane jagia.

قلی قطب شاہ

خبر لیایا ہے ہُد ہُد میرے تئیں اس یارِ جانی کا
خوشی کا وقت ہے ظاہر کروں رازِ نہانی کا
مرے جیو آرسی میں خیال تج مکھ کا سو دستا ہے
کرے او خیال مُنج دل میں نشانی زرفشانی کا
چتا ہو عشق کے جنگل میں بیٹھا ہے دری لے کر
لیا ہے جھانپ سوں آہو مَن دل مُنج ایانی کا
خدا کا شکر ہے تج سلطنت تھے کام پایا ہوں
دندے دشمن کے مکھ پر پیو تا مئے ارغوانی کا
چھبیلے مست ساقی کے پچھیں دوڑیں سو مخموراں
پلا دو مئی ہوا اب نو ہوا ہے گل فشانی کا
دو تنِ افسوں کے بارے تھے ہمن کوں کچھ نہیں ڈر ہے
ہمارے دیوے کوں ہے روشنی صاحب قرانی کا
پڑے دنبال میں میرے سو اس نیناں کے دنبالے
خدایا عشق مشکل ہے بھرم رکھ توں معانی کا

Quli Qutab Shah

The lapwing has brought the news of my darling sweet,
Let me unfold my heart, now the time is meet.

In the mirror of my heart resides your image, dazzling bright,
Dispelling all my inner gloom, spreading like a golden sheet.

There he sits tiger-like, in the wild ambushed,
Set to trap my innocent heart, with his cunning feats.

I can quaff the crimson goblet right in the rival's face,
God be thanked, your regal state has crowned me with success complete.

The cute and carefree Saqi is thus by drinkers teased:
"Give us wine, 'tis springtime, softly blows the breeze".

I'm not scared of the rival's rude breath,
My lamp draws its light from the author of the Quran Majeed.

The sharp arrows of her glance have hit the iris of my eyes,
Love, O Lord, is an uphill task, help Thy Maani his pledge to keep!

Khabar liaya hai hud hud mere taein us yaar-e-jaani ka,
Khushi ka waqt hai zaahir karun raaz-e-nihaani ka.

Mire jeu aarsi mein khayal tuj mukh ka so dista hai,
Kare o khayal munj dil mein nishani zar fishani ka.

Chita ho ishq ke jungle mein baithia hai dari le kar,
Liya hai jhaanp son aahu naman dil mujh ayaani ka.

Khuda ka shukr hai tuj saltanat the kaam paya hun,
Dande dushman ke mukh par peota mai arghawani ka.

Chhabeele mast saqi ke pichhein dauren sau makhmuraan,
Pila do mai hawa ab tau hua hai gul fishani ka.

Do tin afsun ke baare the haman kon kuch nahin dar hai,
Hamare deewe kon hai roshni sahib quraani ka.

Pare dumbaal mein mere so us nainaan ke dumbaale,
Khudaya ishq mushkil hai bharm rakh tu Maani ka.

قلی قطب شاہ

خبر لیا دو کہ میرے تئیں سو اُس بے رحمِ عالم کا
نجانوں ہیں کہ او بے رحم ہے سب جگ میں آدم کا

اگر وہ ملتفت ہووے ہماری بات پر یک چھن
نواروں میں خزینہ اس اپر اس دل کے درہم کا

گدا تج عشق کا ہوں دے زکاتِ عشق مُنج سائیں
کہ ہے اعجاز مُنج من کوں کہ جیوں عیسیٰ مریم کا

فقیر و ناتواں ہوں میں کہاں شاہاں کی مجلس مُنج
مگر اپ خیال میں دیکھوں او صحبت آبِ زمزم کا

مراقد ہے سو تُج ینہ باؤ تھے لرزاں سو جیوں جیغہ
عصا دے ہاتھ میں میرے کہ جیوں موسیٰ محرم کا

توں ہے خورشیدِ خاور ذرہ میں جب ناگنے مُنج کوں
گِنو یا نا گِنو تُج ہات ہے سب حکم خاتم کا

پیا تج بندِ میں ہلجا ہوں کر آزاد مُنج بندے
معانیؔ کوں غلاماں میں خطاب اب دے مکرم کا

Quli Qutab Shah

Bring me, pray, tidings of my dear despot,
Don't I know that this despot resides in every heart?

If he yields to my plea even for a fleeting while,
I'll place at his feet the treasure of my precious heart.

I'm a beggar at your door, dole me out your love, O Lord,
Like the miracle-working Christ, for me your love is magic-fraught.

I'm a poor mendicant, unfit for royal courts,
Still I visit the Mecca's fount, aided by your amorous thought.

The ague of love makes me shake like a waving crest,
Endow me with a staff as prop, like the Moses' rod.

You are the sun sublime, I a speck of humble dust,
You may or mayn't count me so, I count you as my best resort.

I'm a prisoner of your love, break my fetters, set me free,
Assign to me the highest place among the faithful lot.

Khabar liya do keh mere taein so us be rahm-e-aalam ka,
Na jaanun main keh o be-rahm hai sab jag mein aadam ka?

Agar woh multfit howe hamari baat par yak chhin,
Niwaarun main khazina us upar is dil ke darham ka.

Gada tuj ishq ka hun de zakaat-e-ishq munj saaien,
Keh hai aijaaz munj man kon keh jeon issah-e-Mariam ka.

Faqir-o-natawaan hun main kahan shahaan ki majlis munj,
Magar ap khayal mein dekhun o suhbat aab-e-zamzam ka.

Mira qad hai so tuj neh baao the larzaan so jeon jeegha,
Asa de haath mein mere keh jeon musa-e-mohram ka.

Tun hai khurshid-e-khawir, zarra mein jab na gine munj kon,
Gino ya no gino tuj haat hai sab hukam khatim ka.

Piya tuj band mein hilja hun kar aazad munj band the,
Maani kon gulaaman mein khitaab ab de mukarram ka.

Siraj Aurangabadi
(1715-1763)

SIRAJ AURANGABADI
(1715 - 1763)

Siraj was born at Aurangabad (Maharashtra) in 1715 A.D. His early education was taken care of by his father, Sayed Darvesh, who was a man of pronounced literary taste. Siraj was a precocious child. He had read quite a few books of Persian and Arabic at the age of 12, and had published his *Dewan* of Urdu verse at the age of 24. At the age of 13, Siraj had experienced a phase of religious frenzy, a state of psychosis, which lasted for seven years. During this period he used to wander about restlessly, "naked and bare-headed," speaking out Persian couplets. At the return of normalcy Siraj turned to writing Urdu verse, which, however, he gave up at the advice of his religious mentor, Abdul Rahman Chishti. But by this time he had already published his Dewan which contains, in addition to *ghazals, qasidas* and *rubaies,* a long narrative poem *(masnavi),* entitled: *"Bostan-e-Khayaal"*. Siraj is a poet of deep mystic fervour, but he expresses this mysticism through the idiom of love and romance. This makes his poetry universally acceptable and enjoyable. He had also compiled and edited a selection of Persian poets under the title, *Muntekhib Dewanhaa.* In his later life Siraj renounced the world and became a sufi Ascetic. He lived a life of isolation, though a number of younger poets and admirers used to gather at his place for poetic instruction and religious edification.

Siraj may be called a poetic heir of Wali Deccany, for whom he had a great admiration. He is one of the classics of Urdu poetry, who has had an abiding influence on his successors. His *ghazals* are remarkable for the intensity and spontaneity of feeling, depth of thought, and simplicity of style. He was an instinctive poet who sought his inspiration from within. Consequently, there is an element of originality about his style and manner. The opening ghazal of this selection, *"khabr-e-tahayyur-e-ishq sun..."* which is counted among the prized poems of Urdu, contains sufficient evidence of his mystic zeal and poetic power.

سراج اورنگ آبادی

خبرِ تحیرِ عشق سن، نہ جنوں رہا نہ پری رہی
نہ تو تو رہا نہ تو میں رہا جو رہی سو بے خبری رہی

شہِ بے خودی نے عطا کیا مجھے اب لباسِ برہنگی
نہ خرد کی بخیہ گری رہی نہ جنوں کی پردہ دری رہی

چلی سمتِ غیب سیں کیا ہوا کہ چمن ظہور کا جل گیا
مگر ایک شاخِ نہالِ غم جسے دل کہو سو ہری رہی

نظرِ تغافلِ یار کا گلہ کس زباں سیں بیاں کروں
کہ شرابِ صد قدحِ آرزو خُمِ دل میں تھی سو بھری رہی

وہ عجب گھڑی تھی میں جس گھڑی لیا درس نسخۂ عشق کا
کہ کتاب عقل کی تاک میں جوں دھری تھی تیوں ہی دھری رہی

ترے جوشِ حیرتِ حسن کا اثر اس قدر سیں یہاں ہوا
کہ نہ آئینہ میں رہی جلا نہ پری کوں جلوہ گری رہی

کیا خاک آتشِ عشق نے دلِ بے نوائے سراج کوں
نہ خطر رہا نہ حذر رہا مگر ایک بے خطری رہی

Siraj Aurangabadi

Getting wind of love entranced, elfish passions took to heels,
Oblivious of the world I stood, sense of "thee" and "me" had ceased.

Grace transcendent conferred on me nascent, natural robes,
Frenzy needn't rend the cloak, nor sanity mend the sleeve.

The wind blowing from place unseen burnt down every leaf,
But a woeful branch, called the heart, despite the blaze, retained its green.

I can't find adequate words to protest my friend's indifferent glance,
The wine of desire that filled the heart remained suppressed, concealed.

It was at a moment strange that I read the book of love,
The book of reason, brushed aside, remained shelved and sheathed.

Your bewitching beauty, love, such a spell did cast,
The mirror stood bereft of gloss, beauty seemed to freeze.

The fire of love reduced to ashes Siraj's voiceless heart,
Fears and cares got consumed, intrepid courage held the field.

Khabr-e-tahayyur-e-ishq sun na janoon raha na pari rahi,
Na tau tu raha, na tau main raha, jo rahi so be-khabri rahi.

Shah-e-bekhudi ne ita kiya mujhe ab libaas-e-brahnagi,
Na khird ki bakhiya gari rahi, na janoon ki pardah dari rahi.

Chali simat-e-ghaib sein kya hawa ke chaman zahoor ka jal gaya,
Magar ek shaakh-e-nihal-gham, jise dil kaho, so hari rahi.

Nazr-e-taghaful-e-yaar ka gila kis zabaan sein beaan karun,
Ke sharab-e-sad qadah-e-aarzoo khum-e-dil mein thi, so bhari rahi.

Woh ajab ghari thi main jis ghari liya dars nuskha-e-ishq ka,
Ke kitab aqal ki taaq mein jun dhari thi teon hi dhari rahi.

Tire josh-e-hairat-e-husn ka asar qadar sein yahan hua,
Ke na aaeene mein rahi jila, na pari ko jalwa gari rahi.

Kiya khak aatish-e-ishq ne dil-e-be nawa-e-Siraj kon,
Na khatar raha, na hazar raha, magar ek be-khatri rahi.

سراج

عالم کے دوستوں میں مروّت نہیں رہی
شرم و حیا و مہر و شفقت نہیں رہی

ظاہر میں کیا رفیق کہاتے ہیں آپ کوں
لیکن انوں کے دل میں محبت نہیں رہی

ملتے ہیں راستی سیں جو کوئی کج نظر ملے
خوبوں میں پاک بازکی حرمت نہیں رہی

ہر خارِ بوالہوس کی کئے صحبت اختیار
تو حسنِ گل رُخوں میں لطافت نہیں رہی

بھولے ہیں ہر صنم کے کرشمے پہ ہوش کوں
ان زاہدوں میں کشف و کرامت نہیں رہی

مت ہو بہارِ گلشنِ دنیا کا عندلیب
اس پھول بن میں بوئے رفاقت نہیں رہی

اب ذاتِ حق بغیر نہ رکھ دوستی سراج
عالم میں آشنائی و الفت نہیں رہی

Siraj Aurangabadi

Friends in the present age have shed the warmth of olden days,
Honour, shame, love, regard — everything is cast away.

Though they make professions of deep, abiding faith,
Of true love in their hearts, there's not a trace.

The beauties give a straight response to those who archly gaze,
But for those pure-at-heart, they have only scant praise.

Any lusting thorn they can without demur embrace,
The blooming beauties, one infers, have lost their nascent grace.

One glance from the beauteous eye, and they lose their wits,
No more do the priests now spiritual skills display.

Be ye not a nightingale of the worldly glade,
The scent of love and loyalty it no longer exhales.

Befriend not anything else but the Truth divine,
The world, Siraj, is wanting in genuine, friendly ways.

Aalam ke doston mein murawat nahin rahi,
Sharm-o-haya-o-mehar-o-shafqat nahin rahi.

Zahir mein kya rafiq kahate hain aapko,
Lekin unon ke dil mein mahabbat nahin rahi.

Milte hain raasti mein jo koi kaj nazar mile,
Khubon mein pakbaaz ki hurmat nahin rahi.

Har khar-e-bulhawas ki kiye suhbat ikhtiaar,
Tau husn-e-gulrukhon mein litafat nahin rahi.

Bhule hain har sanam ke karishme pe hosh kon,
In zaahidon mein kishf-o-karaamat nahin rahi.

Mat ho bahaar-e-gulshan-e-duniya ka andleeb,
Is phool ban mein boo-e-rafaaqat nahin rahi.

Ab zaat-e-haq baghair na rakh dosti, Siraj,
Aalam mein aashnaai-o-ulfat nahin rahi.

سراجؔ

آئینہ رُو کے شوق میں حیراں ہوا ہوں میں
زلفوں کو اس کی دیکھ پریشاں ہوا ہوں میں

ہے خونِ دل شراب مجھے اور گزک جگر
جب سوں پرت کی بزم میں مہماں ہوا ہوں میں

آبِ حیاتِ وصل سیں دے عمرِ جاوداں
خنجر سوں تجھ فراق کے بے جاں ہوا ہوں میں

مدّت سوں تھا زیارتِ کعبہ کا مجھ کوں ذوق
تیری بھواں کوں دیکھ کے قرباں ہوا ہوں میں

اس ماہ رو کوں دیکھ کے جیوں شمع اے سراجؔ
اپنے عرق کے شرم سیں پنہاں ہوا ہوں میں

Siraj Aurangabadi

The love of that mirror-like face has left me mazed,
With the lustre of her locks, I'm utterly dazed.

My heart's blood serves for wine, my guts serve as snacks,
Since I came as a guest to my love's place.

The sword of separation has denuded me of life,
Make me immortal, love, with thy warm embrace.

For long I had wished for Kaaba's pilgrimage,
Having seen your eyebrows, I kneel down in praise.

Seeing my moon of love, Siraj, like a taper aglow,
In my own sweat, I find myself swathed.

Aaeena-roo ke shauq mein hairaan hua hun main,
Zulfon ko uski dekh pareshaan hua hun main.

Hai khoon-e-dil sharaab mujhe, aur gazak jigar,
Jab son prit ki bazm mein mehmaan hua hun main.

Aab-e-hayaat-e-wasal sein de umr-e-jaawidaan,
Khanjar se tujh firaq ke be-jaan hua hun main.

Muddat son tha zayaarat-e-Kaaba ka mujh ko shauq,
Teri bhawaan ko dekh ke qurbaan hua hun main.

Is maah roo ko dekh ke jeon shama, ai Siraj,
Apne araq ke sharam sein pinhaan hua hun main.

سراج

ہوا ہے مہرباں وو مُو کمر آہستہ آہستہ
کیا مجھ آہ نے شاید اثر آہستہ آہستہ

کیا ہے مسکرا کر بات مثلِ پھول گل رو نے
نہالِ عشق نے لایا ثمر آہستہ آہستہ

طفیلِ سوزشِ دل منزلِ جاناں کوں پہنچا ہوں
ہوئی ہے آہ میری راہبر آہستہ آہستہ

گلی میں اس پری رو کی کیا ہے عزم اوڑنے کا
نکالا مرغِ دل نے بال و پر آہستہ آہستہ

مرے حالِ پریشاں کی حقیقت کوں سنا جا کر
صبا کوچے میں گل رو کے گزر آہستہ آہستہ

Siraj Aurangabadi

That slim-waisted beauty has kinder grown, step by step,
My sighs have impressed her heart, perchance, step by step.

My rose of love has favoured me with a sweet smile,
The plant of love has, at last, borne fruit, step by step.

Thanks to this heartache, I have attained my goal,
My sighs have led me on, slowly, step by step.

To fly to that lane beloved, I'm now resolved,
The bird of heart is fledging forth, lo, step by step.

Go, narrate my woeful tale to my blooming love,
O breeze, blow in her lane, gently, step by step.

Hua hai mehrbaan woh moo kamar, aahista, aahista,
Kiya mujh aah ne shaid asar, aahista, aahista.

Kiya hai muskra ke baat masl-e-phool, gulroo ne,
Nihaal-e-ishq ne laya samr, aahista, aahista.

Tufail-e-sozish-e-dil manzil-e-janaan ko pahuncha hun,
Hui hai aah meri raahbar, aahista, aahista.

Gali mein us pari roo ki kiya hai azm urne ka,
Nikala murgh-e-dil ne baal-o-par, aahista, aahista.

Mere haal-e-pareshan ki haqiqat ko suna ja kar,
Saba kuche mein gulroo ke guzr aahista, aahista.

سراجؔ

بہار ساقی ہے، بزم گلشن، ہیں مطربانِ چمن شرابی
پیالہ گل، سروِ سبز شیشہ، شراب بو اور کلی گلابی
نہیں ہے بلبل کوں ایسے موسم میں درد وغم دھوپ میں خزاں کی
کہ آشیاں اس کوں حسن کا بنگلہ ہے، سایۂ گل ہے آفتابی
ارے چکورو یہ چاندنی نہیں عبث کیے ہو ہجوم تم نے
ہوا ہے جوشِ بہار نسریں سبب دھوپ کا رنگ ماہتابی
ہوا شفق پوش باغ و صحرا محیط ہے رنگِ لالۂ و گل
غبارِ گلگوں ہے آب رنگیں، زمیں ہے سرخ اور ہوا شہابی
سراجؔ اس شوخ چشم کوں کہہ کہ باغ میں منتظر ہے نرگس
ہجومِ شبنم سیں لے کہ موتی نثار کرنے کوں بھر رکابی

Siraj Aurangabadi

Spring is the server, garden the gathering, songsters quaff the bowl,
Flower the cup, cypress the flask, bud, the bottle holds.

The nightingale in this season needn't fear the autumn's heat,
Its nest serves as a house of khas, the rose as a parasol.

O partridges, it's not the moon, why dost thou raise a din?
The riotous bloom of roses white has lent the sun a moony stole.

Desert and grove are dyed in dawn, tulips and roses bloom,
Earth and air are crimson red, water reflects the rose.

Tell that beauty arch-eyed, narcissus lies in wait,
Eager to offer at her feet, a plate of jewels, by dews bestowed.

Bahaar saqi hai, bazm gulshan, hain mutribaan-e-chaman sharabi,
Payala gul, sarw-e-sabz sheesha, sharaab boo, aur kali gulabi.

Nahin hai bulbul kon aise mausim mein dard-o-gham dhoop mein khazaan ki,
Ke aashian iskon khas ka bangla hai, saya-e-gul hai aaftaabi.

Ai chakoro yeh chandni nahin, abas kieye ho hajum tum ne,
Hua hai josh-e-bahaar-e-nasreen mein dhup ka rang maahtaabi.

Hua shafq posh bagh-o-sahara, maheet hai rang-e-lala-o-gul,
Ghubaar-e-gulgoon hai aab-e-rangeen, zamin hai surkh, aur hawa shahaabi.

Siraj is shokh chashm ko kah ke bagh mein muntazir hai nargis,
Hajum-e-shabnam sein le ke moti nissar karne kon bhar rakaabi.

سراج

جاں بلب ہوں، ہے کہاں وو دلبرِ جادو لقب

دل برِ جادو لقب کے ہجر میں ہوں جاں بلب

بے ادب کوں اے صنم ہر گز نہ کر توں رو برو

رو برو تیرے ہوئی ہے آرسی کیا بے ادب

بے سبب ہم بے گنا ہوں پر روامت کر ستم

کر ستم ہم کوں کیا ہے قتل کیوں توں بے سبب

زلف شب ہے اور تیرا عارض ہے رشکِ آفتاب

آفتاب اب ہے ترا رخسار و تیری زلف شب

ہے غضب بے جا ہماری جان پر اے من ہرن

من ہرن تیرِ تغافل حق میں میرے ہے غضب

منتخب ہے مصرعِ موزوں و قدِّ گل بدن

گل بدن کا وو خمِ ابرو ہے فردِ منتخب

مستحب ہے عشق کے مذہب میں ترکِ ماسوا

ماسوا سے باز آنا ہے سراج اب مستحب

Siraj Aurangabadi

I'm on the verge of death, where's my sorcerer sweet,
Absence of my sorcerer sweet has brought me to the verge of death.

Let not a haughty head stare you in the face,
Haughtily it stares at you, your mirrored ornament.

Why are we the innocent subjected to your cruel gaze?
Your cruel gaze has murdered us without a cause, without offence.

Your cheeks are the radiant sun, your locks the sable night,
Sable nights are your looks, your face the sun resplendent.

Unjust is this your wrath, O, enchanting love,
Terrible are your darts, tipped with indifference.

Special are my lines of verse, special too my rose of love,
Special are her eyebrows, uniquely arched and bent.

The creed of love recommends, Siraj, renunciation complete,
Renounce all else besides, if you are on love intent.

Jaan ba-lab hun, hai kahan woh dilbar-e-jaadoo laqab,
Dilbar-e-jaadoo laqab ke hijar mein hun jaan ba-lab.

Be adab kon ai sanam hargiz na kar tu roobaroo,
Roobroo tere hui hai aarsi kya be adab.

Be sabab hum be gunaahon par rawa mat kar sitam,
Kar sitam hum kon kiya hai qatal kyon tun be sabab.

Zulf shab hai aur tera aaraz hai rashk-e-aaftaab,
Aaftaab ab hai tera rukhsaar wa teri zulf shab.

Hai ghazab be ja hamari jaan par ai man-haran,
Man-haran teer-e-taghaaful haq mein mere hai ghazab.

Muntakhib hai misra-e-mauzoon wa qadd-e-gul-badan,
Gul badan ka wo kham-e-abroo hai fard-e-muntakhib.

Mustahib hai ishq ke mazhab mein tark-e-maa siwa,
Maa siwa se baaz aana hai Siraj ab mustahib.

Mirza Mohammed Rafi Sauda
(1713-1781)

MIRZA MOHAMMED RAFI SAUDA
(1713 - 1781)

Mirza Mohammed Rafi Sauda was born in Delhi. His father, Mirza Mohammed Shafi, had come from Kabul to India in search of some business, and had settled down permanently in Delhi. Sauda showed signs of a poetic genius quite early in life. His talent got ample opportunity to develop under the guidance of his poetic mentor, Shah Hatim. The boy poet initially wrote poetry in Persian, but under the influence and advice of Khan Aarzoo, he switched over to Urdu and soon acquired unusual popularity as a poet, so much so that even King Shah Aalam took pride on being included among Sauda's poetic disciples. Later in life, Sauda was compelled by the social and political tensions of Delhi to migrate to Lucknow, where his poetry found a favourable soil under the patronage of Nawab Shaja-ul-Daula and Asaf-ul-Daula. Sauda died in Lucknow in 1781.

Sauda's name is generally mentioned along with Mir's in any discussion of Urdu poetry. Both are the poets of the Delhi School of Poetry, both are contemporaries (Sauda was elder to Mir by eight years), both migrated to Lucknow in the later part of their life, both are counted among the classics of Urdu poetry, and both made a remarkable contribution to the enrichment of poetry and poetic diction. Yet they also present some points of contrast. While Mir Taqi Mir outshines Sauda as a writer of *ghazals,* Sauda's superiority lies in the field of panegyric (*qasida*) and satire. Mir's poetry moves our hearts by its pathos and a haunting wail of melancholy, Sauda's verse is energetic and aggressive, not to be subdued by grief or despair. Correspondingly, Mir's language is simple, natural, speech-like, while Sauda's language is impressive and dignified, embellished occasionally with Persian words and phrases. Such a language is more suited for *qasida* rather than for the *ghazal* which makes its impact through the simplicity and spontaneity of its speech and diction. Moreover, Sauda is fond of using clever conceits and ingenious imagery in his poetry. When asked to spell out the essential difference in the manner of Mir and Sauda, Khwaja Baast of Lucknow, a connoisseur of Urdu poetry, is said to have remarked: "Mir's poetry is 'aah'! (a cry of despair), Sauda's verse is 'waah'! (a voice of exultation)". Be it as it may, both Mir and Sauda are masters of their art, though they speak in their own distinctive voice, moulded by the circumstances of their life and their individual temperaments.

مرزا محمد رفیع سوداؔ

ٹوٹے تیری نگہ سے اگر دل حباب کا
پانی بھی پھر پئیں تو مزا ہے شراب کا
دوزخ مجھے قبول ہے اے منکر و نکیر
لیکن نہیں دماغ سوال و جواب کا
تھا کِس کے دل کو کشمکشِ عشق کا دماغ
یارب برا ہو دیدۂ خانہ خراب کا
زاہد سبھی ہے نعمتِ حق جو ہے اکل و شرب
لیکن عجب مزا ہے شراب و کباب کا
غافل غضب سے ہو کے کرم پر نہ رکھ نظر
پُر ہے شرارِ برق سے دامن سحاب کا
قطرہ گرا تھا جو کے میرے اشکِ گرم سے
دریا میں ہے ہنوز پھپھولا حباب کا
سوداؔ نگاہِ دیدۂ تحقیق کے حضور
جلوہ ہر ایک ذرّے میں ہے آفتاب کا

Mirza Mohammed Rafi Sauda

If you set the bubble aburst with your gaze benign,
Water too will then acquire the taste of foaming wine;
I'm prepared to suffer in hell, O, angels divine,
But to join issue with you I'm not inclined.
My heart was never keen, to court the woes of love,
Accursed be my wretched eyes which got me thus entwined,
Gift of God is everything, whatever we eat or drink,
But, O priest, nothing to beat the joys of meat and wine.
Whelmed by the grace of God, forget ye not His wrath,
Remember that in a vernal cloud rain and fire combine.
There where my scalding tear had dripped into the stream,
You'll find a blistering bubble sparkle still and shine.
A deep discerning eye, Sauda, can easily perceive,
In every grain of dust, the sight of sun sublime.

Toote teri nigah se agar dil habaab ka,
Paani bhi phir piein to maza hai sharaab ka.
Dozakh mujhe qabool, ai, Munkir-o-Nakeer,
Lekin nahin dimagh sawaal-o-jawab ka.
Tha kis ke dil ko kashmkash-e-ishq ka dimagh,
Yaarab bura ho deeda-e-khana-kharaab ka.
Zahid sabhi hai neimat-e-haq jo hai aql-o-sharb,
Lekin ajab maza hai sharaab-o-kabaab ka.
Ghaafil ghazab se ho ke karam par na rakh nazar,
Pur hai sharar-e-baraq se daaman sahaab ka.
Qatra gira tha choo ke mere ashk-e-garam se,
Darya mein hai hanooz phaphola habaab ka.
Sauda, nigah-e-deeda-e-tahqiq ke hazur,
Jalwa har ek zarre mein hai aaftaab ka.

سوداؔ

آدم کا جسم جب کہ عناصر سے مِل بنا
کچھ آگ بچ رہی تھی سو عاشق کا دل بنا

سرگرمِ نالہ ان دنوں میں بھی ہوں عندلیب
مت آشیاں چمن میں مرے متصل بنا

جب تیشہ کوہکن نے لیا ہاتھ، تب یہ عشق
بولا کہ اپنی چھاتی پہ دھرنے کو سِل بنا

جس تیرگی سے روز ہے عشاق کا سیاہ
شاید اُسی سے چہرۂ خوباں پہ تِل بنا

لب زندگی میں کب ملے اُس لب سے اے کلال
ساغر ہماری خاک کو مَتھ کر کے گِل بنا

اپنا ہنر دکھا دیں گے ہم تجھ کو شیشہ گر
ٹوٹا ہوا کسی کا اگر ہم سے دل بنا

سن سن کے عرضِ حال مرا یار نے کہا
سوداؔ نہ باتیں بیٹھ کے یاں متصل بنا

Mohammed Rafi Sauda

When from the elements the human frame was made,
From the little fire that was left, the lover's heart was raised.
Build not your nest beside me, O, thou nightingale,
Wails loud and long nowadays I raise.
When Kohkan lifted the pickaxe, love thus exclaimed:
"Let a heavy stone on your breast be laid."
The darkness that had caused the lover's sable day,
Mayhap, has also fed the mole on the beauty's face.
My lips couldn't close with hers all through my life,
Till out of my kneaded clay the goblet took its shape.
We, too, O, glazier, our might shall display,
If some broken heart we could mend some day.
Fed up with my tale of woe, my friend cut me short:
"Spin no yarns before me, Sauda, finish off your tale."

Aadam ka jism jab ke anaasir se mil bana,
Kuchh aag bach rahi thi, so aashiq ka dil bana.
Sar garam-e-nala in dinon main bhi hoon, andleeb,
Mat aashian chaman mein mere mutsil bana.
Jab teesha Kohkan ne liya haath, tab yeh ishq,
Bola ke apni chhaati pe dharne ko sil bana.
Jis teergi se roz hai ushaaq ka seaah,
Shaaid usi se chehre-e-khubaan pe til bana.
Lab zindagi mein kab mile us lab se, ai kalaal,
Saaghar hamaari khaak ko math karke gil bana.
Apna hunar dikha denge hum tujhko sheesha gar,
Toota hua kisi ka agar hum se dil bana.
Sun sun ke arz-e-haal mera yaar ne kaha,
Sauda na baaten baith ke yaan mutsil bana.

سودا

عاشق کی بھی کٹتی ہیں کیا خوب طرح راتیں
دو چار گھڑی رونا، دو چار گھڑی باتیں

مرتا ہوں میں اس دکھ سے یاد آتی ہیں وہ باتیں
کیا دن وہ مبارک تھے کیا خوب تھیں وہ راتیں

اوروں سے چھٹے دلبر دلدار ہووے میرا
برحق ہیں اگر پیرو کچھ تم میں کراماتیں

کل لڑ گئیں کوچے میں آنکھوں سے مری انکھیاں
کچھ روز ہی آپس میں دو دو ہوئیں سمگھاتیں

اس عشق کے کوچے میں زاہد تو سنبھل چلنا
کچھ پیش نہ جاویں گی یاں تیری مناجاتیں

سودا کو اگر پوچھو احوال ہے یہ اس کا
دو چار گھڑی رونا، دو چار گھڑی باتیں

Mohammed Rafi Sauda

The lover spends his nights in a manner so unique,
A while or two he talks, a while or two he weeps.
Remembering things bygone nostalgic ache evokes,
Delicious were those days, those nights richly sweet!
O Divines, if you can perform miraculous feats,
Save him from the rival's clutches, let him fall for me.
Yesterday in the lane of love our eyes met by chance,
And then ensued some thrusts and passes, rather strong and deep.

In the lane of love, O priest, tread with utmost care,
Bank not on your paens and prayers, nothing would they yield.

How does Sauda fare? Do you want to know?
A while or two he talks, a while or two he weeps.

Aashiq ki bhi kat-tin hain kya khub tarah raaten,
Do chaar ghari rona, do chaar ghari baaten.
Marta hoon main is dukh se, yaad aati hain woh baaten,
Kya din woh mubaarik the, kya khub thin woh raaten!
Auron se chhute dilbar, dildaar hove mera,
Bar haq hain agar peero, kuchh tum mein karaamaaten.
Kal lar gaein kuche mein aankhon se meri ankhian,
Kuchh zor hi aapis mein do do hui samghaaten.
Is ishq ke kuche mein zaahid tu sambhal chalna,
Kuchh pesh na jawengi yaan teri manajaaten.
Sauda ko agar puchho ahwaal hai yeh uska,
Do chaar ghari rona, do chaar ghari baaten.

سودا

دلدار اسکو خواہ دل آزار، کچھ کہو
سنتا نہیں کسی کی مرا یار، کچھ کہو
غمزہ، ادا، نگاہ، تبسم ہے دل کا مول
تم بھی اگر ہو اس کے خریدار کچھ کہو
شیریں نے کوہکن سے منگائی تھی جوئے شیر
گر امتحاں ہے اس سے بھی دشوار کچھ کہو
ہر آن آ مجھی کو ستاتے ہو ناصحو
سمجھا کے تم اسے بھی تو یک بار کچھ کہو
اے ساکنانِ کنج قفس! صبح کو صبا
سنتے ہیں جائیگی سوئے گلزار، کچھ کہو
عالم کی گفتگو سے تو آتی ہے بوئے خوں
بندہ ہے یک نگہ کا گنہگار، کچھ کہو

Mohammed Rafi Sauda

Sweetheart, or a teaser of heart, call him what you will,
My love neither hears nor heeds, tell him what you will.
Glances, graces, guiles and smiles - this is the price of heart,
If you too intend to buy, bid, what you will.
Shirin had asked Kohkan to dig out the milk-canal,
If you propose a harder task, speak out your will.
Why pester me alone, ye counsellors wise,
Expostulate with him as well, try if ye will.
O, inmates of the cage, the morning breeze, we learn,
Would blow towards the garden, convey, what you will.
I can smell the scent of blood in what they think and talk,
I've stolen but a glance, say what you will.

Dildaar usko khwah dil aazaar, kuchh kaho,
Sunta nahin kisi ki mera yaar, kuchh kaho.
Ghamza, ada, nigah, tabassum hai dil ka mol,
Tum bhi agar ho iske kharidaar kuchh kaho.
Shirin ne Kohkan se mangaai thi joo-e-shir,
Gar imtehaan hai is se bhi dushwaar kuchh kaho.
Har aan aa mujhi ko sataate ho naaseho,
Samjha ke tum use bhi tau yak baar kuchh kaho.
Ai saaknaan-e-kunj-e-qafas, subah ko sabaa,
Sunte hain jaaegi soo-e-gulzaar, kuchh kaho.
Aalam ki guftgoo se tau aati hai boo-e-khoon,
Banda hai yak nigah ka gunahgaar, kuchh kaho.

سوداؔ

گُل پھینکے ہیں اوروں کی طرف بلکہ ثمر بھی
اے خانہ براندازِ چمن کچھ تو اِدھر بھی

کیا ضِد ہے خدا جانے مرے ساتھ وگرنہ
کافی ہے تسلّی کو مری ایک نظر بھی

اے ابر قسم ہے تجھے رونے کی ہمارے
تجھ چشم سے ٹپکا ہے کبھو لختِ جگر بھی

اے نالہ صد افسوس جواں مرنے پہ تیرے
پایا نہ تنک دیکھنے میں روئے اثر بھی

کِس ہستئِ موہوم پہ نازاں ہے تو اے یار
کچھ اپنے شب و روز کی ہے تجھ کو خبر بھی

تنہا ترے ماتم میں نہیں شام سیہ پوش
رہتا ہے سدا چاک گریبانِ سحر بھی

سوداؔ تری فریاد سے آنکھوں میں کٹی رات
آئی ہے سحر ہونے کو ٹک تو کہیں مر بھی

Mohammed Rafi Sauda

You have showered flowers on others, even fruits, I see,
O, guardian of the garden, spare something for me.
God knows why with me so adamant is he,
Otherwise one kindly glance would do to gladden me.
Swear by my tears, O cloud, did you ever shed
A broken bit of heart, when you chanced to weep?
Fie on thee, emasculate heart, what a poor show!
Ineffectual we found all your wailing spree.
How can we take pride in this shadowy life?
Ere even we come to know, our days recede.
It's not the eve alone that mourns in black for thee,
Even the white-breasted morn wears a tattered sheet.
Sauda, your night-long wail did not let us sleep,
Now that night is nearly done, get gone and sleep.

Gul phainke hain auron ki taraf balke samar bhi,
Ai khana bar andaaz-e-chaman, kuchh tau idhar bhi.
Kya zid hai Khuda jaane mere saath wagarna,
Kaafi hai tasalli ko miri ek nazar bhi.
Ai abar qasam hai tujhe rone ki hamaare,
Tujh chashm se tapka hai kabhu lakht-e-jigar bhi?
Ai naala, sad afsos jawaan mardi pe tere,
Paaya na tanik dekhne mein roo-e-asar bhi.
Kis hasti-e-mauhoom pe naazaan hai tu ai yaar,
Kuchh apne shab-o-roz ki hai tujh ko khabar bhi.
Tanha tere maatam mein nahin shaam seaah posh,
Rahta hai sada chaak-grebaan sahar bhi.
Sauda, teri faryaad se aankhon mein kati raat,
Aai hai sahar hone ko tuk tu kahin mar bhi.

سوداؔ

جب نظر اس کی آن پڑتی ہے
زندگی تب دھیان پڑتی ہے
جھیل لیتے ہیں عاشق، اے فرہاد
جس کے سر جیسی آن پڑتی ہے
بات اس دل کے درد کی یارو
گفتگو میں ندان پڑتی ہے
ایک کے منھ سے جس گھڑی نکلی
پھر تو سو کی زبان پڑتی ہے
لیکن اتنا کوئی کہے مجھ سے
کبھو اس کے بھی کان پڑتی ہے
منزلت شعر کی ترے سوداؔ
یوں بہ وہم و گمان پڑتی ہے
نہیں عیسیٰ تو، پر سخن سے ترے
تنِ بے جاں میں جان پڑتی ہے

Mohammed Rafi Sauda

When on me he turns his gaze,
Listless life uplifts its face;
O, Farhad, the lovers endure
Whatsoever their fate entails.
To talk about this aching heart,
Is not considered in good taste;
Let it but escape your lips,
The word spreads across space;
But tell me, pray, if my word
My love's ear doth ever invade.
Dubious seem, and hollow, Sauda,
Your poetic worth and state;
You are no Christ, yet your verse
The dead can resuscitate.

Jab nazar uski aan parti hai,
Zindagi tab dhiaun parti hai.
Jhel lete hain aashiq, ai Farhad,
Jiske sar jaisi aan parti hai.
Baat is dil ke dard ki, yaaro,
Gufatgoo mein nidaan parti hai.
Ek ke munh se jis ghari nikli
Phir tau sau ki zabaan parti hai,
Lekin itna koi kahe mujh se
Kabhu us ke bhi kaan parti hai.
Manzalat sher ki tire, Sauda,
Yun bawaham-o-gumaan parti hai,
Nahin Isaah tu, par sukhan se tire,
Tan-e-be jan mein jaan parti hai.

سوداؔ

بدلا تیرے ستم کا کوئی تجھ سے کیا کرے
اپنا ہی تو فریفتہ ہووے خدا کرے

قاتل ہماری نعش کو تشہیر ہے ضرور
آئندہ تا کوئی نہ کسی سے وفا کرے

فکرِ معاش، عشقِ بتاں، یادِ رفتگاں
دو دن کی زندگی میں اب کوئی کیا کیا کیا کرے

عالم کے بیچ پھر نہ رہے رسمِ عاشقی
گر نیم لب کوئی ترے شکوے سے وا کرے

گر ہو شراب و خلوت و محبوب خوب رو
زاہد قسم ہے تجھ کو جو تو ہو تو کیا کرے؟

خاکسترِ پتنگ و مشہد مرے کی خاک
شام و شفق عجب ہو جو مل کر اڑا کرے

اے وائے بر اسیر کہ پر توڑ کر جسے
صیاد فصلِ گل میں چمن سے رہا کرے

Mohammed Rafi Sauda

How should one avenge on you for your tyrannous ways?
O, I wish you fall in love with your own face.
My corpse needs must be publicly displayed
To scare away the lovers from pledging love and faith.
Concerns of life, claims of love, remembering those bygone,
How many things can one do in a life so curtailed?
Creed of love will get dissolved if someone some day,
Even with suppressed lips against his love inveighs.
If wine, seclusion, and a darling cute together lie in wait,
Confess, O, priest, what would you do if you were in my place!
It will be a sight to see if the ashes of my grave,
Mingled with the dust of moth, across the horizon rage.
How accursed the caged bird whom in spring,
The hunter sets at large, with wings clipped away.

Badla tere sitam ka koi tujh se kya kare,
Apna hi tu farefta hove, Khuda kare.
Qaatil hamaari naash ko tash-hir hai zarur,
Aainda ta koi na kisi se wafa kare.
Fikr-e-maash, ishq-e-butaan, yaad-e-raftgaan,
Do din ki zindagi mein ab koi kya kya kiya kare ?
Aalam ke beech phir na rahe rasm-e-aashqi,
Gar neem lab koi tere shikwe se waa kare.
Gar ho sharaab-o-khilwat-o-mahboob-e-khub roo,
Zaahid qasam hai tujh ko jo tu ho tau kya kare ?
Khaakastr-o-patang-o-mashahd meri ki khaak,
Sham-o-shafaq ajab ho jo mil kar ura kare.
Ai waae bar aseer, ke par tor kar jise
Sayyaad fasl-e-gul mein chaman se riha kare.

سوداؔ

جب یار نے اٹھا کر زلفوں کے بال باندھے
تب میں نے اپنے دل میں لاکھوں خیال باندھے

دو دن میں ہم تو ریجھے، اے وائے حال ان کا
گذرے ہیں جن کے دل کو یاں ماہ و سال باندھے

تارِ نگہ میں اس کے کیونکر پھنسے نہ یہ دل
آنکھوں نے جس کی لاکھوں وحشی غزال باندھے

بوسے کی ہے تو خواہش پر کہیے کیوں کے اس سے
جس کے مزاجِ لب پر حرفِ سوال باندھے

مارو گے کس کو جی سے کس پر کمر کسی ہے
پھرتے ہو کیوں پیارے تلوار ڈھال باندھے

دو چار شعر آگے اس کے پڑھے تو بولا
مضموں یہ تو نے اپنے کیا حسبِ حال باندھے

سوداؔ جو ان نے باندھا زلفوں میں دل سزا ہے
شعروں میں، اس کے تو نے کیوں خط و خال باندھے

Mohammed Rafi Sauda

When my love gathered her tresses and tied them into a knot,
I too gathered in my heart many a wishful thought.
We got satiated in a mere day or so, what of those
Who have for years lain embroiled in these locks?
How can my heart escape the snares of those eyes
Which have held in thrall many a maddened heart?
I do crave a kiss, but how to voice my wish?
My petition must await the pleasure of her heart.
Whom art thou out to kill? What these girded loins portend?
Armed with shield and sword, whither art thou marching fast?
As I read out my verse, thus remarked my friend:
How relevant to your case is your theme and thought!
Sauda, she has rightly caught your heart in her locks,
Haven't you, in your verse, her lineaments inwrought?

Jab yaar ne utha kar zulfon ke baal baandhe
Tab main ne apne dil mein laakhon khyal bandhe.
Do din mein hum tau reejhe, ai waae haal unka,
Guzre hain jin ke dil ko yaan maah-o-saal bandhe.
Taar-e-nigah mein uske kyonkar phanse na yeh dil
Aankhon ne jiski laakhon wahshi ghazaal bandhe.
Bose ki hai tau khwahish par kaheye kyonke us se,
Jis ke mizaaj-e-lab par haraf-e-sawaal bandhe.
Maaroge kis ko ji se, kis par kamar kasi hai,
Phirte ho kyon pearey, talwaar dhaal baandhe?
Do chaar sher aage uske parhe tau bola,
Mazmun yeh tu ne apne kya hasb-e-haal baandhe.
Sauda, jo un ne baandha zulfon mein dil, saza hai,
Sheron mein, uske tu ne kyon khat-o-khaal baandhe?

سوداؔ

اب کے بھی دن بہار کے یوں ہی چلے گئے
پھر پھر گل آچکے، پہ سجن تم بھلے گئے

پوچھے ہے پھول پھل کی خبر اب تو عندلیب!
ٹوٹے، جھڑے، خزاں ہوئے، پھولے پھلے گئے

دل خواہ کب کسی کو زمانے نے کچھ دیا
جن کو دیا کچھ، اس میں سے وے کچھ نہ لے گئے

اے شمع! دل گداز کسی کا نہ ہو، کہ شب
پروانہ داغ مجھ سے ہوا، ہم جلے گئے

سوداؔ کوئی بھی دے وے ہے ایسا دل ان کے ہاتھ؟
لاکھوں ہی دل قدم تلے جن کے ملے گئے

Mohammed Rafi Sauda

This time again, spring has gone in vain,
Flower after flower sprang, you, my love, were missed amain.
Would you know, O, nightingale, the fate of flowers and fruits?
They fade, fall, run to seed, bloom, wax, and wane.
Who has ever in this world, all he wished, attained?
Nor did he take along, if aught was ever gained.
May none of us, O taper, be given a sensitive heart!
The moth burned for you at night, I was all aflame.
Who will entrust his heart to such a heartless being?
Who has trampled countless hearts, jilted many a swain.

Ab ke bhi din bahaar ke yunhi chale gaye,
Phir, phir gul aa chuke, pe sajan tum bhale gaye.
Puchhe hai phool phal ki khabar ab tu andleeb,
Tute, jhare, khizaan hue, phule, phale, gaye.
Dil khwah kab kisi ko zamaane ne kuchh diya,
Jin ko diya kuchh, is mein se woh kuchh na le gaye.
Ai shama! dil gudaaz kisi ka na ho, ke shab,
Parwaana dagh tujh se hua, hum jale gaye.
Sauda, koi bhi dewe hai aisa dil un ke haath?
Laakhon hi dil qadam tale jin ke male gaye.

Insha Allah Khan Insha
(1752-1818)

INSHA ALLAH KHAN INSHA
(1752 - 1818)

Insha was born and brought up at Murshidabad. His father, Masha Allah Khan, was a famous hakim and aristocrat, enjoying the patronage of Nawab Siraj-ul-Daula, whose munificence made him the owner of 18 elephants. Masha Allah took deep interest in the education and upbringing of his son. Along with his father, Insha moved from Murshidabad to Delhi in the days of Shah Alam Sani, and later to Lucknow, and at both places the young poet received a phenomenal popularity and royal patronage. Insha was a man of versatile gifts. Apart from writing *ghazals* in Urdu and Persian, Insha also wrote *Dewan-e-Rekhti* (poems written from the woman's point of view), *qasidas, masnavis,* puzzles and satires. Besides being a poet, he was a linguist, conversant with many Indian languages and dialects. He wrote a story in Hindi entitled: *Rani Ketki ki Kahani,* and also the first book on the rules of Urdu language, *Darya-e-Litafat.* Moreover, he was a master of wit and humour and a powerful satirist. His literary skirmishes with Azim Beg in Delhi, and with Mushafi in Lucknow are memorable for their hilarious sarcasm. Imagine the plight of Mushafi when, out of mischievous fun, Insha took out a mock wedding procession through the streets of Lucknow, showing two dolls in a fighting posture, representing Mushafi and Mushafin. Attracted by his brilliant wit and charming conversation, Nawab Saadat Ali Khan of Lucknow grew specially attached to Insha, on whom he generously showered his largesse. But royal favours are fickle and short-lived. When the Nawab got angry with Insha for certain reasons, Insha was divested of all honours and dismissed from the court. Close upon the heels of this disgrace, came the shock of the death of the poet's son, Taala Khan. No wonder, Insha developed symptoms of insanity, and died a heartbroken man in 1818. His most famous *ghazal, Kamar baandhe hue chalne ko yaan sub yaar baithe hain,* is deeply tinged with the gloom of his last days.

But melancholia is not a characteristic strain of Insha's poetry. Unlike Mir or Ghalib, Insha is a poet of light-hearted romancing, not of deep, passionate love, which often entails frustration and despair. He is a man of verve and vitality, which he has also injected into his poetry.

انشاء اللہ خاں انشاءؔ

جگر کی آگ بجھے جلد جس میں وہ شے لا
لگا کے برف میں ساقی صراحیِ مے لا

قدم کو ہاتھ لگاتا ہوں، اٹھ کہیں گھر چل
خدا کے واسطے اتنا تو پاؤں مت پھیلا

نکل کے وادیِ وحشت سے دیکھ اے مجنوں
کہ زور دھن میں اب آتا ہے ناقۂ لیلا

گرا جو ہاتھ سے فرہاد کے کہیں تیشہ
درونِ کوہ سے نکلی صدائے واویلا

نزاکت اس کے مکھڑے کی دیکھیو انشاؔ
نسیمِ صبح جو چھو جائے رنگ ہو میلا

Insha Allah Khan Insha

Saqi, bring the thing that may, at once quench the fire of heart,
Bring the flask of wine, kept in a frozen cask.

I touch your feet, bestir yourself, 'tis time to go home,
For God's sake, do not, pray, stretch your feet so far.

Come out of the wilds of frenzy, Majnun, look around,
Driven by the force of love, comes your Laila, riding fast.

When somewhere in the wilds Farhad's pickaxe did fall,
The rocks raised a hue and cry, that was heard afar.

Mark, Insha, the exquisite grace of her lovely face!
Even a whiff of morning breeze, its gloss would mar.

Jigar ki aag bujhe jald jismen woh shai laa,
Laga ke barf mein, saqi, surahi-e-mai laa.

Qadam ko haath lagaata hun, uth kahin, ghar chal,
Khuda ke waste, itne tau paaon mat phaila.

Nikal ke wadi-e-wahshat se dekh, ai Majnun,
Ke zor dhun mein ab aata hai naaqa-e-Laila.

Gira jo haath se Farhad ke kahin teesha,
Daroon-e-koh se nikli sada-e-wavela.

Nazakat uske mukhre ki dekhio, Insha,
Naseem-e-subah jo chhoo jaae, rang ho maila.

انشاء

مجھے کیوں نہ آوے ساقی نظر آفتاب الٹا
کہ پڑا ہے آج خُم میں قدحِ شراب الٹا

عجب الٹے ملک کے ہیں اجی آپ بھی کہ تم سے
کبھی بات کی جو سیدھی تو ملا جواب الٹا

چلے تھے حرم کو، رہ میں ہوئے اک صنم کے عاشق
نہ ہوا ثواب حاصل، یہ لیا عذاب الٹا

یہ شب گزشتہ دیکھا، وہ خفا سے کچھ ہیں گویا
کہیں حق کرے کہ ہووے یہ ہمارا خواب الٹا

ابھی جھڑی لگا دے بارش، کوئی مست بھر کے نعرہ
جو زمین پہ پھینک مارے قدحِ شراب الٹا

ہوئے وعدے پر جو جھوٹے تو نہیں ملاتے تیور
اے لو اور بھی تماشہ یہ سنو حجاب الٹا

غزل اور قافیوں میں نہ کہے سو کیوں کر انشا
کہ ہوا نے خود بخود آ، ورق کتاب الٹا

Insha Allah Khan Insha

Why shouldn't the sun appear inverted now to me,
The cup lies inverted in the wine-jar, I see.

You must have come, it seems, from the antipodes,
Even my straight talk a crooked response receives.

I had set out for the mosque, but got enticed en route,
Instead of winning grace divine a sea of troubles me besieged.

Yesternight in my dream I found him somewhat cross,
I wish to God that my dream the contrary thing reveals.

It will unleash a flood of rain, if some reveller drunk,
Shouts and flings his brimming cup, upside down beneath.

Embarrassed by his word belied, he shrinks from my side,
Instead of showing remorse, lo, he veils his face from me.

Why shouldn't Insha write a ghazal in a different rhyme,
The breeze has of itself turned o'er this leaf.

Mujhe kyon na aawe saqi nazar aaftaab ulta,
Ke para hai aaj khum mein qadah-e-sharab ulta.

Ajab ulte mulk ke hain aji aap bhi ke tum se,
Kabhi baat ki jo seedhi tau mila jawab ulta.

Chale the haram ko, rah mein hue ik sanam ke aashiq,
Na hua sawab haasil, yeh liya azaab ulta.

Yeh shab guzashta dekha, woh khafa se kuchh hain, goya,
Kahin haq kare ke howe yeh hamara khwab ulta.

Abhi jhari laga de baarish, koi mast bhar ke naara,
Jo zamin pe phaink maare qadah-e-sharab ulta.

Hue waada par jo jhute tau nahin milate tewar,
Ai lo, aur bhi tamasha, yeh suno hijab ulta.

Ghazal aur qaafion mein na kahe so kyonkar, Insha,
Ke hawa ne khud bakhud aa, warq-e-kitab ulta.

انشاء

آدمی چیز ہے کیا ان نے نہ چھوڑے پتھر
پھوٹ نکلے جس جلوے نے سب طور کے روڑے پتھر

چادرِ آب کا گرنا تو پہاڑوں پر دیکھ
واہ کیا حکم ہے یوں جس نے نچوڑے پتھر

کر نظر لعل و زمرّد کی طرف، پہنے ہیں
سُرخ اور سبز عجب رنگ کے جوڑے پتھر

آتشِ عشقِ الٰہی سے ہے خالی کب شے
یہ شرر رکھتے ہیں سب، سینے میں روڑے پتھر

آبلے ہیں دلِ دریا کے حباب ایسے ہی
جس طرح کوہ کی چھاتی پہ دوڑیں پتھر

کہہ غزل اور بدل قافیہ، انشا کہ شرار
نکل آئے ہیں بہت تو نے جو توڑے پتھر

Insha Allah Khan Insha

Man is a trivial thing, He hasn't spared the stones,
His wondrous glimpse had set ablaze Sinai's rocky dome.
Watch the sheets of water rolling down the hills,
Ah! His supernal might can squeeze even the stones.
Mark the rubies and emeralds studded in the rocks,
In robes of red and green the quarries lie adorned.
What is it that doesn't throb with the fire divine,
Every stone at its heart a spark of fire doth own.
The bubbles on the river's breast are blisters of its heart,
Like the stones and pebbles, on the mounts bestrewn.
Insha, write another *ghazal,* pray change the rhyme,
The air is hot with the sparks, since you broke the stones.

Aadmi cheez hai kya un ne na chhore pathhar,
Phoonke jis jalwe ne sub Tur ke rore, pathhar.
Chaadar-e-aab ka girna tu pahaaron par dekh,
Waah, kya hukam hai yun jis ne nichore pathhar.
Kar nazar laal-o-zamurrad ki taraf, pahne hain,
Surkh aur sabaz ajab rang ke jore pathhar.
Aatish-e-ishq-e-ilahi se hai khali kya shai,
Yeh sharar rakhte hain sub seene mein rore pathhar.
Aable hain dil-e-darya ke habab aise hi,
Jis tarah koh ki chhati pe dauren pathhar.
Kah ghazal aur badal qafia, Insha, ke sharaar,
Nikal aae hain bahut tu ne jo tore pathhar.

انشاؔ

کہتے ہو تم تو دم لے، پرے ہٹ، ابھی نہیں
اور آنہ جاوے کوئی، مرے جی میں جی نہیں

"ہاں ہاں" ہے سب سے اور ہمیں سے "نہیں نہیں" سو کیوں
کیوں کر "نہیں نہیں نہیں" کیوں ایسے جی نہیں

گر یار مئے پلاوے تو کیوں کر نہ پیجیے
زاہد نہیں، میں شیخ نہیں، کچھ ولی نہیں

خلوت میں یوں جو چاہئے کہہ لیجئے مجھے
لوگوں میں لیکن آپ کے میرے ہنسی نہیں

کیوں پاس میرے آکے نہیں بیٹھتے اگر
غیروں کے ساتھ رات کو مے تم نے پی نہیں

میں نے کہا کہ آئیے گا میرے پاس کب
بولے نہیں نہیں، ہرگز کبھی نہیں

ذرّہ سی بات پر رہے انشاؔ سے یوں خفا
"کیا جانے کیا بلا ہے؟ تو کچھ آدمی نہیں"

Insha Allah Khan Insha

"Hold on, keep off, not yet," this is all you say,
"Lest someone drops in, my heart is pounding away."
"Yes, yes," to everyone, why "nay" to me?
Why can't you stop this "nay", so I have my way?
If my love proffers wine, how can I say, "no"?
I'm not a priest or prophet, nor a holy sage.
Treat me the way you like, when we are alone,
But in public no pranks on me should you play.
Why dost thou avoid me, if yesternight,
You didn't join the drinking bout at the rival's place?
When I ask, when should I expect you at my place,
"No, no, never at all," is all he has to say.
Taking offence to a trivial thing you snubbed Insha in vain,
"What are you, a jinn or demon, not a man, anyway."

Kahte ho tum, tu dam le, pare hat, abhi nahin,
Aur aa na jaawe koi, mire ji mein ji nahin.
"Haan, "haan", hai sub se, aur hameen se "nahin", so kyon?
Kyonkar "nahin, nahin, nahin", kyon aise ji nahin.
Gar yaar mai pilaawe tau kyonkar na peejeye,
Zaahid nahin, main sheikh nahin, kuchh wali nahin.
Khilwat mein yun jo chaaheye kah leejeye mujhe,
Logon mein lekin aap ke mere hansi nahin.
Kyon pass mere aa ke nahin baithte agar,
Ghairon ke saath raat ko mai tum ne pee nahin.
Main ne kaha ke aaeye ga mere paas kab,
Bole nahin, nahin, nahin, hargiz kabhi nahin.
Zara si baat par hai Insha se yun khafa :
"Kya jaaneye kya bala hai tu, kuchh aadmi nahin."

انشاء

کمر باندھے ہوئے چلنے کو یاں سب یار بیٹھے ہیں
بہت آگے گئے باقی جو ہیں تیار بیٹھے ہیں

نہ چھیڑ اے نکہتِ بادِ بہاری راہ لگ اپنی
تجھے اٹھکیلیاں سوجھی ہیں ہم بےزار بیٹھے ہیں

تصور عرش پر ہے اور سر ہے پائے ساقی پر
غرض کچھ اور دھن میں اس گھڑی میخوار بیٹھے ہیں

بسانِ نقش پائے رہرواں کوئے تمنا میں
نہیں اٹھنے کی طاقت کیا کریں لاچار بیٹھے ہیں

یہ اپنی چال ہے افتادگی سے اب کہ پہروں تک
نظر آیا جہاں پر سایۂ دیوار بیٹھے ہیں

کہاں صبر و تحمل، آہ! ننگ و نام کیا شے ہے
یہاں رو پیٹ کر ان سب کو ہم یکبار بیٹھے ہیں

بھلا گردش فلک کی چین دیتی ہے کسے انشا
غنیمت ہے کہ ہم صورت یہاں دو چار بیٹھے ہیں

Insha Allah Khan Insha

All of us with loins girt are waiting for the bark,
A good many have gone before, the rest will soon embark.
Vex us not, O fragrant breeze, go, mind your task,
You are in a mood to tickle, we feel distraught.
Their heads rest at the Saqi's feet, their fancy skyward soars,
The drinkers are at present in a different mood absorbed.
Fagged out, we sink and squat, too weak to stand,
Stuck in the street of desire, like footprints on the path.
Such is our crippled state, by weariness waylaid,
For hours on end listless we lie, wherever a shade doth fall.
Who cares for poise and patience, what is name or fame?
We have mourned over this stuff, buried it once for all.
The whirlwheel of Time, Insha, spares not a soul,
God be thanked, some friends are left to sit together and talk.

Kamar baandhe hue chalne ko yaan sub yaar baithe hain,
Bahut aage gaye, baqi jo hain tayyaar baithe hain.
Na chher, ai, nikhat-e-baad-e-bahari raah lag apni,
Tujhe athkelian sujhi hain, hum bezaar baithe hain.
Tasawwur arsh par hai, aur sar hai paae saqi par,
Garz kuchh aur dhun mein is ghari maikhwaar baithe hain.
Basaan-e-naqsh-e-paae rahrawan koo-e-tamanna mein,
Nahin uthne ki taqat, kya karen, lachaar baithe hain.
Yeh apni chaal hai uftaadgi se ab ke pahron tak,
Nazar aaya jahan par saaya-e-deewar baithe hain.
Kahan sabar-o-tahammal, ah! nang-o-naam kya shai hai,
Yahan ro peet kar in sub ko hum yak baar baithe hain.
Bhala gardish falak ki chain deti hai kise, Insha,
Ghanimat hai ke hum surat yahan do chaar baithe hain.

انشاؔ

لہرا دیا صبا نے جو کل سبزہ زار کو
وو ہیں گھٹا نے گھیر لیا چشمہ سار کو

جوش و خروشِ رعد نے یہ دھوم دھام کی
ہرگز کوئی کسی کی نہ پہنچا پکار کو

کچھ لکّہ ہا ابرِ سفید و سیاہ پھر
مستانہ جھوم جھوم چلے کوہسار کو

شادابیِ ہوا نے یہ چاہا کہ کیجیے
محبوس، کوچۂ رگِ گل میں بہار کو

اڑنے لگیں ملار کی تانیں فلک تلک
سازندے چھیڑنے لگے بین و ستار کو

ہم مشرب اپنے چند جواں تھے، سو نہر پر
تشریف لے گئے بطِ مے کے شکار کو

بولی یہ عندلیب کہ باقی نہ چھوڑیو
ایسے سمے میں خواہشِ بوس و کنار کو

Insha Allah Khan Insha

When yesterday the meadows were bestirred by the breeze,
Then were the cataracts by dark clouds besieged.
The fire and flash of thunder raised such a din,
None could hear or heed what others did beseech.
Flocks of clouds, black and white, emerged in the sky,
Marching like a drunken throng to the mountain peak.
The freshening wind seemed intent on capturing the spring,
And sealing it in floral veins, slowly to release.
Songs of rains filled the air and shot up to the sky,
With commingled strains of lute and flute the musicians charmed and pleased.
I and my fellow revellers made for the stream
To chase the flask with clanking cups, squatting on the beach.
The nightingale counsel gave: 'tis the fittest time
To indulge romantic longings, to hold amorous meets.

Lahra diya saba ne jo kal sabza zaar ko,
Wohin ghata ne gher liya chashma saar ko.
Josh-o-kharosh-e-raad ne yeh dhoom dhaam ki,
Hargiz koi kisi ki na pauhncha pukar ko.
Kuchh lukkahaae abar-e-safed-o-seaah phir,
Mastana jhoom jhoom chale kohsaar ko.
Shaadaabi-e-hawa ne yeh chaaha ke kijeye,
Mahboos, kucha-e-rag-e-gul mein bahar ko.
Urne lagin malhar ki taanen falak talak,
Saazinde chherne lage been-o-sitar ko.
Hum mashrab apne chand jawan the so nahar par,
Tashrif le gaye bat-e-mai ke shikar ko;
Boli yeh andleeb ke baaqi na chhorio
Aise same mein khwahish-e-bos-o-kinaar ko.

انشاء

شب خانۂ رقیب میں تا صبح سو چکے
اب فائدہ مکرنے سے؟ ہم دیکھ تو چکے

کہتے ہو جنسِ دل کو ہماری بغل میں دیکھ
بولو نہ بیچتے ہو تو قیمت کہو، ہا چکے

قیمت ہے ایک بوسہ درمِ نقد ایسے جی
تم چاہتے ہو مفت میں کچھ لو نہ دو، چکے

رونا ہی تھا یہ موجبِ افشائے رازِ عشق
یہ مردمانِ چشم مجھے تو ڈبو چکے

پھر جان بوجھ کہتے ہو جاتا ہوں جائیے
تشریف لے سدھاریئے ہم دل کو رو چکے

میں جانتا ہوں آپ کو، ہرگز نہ مول لیں
قیمت جو دل کی ایک ہی بوسہ پہ گو چکے

خوابِ عدم سے شورِ جنوں نے جگادیا
انشاؔ بس اور نیند کہاں، خوب سو چکے

Insha Allah Khan Insha

You were at the rival's place right from night till day,
We have seen for ourselves, deny though you may.
Seeing the heart under my arm, this is what you say:
"Will you sell it? Name the price, so that I may pay."
A single kiss is its price, cash and carry away,
But you want to grab it without having to pay.
The pupils of my eyes have brought me disgrace,
My tears were the culprits that gave my heart away.
Though you know everything, yet you say: "I go,"
I've already rued my heart, you may go your way.
I know you will not buy it, even if my heart,
Just for a single kiss, I should throw away.
The frenzied din shocked me out of eternal sleep,
"Wake up, Insha, sleep no more, enough for the day."

Shab khana-e-raqeeb mein ta subah so chuke,
Ab faida mukarne se, hum dekh tau chuke.
Kahte ho jins-e-dil ko hamari baghal mein dekh,
"Bolo na, bechte ho tau qeemat kaho, chuke."
Qeemat hai ek bosa dam-e-naqd aise ji,
Tum chaahte ho muft mein kuchh lo na do, chuke.
Rona hi tha yeh moojab-e-afsha-e-raz-e-ishq,
Yeh mardumaan-e-chashm mujhe tau dabo chuke.
Phir jaan boojh kahte ho, "jaata hun" jaaeye,
Tashreef le sadhaareye, hum dil ko ro chuke.
Main jaanta hun aapko, hargiz na mol lein,
Qeemat jo dil ki ek hi bosa pe go chuke.
Khwab-e-adam se shor-e-janoon ne jaga diya,
Insha, bas aur neend kahan, khub so chuke.

Bahadur Shah Zafar
(1775-1862)

BAHADUR SHAH ZAFAR
(1775 - 1862)

Bahadur Shah Zafar was the last Moghul King of Delhi. When he ascended the throne in 1837, the Moghul empire had all but fallen, and the king's command had ceased to carry weight beyond the four walls of the Red Fort. Zafar lived a long life of 87 years, but his life was a tale of unbroken suffering and humiliation. The events took a tragic turn when in 1857 Zafar was accused of complicity in the rebellion against the British rulers, and was deported to Rangoon, where he died in 1862, a helpless prisoner of Imperial tyranny. But the loss of Zafar the King was the gain of Zafar the poet. As he had no regal functions to perform, no battles to fight, and no affairs of state to manage, Zafar sought strength and consolation in the world of art and poetry, and soon acquired proficiency not only in the field of poetry, but also in painting and calligraphy. It deserves remembering that while the age of Zafar was the time of social and political holocaust, it was also the golden age of Urdu poetry. The court of Zafar was the hub of poetic activity, adorned by a galaxy of famous poets, such as Aazurda, Shefta, Ghalib, Momin and Zauq. Getting together of such brilliant talent for participation in *mushairas* brought out the best in Urdu poetry and created an atmosphere highly favourable to the Muse. Moreover, the all-pervasive sense of defeat and distress touched the inmost chords of the poets and inspired them to convert their suffering into song. This was particularly true of Zafar, a bulk of whose poetry is built around his personal experience of loss, defeat and despair. His famous couplet: *Lagta nahin hai ji mera ujre dayaar mein, Kis ki bani hai aalam-e-na paidaar mein* (I feel ill-at-ease on this wasted heath; Who, in this ephemeral world, hath ever been at peace?) sums up the one important theme of his poetry; the theme of the callousness of life and time, of the inconstancy of friends, and of the helplessness of man. This feeling of melancholia reminds us of Mir, the master poet of pathos, but there is a difference. While Mir's suffering is the suffering of a sensitive poet who shares his lot with most of us, Zafar's poetry tells the tale of a king who has been ruthlessly denuded of his power and position, whose sons and relations were done to death before his eyes, and who was forced to live in exile far from his beloved land.

Among the other important themes of Zafar's poetry may be mentioned his impressive handling of didactic and ethical subjects, and his sensitive concern for the universal process of change and decay constantly operative in the world. This last concern, incidentally, links Zafar with the imaginative writers of Victorian England, like Tennyson, for instance, who, influenced by the Evolutionary ideas of the day, repeatedly dwell upon the phenomenon of geological change and its implications for the traditional religious faith.

There is disagreement in literary circles about the actual authorship of some of Zafar's *ghazals.* According to Mohammed Hussain Azad, the author of *Aab-e-Hyaat,* many of these poems were actually written by Zauq, who generously passed them on to his royal disciple, Zafar. Some of the modern critics, however, dispute this view. They feel that Azad's assertion is based more on his personal regard for his poetic mentor, Zauq, than on actual fact. Zafar was a poet of no mean merit. He could legitimately get his verse corrected from Zauq, but he would not attribute to himself what was actually written by others. It will be unfair, therefore, to call him a plagiarist.

بہادر شاہ ظفرؔ

نہیں عشق میں اسکا تو رنج ہمیں کہ قرار و شکیب ذرا نہ رہا
غمِ عشق تو اپنا رفیق رہا، کوئی اور بلا سے رہا نہ رہا
دیا اپنی خودی کو جو ہم نے مٹا، وہ جو پردہ سا بیچ میں تھا نہ رہا
پردے میں اب نہ وہ پردہ نشیں، کوئی دوسرا اسکے سوا نہ رہا
نہ تھی حال کی جب ہمیں اپنے خبر، رہے دیکھتے اوروں کے عیب و ہنر
پڑی اپنی برائیوں پر جو نظر تو نگاہ میں کوئی بُرا نہ رہا
ہمیں ساغر و بادہ کے دینے میں اب کرے دیر جو ساقی تو ہائے غضب
کہ یہ عہدِ نشاط یہ دورِ طرب رہے گا جہاں میں سدا نہ رہا
لگے یوں تو ہزاروں ہی تیرِ ستم، کہ تڑپتے رہے پڑے خاک پہ ہم
وہ لے ناز و کرشمہ کی تیغِ دو دُم، لگی ایسی کہ تسمہ لگا نہ رہا
کئی روز میں آج وہ ماہِ لقا ہوا میرے جو سامنے جلوہ نما
مجھے صبر و قرار ذرا نہ رہا، اسے پاسِ حجاب و حیا نہ رہا
ظفرؔ آدمی اس کو نہ جانیے گا وہ ہو کتنا ہی صاحبِ فہم و ذکا
جسے عیش میں یادِ خدا نہ رہی، جسے طیش میں خوفِ خدا نہ رہا

Bahadur Shah Zafar

I don't regret that in love, I lost my poise, my calm,
At least the grief of love was mine, who cares for other balms?
To shed the ego is to lift the blinds that blur the vision sublime,
The veiled beauty discards its veil, otherness gets disarmed.
Oblivious of our own faults, we find fault in others,
Once we see the flaws within, none else seems deformed.
If the Saqi holds his hand, how tragic it would be,
Youth and pleasure wait for none, transient is their form.
Though I bore a million darts that made me writhe in pain,
The two-edged sword of coquettish glance did me mortal harm.
After many a lonesome day, when I met my moon of life,
I couldn't retain my self-restraint, nor she her coyish form.
Call him not a man, Zafar, howsoever wise,
Who, in joy, forgets his Lord, in rage respects no qualms.

Nahin ishq mein iska tau ranj hamen ke qarar-o-shakeb zara na raha,
Gham-e-ishq tau apna rafiq raha, koi aur bala se raha, na raha.
Diya apni khudi ko jo hum ne mita, woh jo parda sa beech mein tha na raha,
Parde mein ab na woh pardah nashin, koi doosra uske siwa na raha.
Na thi haal ki jab hamen apne khabar, rahe dekhte auron ke aib-o-hunar,
Pari apni buraion par jo nazar, tau nigah mein koi bura na raha.
Hamen saagir-o-bada ke dene mein ab kare der jo saqi tau haae ghazab,
Ke yeh ahd-e-nishat, yeh daur-e-tarab, rahega jahan mein sada na raha.
Lage yun tau hazaaron hi tir-e-sitam, ke tarpte rahe pare khak pe hum,
Wale naz-o-karishma ki tegh-e-do dum, lagi aisi ke tasma laga na raha.
Kai roz mein aaj woh maah-e-laqa, hua mere jo samne jalwa numa,
Mujhe sabr-o-qarar zara na raha, use paas-e-hijab-o haya na raha.
Zafar aadmi usko na jaaneeyga, woh ho kitna hi sahib-e-fahm-o-zaka,
Jise aish mein yaad-e-Khuda na rahi, jise taish mein khauf-e-Khuda na raha.

ظفؔر

بات کرنی مجھے مشکل کبھی ایسی تو نہ تھی
جیسی اب ہے، تری محفل کبھی ایسی تو نہ تھی

لے گیا چھین کے کون آج ترا صبر و قرار
بیقراری تجھے اے دل کبھی ایسی تو نہ تھی

اس کی آنکھوں نے خدا جانے کیا کیا جادو
کہ طبیعت مری مائل کبھی ایسی تو نہ تھی

عکسِ رخسار نے کس کے ہے تجھے چمکایا
تاب تجھ میں مہِ کامل کبھی ایسی تو نہ تھی

پائے کوباں کوئی زنداں میں نیا ہے مجنوں
آتی آوازِ سلاسل کبھی ایسی تو نہ تھی

نگہِ یار کو اب کیوں ہے تغافل اے دل
وہ ترے حال سے غافل کبھی ایسی تو نہ تھی

کیا سبب تو جو بگڑتا ہے ظفؔر سے ہر بار
خُو تری حُور شمائل کبھی ایسی تو نہ تھی

Bahadur Shah Zafar

Never before was it so hard to articulate my thought,
Your court too, I can see, has now changed a lot.
Who has robbed thee, O heart, of thy inward calm,
Never wert thou as disturbed as now thou art.
God knows what strange spell those eyes did cast,
Never before did my heart feel so distraught.
Whose reflected visage has illuminated your orb,
Never before, you were, O moon, with such splendour shot.
A fresh Majnun is stamping about inside the cage,
The clinking of the chains strikes a different chord.
Why doth your love, O, heart, thus coldly glance?
Never was her gaze so indifference-fraught.
Why dost thou so oft grow cross with Zafar?
You weren't, O, fairy-face, fretful in the past.

Baat karni mujhe mushkil kabhi aisi tau na thi,
Jaisi ab hai, teri mehfil kabhi aisi tau na thi.
Le gaya chheen ke kaun aaj tera sabar-o-qarar,
Beqarari tujhe ai dil kabhi aisi tau na thi.
Uski aankhon ne khuda jaane kiya kya jaadu,
Ke tabeeat meri mayal kabhi aisi tau na thi.
Aks-e-rukhsaar ne kis ke hai tujhe chamkaya,
Taab tujh mein mah-e-kaamil kabhi aisi tau na thi.
Paae kooban koi zindaan mein naya hai Majnun,
Aai aawaaz-e-salaasal kabhi aisi tau na thi.
Nigah-a-yaar ko ab kyon hai taghaful, ai dil,
Woh tere haal se ghaafil kabhi aisi tau na thi.
Kya sabab tu jo bigarta hai Zafar se har baar,
Khu tiri hur shamayal kabhi aisi tau na thi.

ظفرؔ

کہیں میں غنچہ ہوں وا شد سے اپنے خود پریشاں ہوں
کہیں گوہر ہوں اپنی موج میں میں آپ غلطاں ہوں
کہیں میں ساغرِ گل ہوں کہیں میں شیشۂ مُل ہوں
کہیں میں شورِ قلقل ہوں کہیں میں شورِ مستاں ہوں
کہیں میں جوشِ وحشت ہوں، کہیں میں محوِ حیرت ہوں
کہیں میں آبِ رحمت ہوں، کہیں میں داغِ عصیاں ہوں
کہیں میں برقِ خرمن ہوں، کہیں میں ابرِ گلشن ہوں
کہیں میں اشکِ دامن ہوں، کہیں میں چشمِ گریاں ہوں
کہیں میں عقل آرا ہوں، کہیں مجنوں ہوں رسوا ہوں
کہیں میں پیرِ دانا ہوں، کہیں میں طفلِ ناداں ہوں
کہیں میں دستِ قاتل ہوں، کہیں میں حلقِ بسمل ہوں
کہیں زہرِ ہلاہل ہوں، کہیں میں آبِ حیواں ہوں
کہیں میں سروِ موزوں ہوں، کہیں میں بیدِ مجنوں ہوں
کہیں گل ہوں ظفرؔ میں اور کہیں خارِ بیاباں ہوں

Bahadur Shah Zafar

Somewhere I am a bud, worried about my bloom,
Somewhere a precious pearl in its waves entombed.
Somewhere I'm a floral cup, somewhere the crystal ball,
Somewhere the gurgling flask, somewhere the revellers' boom.
Somewhere I'm the frenzy wild, somewhere silence stunned,
Somewhere the kindly shower, somewhere the guilty gloom.
Somewhere I'm the lightning blast, somewhere the vernal cloud,
Somewhere the dripping tear, or the eye drowned in gloom;
Now I'm the wise sage, now a Majnun, out of grace,
Somewhere a hoary wizard, a silly child eftsoon.
Here I'm the assassin's hand, there the throat aslit,
Here the deadly poison, there ambrosial boon;
Here I'm a stately cypress, there the willow bent,
Here, Zafar, the scented rose, there the bristling broom.

Kahin main ghuncha hun washud se apne khud pareshan hun,
Kahin gohar hun apni mauj mein main aap ghaltan hun.
Kahin main saghir-e-gul hun, kahin main sheesha-e-mul hun,
Kahin main shor-e-qulqul hun, kahin main shor-e-mastan hun.
Kahin main josh-e-wahshat hun, kahin main mahw-e-hairat hun,
Kahin main aab-e-rahmat hun, kahin main dagh-e-isian hun;
Kahin main barq-e-khirman hun, kahin main abr-e-gulshan hun,
Kahin main ashk-e-daman hun, kahin main chashm-e-giryan hun.
Kahin main aql aara hun, kahin Majnun hun, ruswa hun,
Kahin main peer-e-dana hun, kahin main tifal-e-nadan hun.
Kahin main dast-e-qatil hun, kahin main halq-e-bismal hun,
Kahin zahr-e-halahal hun, kahin main aab-e-haiwan hun.
Kahin main sarv-e-mauzoon hun, kahin main baid-e-Majnun hun,
Kahin gul hun Zafar main, aur kahin khaar-e-beeaban hun.

ظفرؔ

جہاں ویرانہ ہے پہلے کبھی آبادیاں گھر تھے
شغال اب ہیں جہاں بستے کبھی بستے بشر یاں تھے

جہاں چٹیل ہے میداں اور سراسر ایک خارستاں
کبھی یاں قصر و ایواں تھے چمن تھے اور شجر یاں تھے

جہاں پھرتے بگولے ہیں اڑاتے خاک صحرا میں
کبھی اڑتی تھی دولت رقص کرتے سیم بر یاں تھے

جہاں ہیں سنگریزے، تھے یہاں یاقوت کے تودے
جہاں کنکر پڑے ہیں اب، کبھی رلتے گہر یاں تھے

جہاں سنسان اب جنگل ہے اور ہے شہرِ خموشاں
کبھی کیا کیا تھے ہنگامے یہاں اور شور و شر یاں تھے

جہاں اب خاک پر ہیں نقشِ پائے آہوئے صحرا
کبھی محوِ تماشا دیدۂ اہلِ نظر یاں تھے

ظفرؔ احوالِ عالم کا کبھی کچھ ہے کبھی کچھ ہے
کہ کیا کیا رنگ اب ہیں اور کیا کیا پیشتر یاں تھے

Bahadur Shah Zafar

There where you see the wilds, bustling towns did once abide,
Where jackals prowl and roar, men and women lived in pride.
Stately palaces, trees and gardens once marked the site,
Where barren wastes and brambly bushes now meet the eye.
Where whirlwinds reign supreme and desert sands do blow,
Gold and riches flowed unchecked, beauty did the fun provide.
Where broken bits of rock spread, rubies lay interred,
Where you see the pebbles, precious pearls were rife.
Where lonesome wilds and desolate graves make a fearsome sight,
What riotous scenes and revelry, what thrills gave delight.
Where you see the pug-prints of the desert deer,
Wise, discerning folk had once stood surprised.
The world goes on changing, Zafar, with the changing times,
What sights it then displayed, what it now provides!

Jahan weeraana hai pahle kabhi aabad yaan ghar the,
Shaghaal ab hain jahan baste, kabhi baste bashar yaan the.
Jahan chatial hai maidan aur sarasar ek khaaristan,
Kabhi yaan qasar-o-oaiwan the, chaman the aur shajar yaan the.
Jahan phirte bagoole hain, uraate khak sahra mein,
Kabhi urti thi daulat, raqas karte seembar yaan the.
Jahan hain sang reze, the yahan yaaqut ke taude,
Jahan kankar pare hain ab, kabhi rulte gohar yaan the.
Jahan sunsaan ab jungle hai aur hai shar-e-khamoshan,
Kabhi kya kya the hangaame yahan, aur shor-o-shar yaan the,
Jahan ab khak par hain naqash-e-paae-aahu-e-sahra,
Kabhi mahw-e-tamasha deeda-e-ahl-e-nazar yaan the.
Zafar ahwaal aalam ka kabhi kuchh hai, kabhi kuchh hai,
Ke kya kya rang ab hain aur kya kya peshtar yaan the.

ظفرؔ

یا مجھے افسرِ شاہانہ بنایا ہوتا
یا مِرا تاج گدایانہ بنایا ہوتا

خاکساری کے لیے گرچہ بنایا تھا مجھے
کاش خاکِ درِ جانانہ بنایا ہوتا

نشۂ عِشق کا گر ظرف دیا تھا مجھکو
عمر کا تنگ نہ پیمانہ بنایا ہوتا

دلِ صد چاک بنایا تو بلا سے لیکن
زلفِ مشکیں کا تیری شانہ بنایا ہوتا

صوفیوں کے جو نہ تھا لائقِ صحبت تو مجھے
قابلِ جلسۂ رندانہ بنایا ہوتا

تھا جلانا ہی اگر دوریٔ ساقی سے مجھے
تو چراغِ درِ مےخانہ بنایا ہوتا

روز معمورۂ دنیا میں خرابی ہے ظفرؔ
ایسی بستی کو تو ویرانہ بنایا ہوتا

Bahadur Shah Zafar

You should have invested me either with a crown,
Or wrapped my body in a lowly, beggar's gown.

I wish I were turned to dust and strewn at love's door,
If I was meant to be humbled to the ground.

If I was endowed with insatiate thirst for love,
I wish I were given a life unlimited, unbound.

That my heart is rent apart, I do not care,
Provided the pillow of your locks serves as its resting ground.

If I'm not worthy of the company of the saints,
In the revellers' throng at least let my voice resound.

Bereft of the Saqi's grace, if I am to burn alone,
Make me a tavern lamp, burning at the tavern ground.

Everything is always wrong in this mundane world,
Such a place had better been a wild barren ground.

Ya mujhe afsar-e-shahana banaya hota,
Ya mera taj gadayana banaya hota.

Khaksaari ke lieye garche banana tha mujhe,
Kaash khak-e-dar-e-janana banaya hota.

Nasha-e-ishq ka gar zarf diya tha mujh ko,
Umr ka tang na paimana banaya hota.

Dil-e-sud chaak banaya tau bala se lekin,
Zulf-e-mushkeen ka tiri shana banaya hota.

Sufion ke jo na tha laiq-e-suhbat tau mujhe,
Qaabil-e-jalsa-e-rindaana banaya hota.

Tha jalana hi agar doori-e-saqi se mujhe,
Tau chiragh-e-dar-e-mai khana banaya hota.

Roz maamura-e-duniya mein kharabi hai, Zafar,
Aisi basti ka tau weerana banaya hota.

ظفر

نہ کسی کی آنکھ کا نور ہوں، نہ کسی کے دل کا قرار ہوں
جو کسی کے کام نہ آسکے میں وہ ایک مشتِ غبار ہوں

میرا رنگ روپ بگڑ گیا، مرا یار مجھ سے بچھڑ گیا
جو چمن خزاں سے اجڑ گیا، میں اسی کی فصلِ بہار ہوں

نہ تو میں کسی کا حبیب ہوں، نہ تو میں کسی کا رقیب ہوں
جو بگڑ گیا وہ نصیب ہوں، جو اجڑ گیا وہ دیار ہوں

پئے فاتحہ کوئی آئے کیوں، کوئی چار پھول چڑھائے کیوں
کوئی آکے شمع جلائے کیوں میں وہ بے کسی کا مزار ہوں

میں نہیں ہوں نغمۂ جانفزا، مجھے سن کے کوئی کرے گا کیا
میں بڑے بروگ کی ہوں صدا میں بڑے دکھی کی پکار ہوں

Bahadur Shah Zafar

I am not the apple of any eye, nor the joy of any heart,
A handful of useless dust, no purpose I discharge.
I've lost my strength and shape, I'm severed from my friend,
I'm the spring of the garden, laid waste by fall.
I'm a friend to no one, nor a foe to aught,
I'm the star-crossed fate, I'm the ruined resort.
Why should someone sing my dirge, or come to lay a wreath?
I'm the tomb of helplessness, better left in dark.
I'm not a lilting song, which others may hear or heed,
I'm the wail by severance caused, a cry of anguished heart.

Na kisi ki aankh ka nur hun, na kisi ke dil ka qarar hun,
Jo kisi ke kam na aa sake, main woh ek musht-e-ghubar hun.
Mera rang roop bigar gaya, mera yaar mujh se bichhar gaya,
Jo chaman khazaan se ujar gaya, main usi ki fasl-e-bahar hun.
Na tau main kisi ka habib hun, na tau main kisi ka raqib hun,
Jo bigar gaya woh naseeb hun, jo ujar gaya woh dayaar hun.
Paie faateha koi aae kyaon, koi chaar phool charhaae kyon,
Koi aake shama jalaay kyon, main woh be-kasi ka mazaar hun.
Main nahin hun naghmaa-e-jaanfaza, mujhe sun kae koi karega kya,
Main bare barog ki hun sada, main bare dukhi ki pukar hun.

ظفرؔ

بلائیں زلفِ جاناں کی اگر لیتے تو ہم لیتے
بلا یہ کون لیتا جان پر لیتے تو ہم لیتے

اسے کیا کام تھا وہ بے خبر کیوں پوچھتا پھرتا
دلِ گم گشتہ کی اپنے خبر لیتے تو ہم لیتے

نہ لیتا مول سودا کوئی بازارِ محبت کا
مگر کچھ جان اپنی بیچ کر لیتے تو ہم لیتے

نہ ہوتا کوئی منت کش تیری شمشیر کا ہرگز
یہ احساں سر پہ اے بیداد گر لیتے تو ہم لیتے

لگایا جامِ مے ہونٹوں سے اُس نے ہم کو رشک آیا
کہ بوسہ اُس کے لب کا اے ظفرؔ لیتے تو ہم لیتے

Bahadur Shah Zafar

None but I should woo and bless those darling locks,
None but I can bear the brunt of her deadly darts.
Why should he be looking about, what is his concern?
It is for us to search the heart, now for ever lost.
None would buy the merchandise in the love's mart,
We alone, at the cost of life, could have something bought.
None would have come forth to bow beneath your sword,
I alone, O despot, would have your debt discharged.
When he raised the cup to his lips, I was, Zafar, by envy gripped,
Wishing I should kiss the lips, and not the purple draught.

Balaaen zulf-e-janan ki agar lete tau hum lete,
Bala yeh kaun leta jaan par, lete tau hum lete.
Use kya kaam tha woh be-khabar kyon puchhta phirta,
Dil-e-gum-gashta ki apne khabar lete tau hum lete.
Na leta mol sauda koi bazaar-e-muhabbat ka,
Magar kuchh jaan apni bech kar lete tau hum lete.
Na hota mannat kash koi tiri shamsheer ka hargiz,
Yeh ahsaan sar pe, ai bedadgar, lete tau hum lete.
Lagaya jaam-e-mai honton se us ne, hum ko rashk aaya,
Ke bosa uske lab ka, ai Zafar, lete tau hum lete.

ظفؔر

لگتا نہیں ہے جی مرا اجڑے دیار میں
کِس کی بنی ہے عالمِ ناپائیدار میں

بلبل کو پاسباں سے نہ صیاد سے گلہ
قسمت میں قید تھی لکھی فصلِ بہار میں

کہہ دو یہ حسرتوں سے کہیں اور جا بسیں
اتنی جگہ کہاں ہے دلِ داغدار میں

عمرِ دراز مانگ کے لائے تھے چار دن
دو آرزو میں کٹ گئے دو انتظار میں

دن زندگی کے ختم ہوئے شام ہو گئی
پھیلا کے پاؤں سوئیں گے کُنجِ مزار میں

کتنا ہے بدنصیب ظفؔر دفن کے لئے
دو گز زمین بھی نہ ملی کوئے یار میں

Bahadur Shah Zafar

I feel ill-at-ease on this wasted heath,
Who in this ephemeral world has ever found relief?
The nightingale has no complaint against the hunter or the watch,
It is her fate to lie in cage, and spring in every mead!
My desires were better advised to find a new resort,
Where in my scalded heart is space enough to breathe?
We had borrowed this long life on a four-day lease,
Two were spent in yearnings vain, two by waiting seized.
The day of life is nearly done, the shades of night approach,
We shall sleep in the grave, stretching both our feet.
How unlucky is Zafar, mark! for his burial place,
He couldn't find two yards of ground in his love's street.

Lagta nahin hai ji mira ujre dyaar mein,
Kis ki bani hai aalam-e-na-paidar mein ?
Bulbul ko paasbaan se na sayyaad se gila,
Qismat mein qaid likhi thi fasl-e-bahar mein.
Kah do yeh hasraton se kahin aur ja basen,
Itni jagah kahan hai dil-e-daghdaar mein.
Umr-e-daraaz maang ke laaey the chaar din,
Do aarzoo mein kat gaye, do intezaar mein.
Din zindagi ke khatam hue, shaam ho gai,
Phaila ke paaon soeynge kunj-e-mazaar mein.
Kitna hai bud naseeb, Zafar, dafan ke lieye,
Do gaz zameen bhi na mili koo-e-yaar mein.

Khwaja Hyder Ali Aatish
(1777-1847)

KHWAJA HYDER ALI AATISH
(1777 - 1847)

Aatish belonged to Faizabad. Due to the death of his father in childhood, he was denied the opportunity of regular instruction in a school. But he had a deep, instinctive taste for poetry which gave him easy access to the court of Nawab Mohammed Taqi Khan Taraqqi, who, in turn, took him to Lucknow. At Lucknow he sought poetic instruction from Mushafi, an important poet of the Lucknow school. On the strength of his poetic abilities and performance, Aatish soon established his reputation in literary circles, and came to be regarded a top-ranking poet of Lucknow, and a worthy rival of Nasikh. Aatish was a contented, self-respecting man who led a simple and stringent life, and never stooped before nobility to gain personal favours. This independence of spirit and ascetic- like unconcern with worldly comforts, is also reflected in his poetry.

Although Aatish belongs unmistakably to the Lucknow school, his poetry is generally free from the faults of affectation, sensuality, and linguistic jugglery, associated with this school. He is generally bracketed with Nasikh for purposes of poetic comparison. Both of them were good friends and poetic rivals, both of them were representatives of the Lucknow school, and both of them were acknowledged masters in the field. Again, both of them respected each other, so much so, that after the death of Nasikh, Aatish stopped writing poetry. However, when we are asked to make the choice, we must award the palm to Aatish. Some critics rank him next to Mir and Ghalib. His ghazals are built round the traditional themes of love and mysticism, and his sentiment is noble and refined. He writes familiar, speech-like language, and his words are carefully chosen and artistically arranged. He also makes an apt use of the contemporary idiom, so that some of his lines, like the following, have become popular quotations:

اگر بخشے زہے رحمت ! نہ بخشے تو شکایت کیا
سرِ تسلیم خم ہے ، جو مزاجِ یار میں آئے

Let him punish or forgive, we'll not demur,
He who comes to the court of love, must submit and bend.

خواجہ حیدر علی آتش

دہن پر ہیں اُنکے گماں کیسے کیسے
کلام آتے ہیں درمیاں کیسے کیسے

زمینِ چمن گل کھلاتی ہے کیا کیا
بدلتا ہے رنگ آسماں کیسے کیسے

نہ گورِ سکندر نہ ہے قبرِ دارا
مٹے نامیوں کے نشاں کیسے کیسے

بہارِ گلستاں کی ہے آمد آمد
کہ پھرتے ہیں خوش باغباں کیسے کیسے

توجہ نے تیری ہمارے مسیحا
توانا کئے ناتواں کیسے کیسے

دلِ و دیدۂ اہلِ عالم میں گھر ہے
تمہارے لئے ہیں مکاں کیسے کیسے

غم و غصہ و رنج و اندوہ و حرماں
ہمارے بھی ہیں مہرباں کیسے کیسے

کرے جس قدر شکرِ نعمت وہ کم ہے
مزے لوٹتی ہے زباں کیسے کیسے

Khwaja Hyder Ali Aatish

His mouth inscrutable what various doubts doth raise,
Who knows what sort of words are loosened from its cage!
What diverse flowers bloom and blossom on the soil beneath,
What varied hues the sun reflects in its changing face!
Where's the grave of Darius gone, where Alexander's tomb?
What glorious names from the earth hath Time effaced.
The flush and blush of bud and bloom announces the spring,
How the gardeners strut about, contented and elate!
Your gracious glance, my Saviour, my Christ,
Many a broken spirit has raised.
Your home is in our hearts and eyes,
What wondrous lodges for your grace!
Grief, gloom and care, anger and despair,
Benefactors galore upon me wait.
No praise is too much for God's bounteous ways,
How the tongue enjoys a thousand different tastes!

Dahan par hain unke gumaan kaise kaise,
Kalaam aate hain darmiaan kaise kaise.
Zamin-e-chaman gul khilati hai kya kya,
Badalta hai rang aasmaan kaise kaise.
Na gor-e-Sikander, na hai qabar-e-Dara,
Mite naamion ke nishaan kaise kaise.
Bahar-e-gulistan ki hai aamad, aamad,
Keh phirte hain khush baagbaan kaise, kaise.
Tawajjuh ne teri hamaare Maseeah,
Tawaana Kieye naatwaan kaise kaise.
Dil-o-deeda-e-ahl-e-alaam mein ghar hai,
Tumhaare lieye hain makaan kaise kaise.
Gham-o-ghussa-o-ranj-o-andoh-o-hirman,
Hamaare bhi hain mehrbaan kaise kaise.
Kare jis qadar shukr-e-naimat woh kam hai,
Maze loot-ti hai zabaan kaise kaise.

آتش

تصوّر سے کسی کے میں نے کی ہے گفتگو برسوں
رہی ہے ایک تصویرِ خیالی روبرو برسوں

برابر جان کے رکھا ہے اُسکو مرتے مرتے تک
ہماری قبر پر رویا کرے گی آرزو برسوں

ملی ہے ہم کو بھی کُنجِ خانۂ افلاک میں راحت
سرہانے ہاتھ رکھ کر سوئے ہیں زیرِ سُبو برسوں

بسر کی مدّت العمر اپنی یکسر باغ وبستاں میں
سنگھائی گُل نے اُس گل پیرہن کی ہم کو بُو برسوں

فنا ہو جائے گی جاں اپنی وہ نازک طبیعت ہوں
دُکھا کر دل مرا پچھتائیگا وہ تُند خُو برسوں

اگر میں خاک بھی ہُونگا تو آتش گردِ باد آسا
رکھے گی مجھ کو سرگشتہ کسی کی جُستجو برسوں

Hyder Ali Aatish

For years have I held converse with someone in my thoughts,
For long has a pictured visage lodged within my heart.

I had held it all through as dear as life,
My desire will weep for me for years in the burial yard.

I too once drank the draughts from the fount of life,
I too slept for long in peace, sheltered by the flask.

For long did I stroll about in gardens and groves,
For long could I smell my rose in the roses of the park.

Such a sensitive being am I, it will cause my death,
For years shall that shrew regret having hurt my heart.

Even if reduced to ashes, like the wind-borne dust,
For years I'll eddy around questing someone lost.

Tasawur se kisi ke main ne ki hai guftgoo barson,
Rahi hai ek tasvir-e-khayaali roo-baroo barson.

Barabar jaan ke rakha hai usko marte marte tak,
Hamari qabar par roya karegi aarzoo barson.

Mili hai humko bhi khumkhana-e-iflaak mein rahat,
Sarhaane haath rakh kar soe hain zer-e-saboo barson.

Basar ki muddat-ul-umar apni sair-e-baagh-o-bastaan mein,
Sunghaai gul ne us gul-parahan ki hum ko boo barson.

Fana ho jaaegi jaan apni woh naazuk tabiat hun,
Dukha kar dil mira pachhtaaega woh tund-khu barson.

Agar main khaak bhi hunga, tau Aatish, gard-e-baad aasa,
Rakhegi mujhko sargashta kisi ki justjoo barson.

آتش

خوشا وہ دل کہ ہو جس میں آرزو تیری
خوشا دماغ جسے تازہ رکھے بُو تیری

یقیں ہے اٹکے گی جاں اپنی آکے گردن میں
سُنا ہے جا ہے قریبِ رگِ گلو تیری

شبِ فراق میں اے روزِ وصل تا دمِ صبح
چراغ ہاتھ میں ہے اور جستجو تیری

میری طرف سے صبا کہیو میرے یوسف سے
نکل چلی ہے بہت پیرہن سے بو تیری

جو ابر گریہ زناں ہے تو برق خندہ زناں
کسی میں خُو ہے ہماری، کسی میں خُو تیری

زمانہ میں کوئی تجھ سا نہیں سیف زباں
رہے گی معرکہ میں آتش آبرو تیری

Hyder Ali Aatish

Happy is the heart which nurtures your desire,
Happy is the head by your scent inspired.

My dying breath will sure be stuck near the neck,
For close to the jugular vein is located Thy empire.

I look for thee, O union day, throughout the severance night,
Lamp in hand I search the land and everywhere inquire.

Go gentle breeze, address my Yousaf thus on my behalf,
Your fragrance which enriched my robes has well-nigh expired.

If the cloud is shedding tears, lightning giggles and laughs,
One represents my gloomy cast, the other, your verve and fire.

You, Aatish, have the sharpest tongue in the world entire,
This tongue will harm your honour, fuel the people's ire.

Khusha woh dil ke ho jis mein aarzoo teri,
Khusha dimagh jise taaza rakhe boo teri.

Yaqin hai atke gi jaan apni aa ke gardan mein,
Suna hai jaa hai qarib rag-e-gulu, teri.

Shab-e-faraq mein ai roz-e-wasal taa dam-e-subah,
Chiraagh haath mein hai aur justjoo teri.

Meri taraf se saba kahio mere Yousaf se,
Nikal chali hai bahut parahan se boo teri.

Jo abar girya zanaan hai tau barq khanda zanaan,
Kisi mein khoo hai hamari, kisi mein khoo teri.

Zamana mein koi tujh saa nahin saif-zabaan,
Rahegi maarka mein, Aatish, aabroo teri.

آتش

سن تو سہی جہاں میں ہے تیرا فسانہ کیا
کہتی ہے تجھ کو خلقِ خدا غائبانہ کیا

زیرِ زمین سے آتا جو گُل سو زر بکف
قاروں نے راستہ میں لٹایا خزانہ کیا

اُڑتا ہے شوقِ راحتِ منزل سے اسپِ عمر
مہمیز کس کو کہتے ہیں اور تازیانہ کیا

طبل و علم ہی پاس ہے اپنے نہ مُلک و مال
ہم سے خلاف ہو کے کریگا زمانہ کیا

آتی ہے کس طرح سے مری قبضِ روح کو
دیکھوں تو مَوت ڈھونڈ رہی ہے بہانہ کیا

صیّاد اسیرِ دامِ رگِ گل ہے عندلیب
دِکھلا رہا ہے چھپ کے اسے آب و دانہ کیا

یاں مدعی حسد سے نہ دے داد تو نہ دے
آتش غزل یہ تُو نے کہی عاشقانہ کیا

Hyder Ali Aatish

You should but hear your tale as the folks propound,
What they talk in secret, you should have but found.

Every flower springing forth, comes crowned with gold,
Qarun's wealth lies, mayhap, strewn, underground.

The steed of life is galloping fast attracted by the bliss beyond,
It dosen't need the spur or lash to make it leap and bound.

We have neither fame nor name, wealth nor estate,
What for should the world then fell us to the ground?

There he comes to seize my soul, the all-consuming shade,
Let's see how I'm floored in the final round.

The nightingale, O fowler, is by the rose enthralled,
Tempt her not with grub or grain, slyly sitting around.

Envy might compel the rival to withhold his praise,
How romantic is your *ghazal*, both in sense and sound!

Sun tau sahi jahaan mein hai tera fasana kya,
Kahti hai tujhko khalq-e-Khuda ghaaibana kya.

Zer-e-zamin se aata hai jo gul so zar-ba-kaf,
Qarun ne raaste mein lutaaya khazana kya?

Urta hai shauq-e-rahat-e-manzil se asp-e-umr,
Mahmeez kis ko kahte hain aur taaziana kya.

Tabal-o-alam hi paas hai apne, na mulk-o-maal,
Hum se khilaf ho ke karega zamana kya.

Aati hai kistarah se miri qabz-e-rooh ko,
Dekhun tau maut dhoond rahi hai bahana kya.

Sayyad asir-e-daam-e-rag-e-gul hai andleeb,
Dikhla raha hai chhup ke ise aab-o-dana kya.

Yaan muddai hasad se na de daad tau na de,
Aatish ghazal yeh tu ne kahi aashiqaana kya!

آتش

بدن سا شہر نہیں دل سا بادشاہ نہیں
حواس خمسہ سے بہتر کوئی سپاہ نہیں
وہ آب و رنگ کہاں روئے یار کا گل پر
ہزار آنکھ ہو نرگس کی وہ نگاہ نہیں
صدا یہ قبر سے بیدار دل کو آتی ہے
عمل جو نیک ہوں تو ایسی خواب گاہ نہیں
نہ پاک ہوگا کبھی حسن و عشق کا جھگڑا
وہ قصہ ہے یہ کہ جس کا کوئی گواہ نہیں
فقیر بن کے قدم مار اس میں اے آتش
طریقِ احمدِ مرسل سی شاہراہ نہیں

Hyder Ali Aatish

No city like the body, no emperor like the heart,
Our five senses provide the best armed escort.

Can the rose ever reflect my darling's glow and grace?
The narcissus may have a thousand eyes, can they flash and dart?

The wakeful heart hears a voice proceeding from the grave,
No better place than this for sleep, if you own a blameless past.

The dispute betwixt love and beauty will never be resolved,
None is there to testify the affairs of the heart.

Tread this path without a thought like a saint of God,
No better way in the world than that by Prophet taught.

Badan saa shahr nahin, dil saa baadshaah nahin,
Hawaas-e-khamsa se behtar koi sipaah nahin.

Woh aab-o-rang kahaan, roo-e-yaar ka gul par,
Hazaar aankh ho nargis ki woh nigaah nahin.

Sadaa yeh qabar se be-daar dil ko aati hai,
Amal jo nek hon tau aisi khwab-gaah nahin.

Na paak hoga kabhi husn-o-ishq ka jhagra,
Woh qissa hai yeh ke jiska koi gawaah nahin.

Faqir ban ke qadam maar is mein, ai Aatish,
Tariq-e-Ahmed-e-Mursil si shaahraah nahin.

آتشؔ

عدم سے جانبِ ہستی تلاشِ یار میں آئے!
کھلی آنکھیں تو دیکھا، وادیٔ پُرخار میں آئے!

یقین ہے کچھ نہ کچھ رحمت مزاجِ یار میں آئے!
ادب سے ہاتھ باندھے ہم تیرے دربار میں آئے!

اگر بخشے زہے رحمت! نہ بخشے تو شکایت کیا؟
سرِ تسلیم خم ہے۔ جو مزاجِ یار میں آئے

نہ پوچھو اہلِ محشر ہم سے دیوانہ کی بے تابی
یہاں مجمع سنا۔ یاں بھی تلاشِ یار میں آئے

عدم کے جانے والو۔ بزمِ جاناں تک اگر پہنچو
ہمیں بھی یاد رکھنا۔ ذکر جو دربار میں آئے

نہ مانگو بوسہ اے آتشؔ بگاڑے منھ وہ بیٹھے ہیں
قیامت ہے اگر بل ابروئے خمدار میں آئے

Hyder Ali Aatish

Hither we came from the world celestial questing for o'r friend,
It was but a vale of thorns, we realised in the end.

A little bit of mercy, sure, will ooze out of his heart,
With folded hands, in deep respect, we his court attend.

Let him punish or forgive, we'll not demur,
He who comes to the court of love, must submit and bend.

O denizens of the land of dead, imagine o'r restless state,
Hearing about a gathering here, we came to find o'r friend.

Travellers of the world beyond, if you reach my love's court,
Forget not to mention us, if a chance presents.

Ask her not for a kiss, she is in an angry mood,
If her curling locks are ruffled, a doom shall on earth descend.

Adam se jaanib-e-hasti talaash-e-yaar mein aae,
Khuli aankhen tau dekha, waadi-e-pur khaar mein aae.

Yaqin hai kuchh na kuchh rahmat mizaaj-e-yaar mein aae,
Adab se haath baandhe hum tere darbaar mein aae.

Agar bakhshe zahe rehmat, na bakhshe tau shikaait kya,
Sar-e-taslim khum hai, jo mizaaj-e-yaar mein aae.

Na puchho ahl-e-mahshar, hum se diwaana ki be-taabi,
Yahaan majma suna, yaan bhi talaash-e-yaar mein aae.

Adam ke jaane waalo, bazm-e-jaanaan tak agar pahuncho,
Hamen bhi yaad rakhna, zikar jo darbaar mein aae.

Na maango bosa, ai Aatish, bigaare munh woh baithe hain,
Qayaamat hai agar bal abroo-e-khamdaar mein aae.

Sheikh Mohammed Ibrahim Zauq
(1788-1855)

SHEIKH MOHAMMED IBRAHIM ZAUQ
(1788 - 1855)

Sheikh Mohammed Ibrahim Zauq was born in Delhi in 1788. His father, Sheikh Mohammed Ramzan, was an ordinary soldier who had served in the court of Bahadur Shah Zafar, the last Moghul emperor of Delhi. Zauq received his early education at the private school of Hafiz Ghulam Rasul, who was a poet in his own right, writing under the pen-name of Shauq. It is believed that Zauq's own poetic name (Zauq), is a variant of his mentor's pseudonym, Shauq. In the school of Mian Abdul Razzaq which he next attended, Zauq contracted a lifelong friendship with Maulana Mohammed Baqar. After finishing his formal education Zauq devoted himself wholeheartedly to the pursuit and perfection of his poetic talent. He became the poetic disciple of Shah Naseer, a famous poet who was also the poetic preceptor of Bahadur Shah Zafar. When Shah Naseer migrated to Deccan, Zafar chose Zauq as his poetic mentor. This gave a big boost to Zauq's reputation, and his circle of admirers and disciples suddenly swelled. Among his reputed disciples may be mentioned, in addition to Bahadur Shah Zafar, Mohammed Hussain Azad and Dagh Dehlvi. Proximity to the king and the court also proved highly beneficial for the development of Zauq's art and mind. Zafar's court was the centre of literary meets and *mushairas,* which attracted all the important poets of the day, including Ghalib, Momin, Aazurda and Shefta. In sheer poetic merit, Zauq lags behind both Ghalib and Momin. He lacks the philosophic depths of Ghalib, as also Momin's masterly handling of romantic love, rooted in the reality of emotional experience. Zauq's characteristic merit lies not so much in the originality of thought or freshness of emotion as in the aptness and alacrity of expression. He is the master of the living language of Delhi which he skilfully employs in the service of poetry. Moreover, like Sauda before him, Zauq is a writer par excellence of *qasida.* His panegyrics written in praise of Akbar Shah Saani won him the title of "Khaqani-e-Hind", while Zafar conferred on him the title of "Malik-ul-Shora".

Zauq did not give much thought to the publication of his works in his lifetime, so pre-occupied he was in correcting and improving the verse of his disciples, in particular, of Bahadur Shah Zafar. Consequently, his poetic works were published posthumously in 1863, eight years after his death.

شیخ محمد ابراہیم ذوقؔ

جینا نظر اپنا ہمیں اصلا نہیں آتا
گر آج بھی وہ رشکِ مسیحا نہیں آتا

مذکور تری بزم میں کس کا نہیں آتا
پر ذکر ہمارا نہیں آتا، نہیں آتا

آتا ہے دم آنکھوں میں دمِ حسرتِ دیدار
پر لب پہ کبھی حرفِ تمنا نہیں آتا

بے جا ہے دلا! اس کے نہ آنے کی شکایت
کیا کیجئے گا فرمایئے، اچھا نہیں آتا

قسمت ہی سے لاچار ہوں اے ذوقؔ وگرنہ
سب فن میں ہوں میں طاق مجھے کیا نہیں آتا

Sheikh Mohammed Ibrahim Zauq

I fear today I mayn't survive,
Unless my Christ-like love arrives.
All and sundry find a mention at your nightly meets,
To me alone, alas, is this privilege denied.
Though my strong desire seems to choke my breath,
Not a word about my wish on my lips arrives.
To complain that he does not come, is, O heart, futile,
What would you do, tell me, sir, if he doesn't oblige?
Fate has bowed me down, otherwise, O, Zauq!
What is it I do not know, who can my skills deny?

Jeena nazar apna hamen asla nahin aata,
Gar aaj bhi woh rashk-e-Masiha nahin aata.
Mazkur teri bazam mein kiska nahin aata,
Par zikar hamara nahin aata, nahin aata.
Aata hai dam aankhon mein dam-e-hasrat-e-deedar,
Par lab pe kabhi harf-e-tamannaa nahin aata.
Be ja hai dila, uske na aane ki shikaayat,
Kya kijieye ga, farmaieye, achha nahin aata.
Qismat se hi laachar hun, ai Zauq, wa garna,
Sab fan meịn hun main taaq, mujhe kya nahin aata.

ذوقؔ

آنکھیں مری تلووں سے وہ مل جائے تو اچھا
ہے حسرتِ پابوس، نکل جائے تو اچھا

جو چشم کہ بے نم ہو، وہ ہو کور تو بہتر
جو دل کہ ہو بے داغ، وہ جل جائے تو اچھا

فرقت میں تری، تارِ نفس سینے میں مرے
کانٹا سا کھٹکتا ہے، نکل جائے تو اچھا

وہ صبح کو آئے، تو کروں باتوں میں دوپہر
اور چاہوں کہ دن تھوڑا سا ڈھل جائے تو اچھا

ڈھل جائے جو دن بھی تو اسی طرح کروں شام
اور چاہوں کہ گر آج سے کل جائے تو اچھا

جب کل ہو تو پھر وہی کروں کل کی طرح سے
گر آج کا دن بھی یوں ہی ٹل جائے تو اچھا

القصہ نہیں چاہتا میں، جائے وہ یاں سے
دِل اُس کا یہیں گرچہ بہل جائے تو اچھا

Mohammed Ibrahim Zauq

If with his soles he rubs my eyes, it would be so nice!
A desire I have to kiss his feet, let it be realised.
The eye that can shed no tear, better were it blind,
The heart that's without a scar, should be burnt alive.
In your absence this throbbing heart like a thorn pricks my breast,
How I wish that this thorn is plucked and cast aside!
If he arrives in the morn, I talk with him till noon,
Wishing that he stays on till the day abides.
As the day declines, I look towards the eve,
Thinking how great it were, if he stayed o'ernight!
Next day again, I repeat the same, wishing all the while,
If another day passes this way, what a great delight!
In short, I want him never to go, thinking in my heart,
It would be a treat indeed if he for aye with me abides.

Aankhen meri talwon se woh mul jaae tau achha;
Hai hasrat-e-pa bose nikal jaae tau achha.
Jo chashm ke be-num ho, woh ho kor to behtar,
Jo dil ke ho be-dagh, woh jal jaae tau achha.
Furqat mein teri taar-e-nafas seene mein mere,
Kaanta sa khatakta hai, nikal jaae tau achha.
Woh subah ko aae tau karun baaten main dopahar,
Aur chaahun ke din thora sa dhal jaae tau achha.
Dhal jaae jo din bhi tau isi tarah karun shaam,
Aur chaahun ke gar aaj se kal jaae tau achha,
Jab kal ho tau phir wohi karun kal ki tarah se,
Gar aaj ka din bhi yunhi tal jaae tau achha;
Alqissa nahin chaahta main, jaae woh yaan se,
Dil uska yahin garche bahal jaae tau achha.

ذوقؔ

وقتِ پیری شباب کی باتیں
ایسی ہیں جیسے خواب کی باتیں
پھر مجھے لے چلا اُدھر دیکھو
دلِ خانہ خراب کی باتیں!
سنتے ہیں اُسے چھیڑ چھیڑ کے ہم
کس مزے سے عتاب کی باتیں
مجھ کو رسوا کریں گی خوب اے دل
یہ تری اضطراب کی باتیں
جاؤ، ہوتا ہے اور بھی خفقان
سُن کے ناصح جناب کی باتیں
ذکر کیا جوشِ عشق میں اے ذوقؔ
ہم سے ہوں صبر و تاب کی باتیں

Mohammed Ibrahim Zauq

To talk of youth in hoary age,
Recalls a dream of distant days;
Lo, it drags me thither again,
How my rootless heart behaves!
First I tease him and provoke,
Then relish his flights of rage.
Surely they would embarrass me,
These, O heart, your restive ways.
Vex me not, off you go!
The priestly sermons me dismay.
Talk not, Zauq, of wise restraint
To us who are by passion crazed.

Waqt-e-peeri shabab ki baaten
Aisi hain jaise khwab ki baaten;
Phir mujhe le chala udhar, dekho
Dil-e-khana kharab ki baaten.
Sunten hain use chher chher ke hum
Kis maze se itaab ki baaten.
Mujh ko ruswa karengi khub, ai dil,
Yeh teri iztaraab ki baaten;
Jaao hota hai aur bhi khafqaan,
Sun ke naaseh janab ki baaten;
Zikar kya josh-e-ishq mein, ai Zauq,
Hum se hon sabar-o-taab ki baaten.

ذوق

لیتے ہی دِل جو عاشقِ دل سوز کا چلے
تم آگ لینے آئے تھے کیا آئے کیا چلے

بل بے غرورِ حسن ! زمیں پر نہ رکھے پاؤں
مانندِ آفتاب وہ بے نقشِ پا چلے

کیا اے چلے گلی سے تری ہم کہ جوں نسیم
آئے تھے سر پہ خاک اُڑاتے، اُڑا چلے

آلودہ چشم میں نہ ہوئی سُرمہ سے نگاہ
دیکھا، جہاں سے صاف ہی اہلِ صفا چلے

ساتھ اپنے لے کے توسنِ عمرِ رواں کو آہ
ہم اس سرائے دہر میں کیا آئے کیا چلے

فکرِ قناعت ان کو میسّر ہوئی کہاں
دنیا سے دل میں لے کے جو حرص و ہوا چلے

اے ذوق، ہے غضب نگہِ یار، الحفیظ!
وہ کیا بچے کہ جس پہ یہ تیرِ قضا چلے

Mohammed Ibrahim Zauq

Grabbing the heart of the heart-sick lover, you're slipping away,
You had come to fetch the fire, now you slink away !
Mark the beauty's heady pride, she hates to tread on earth,
Sun-like she struts in space, printless all the way.
What did we get in your street? Like the morning breeze,
Having blown about the dust, we wing back our way.
Collyrium can't restore the vision of the blemished eye,
Behold the virtuous quit the world with a clean slate.
Riding astride the winged horse, we come into this world,
What a way to come and go, we aren't allowed to stay.
When have they found peace on earth?
The folks by lusts and greeds assailed.
What a fatal thing, my God, is her deadly glance!
Who can save the man, Zauq, to such a dart a prey?

Lete hi dil jo aashiq-e-dil soz ka chale,
Tum aag lene aae the, kya aae kya chale.
Bal be gharoor-e-husn, zamin par na rakhe paaon,
Maanind-e-aaftaab woh be naqsh-e-pa chale.
Kya le chale gali se teri hum ke jun naseem,
Aae the sar pe khak urane, ura chale.
Aaluda chashm mein na hui surma se nigah,
Dekha, jahan se saaf hi ahl-e-safa chale.
Saath apne le ke tausan-e-umr-e-rawan ko, aah!
Hum is sarai dahar mein kya aae, kya chale.
Fikr-e-qanayat unko muyassar hui kahan,
Dunya se dil mein le ke jo hirs-o-hawa chale.
Ai Zauq, hai ghazab nigah-e-yaar, alhafeez!
Woh kya bache ke jis pe yeh teer-e-qaza chale.

ذوقؔ

لائی حیات، آئے، قضا لے چلی چلے
اپنی خوشی نہ آئے نہ اپنی خوشی چلے

ہو عمرِ خضر بھی تو ہو معلوم وقتِ مرگ
ہم کیا رہے یہاں، ابھی آئے ابھی چلے

ہم سے بھی اس بساط پہ کم ہوں گے بدقمار
جو چال ہم چلے سو نہایت بُری چلے

بہتر تو ہے یہی کہ نہ دنیا سے دل لگے
پر کیا کریں جو کام نہ بے دل لگی چلے

نازاں نہ ہو خرد پہ جو ہونا ہے، ہو وہی
دانش تیری نہ کچھ مری دانشوری چلے

دنیا نے کس کا راہِ فنا میں دیا ہے ساتھ
تم بھی چلے چلو یُونہیں جب تک چلی چلے

جاتے ہوائے شوق میں ہیں اس چمن سے ذوقؔ
اپنی بلا سے بادِ صبا اب کبھی چلے

Mohammed Ibrahim Zauq

Commissioned by life we come, commanded by death we go,
Sans our will we come, sans will we go.

Even if given Khizar's life, we will but complain:
"A while ago here we came, in another while we go."

What a poor player am I in the game of life!
Every move on my part makes a dismal show.

Good, if the world doesn't engage our heart and soul,
But what to do? Uninvolved, we cannot run this show.

Declaim not your virtues, too strong is Fate,
Your wit and my wisdom must before her bow.

Has the world been faithful to anyone on earth?
Move along the tide of time as it ebbs and flows.

Carried on the wings of love, here we quit this grove,
What care we whether or not the morning breeze now blows.

Laai hyat aae, qaza le chali, chale,
Apni khushi na aae, na apni khushi chale.
Ho umr-e-Khizar bhi tau ho maalum waqt-e-marg,
Hum kya rahe yahan, abhi aae, abhi chale.
Hum se bhi is basat pe kam honge bud-qamar,
Jo chaal hum chale, so nihaayat buri chale.
Behtar tau hai yahi ke na duniya se dil lage,
Par kya karen jo kam na be dil lagi chale.
Naazaan na ho khirad pe, jo hona hai, ho wohi,
Daanish teri na kuchh meri daanishwari chale.
Duniya ne kis ka raah-e-fana mein diya hai saath ?
Tum bhi chale chalo yunhin, jab tak chali chale.
Jaate hawai-e-shauq mein hain is chaman se, Zauq,
Apni bala se baad-e-saba ab kabhi chale.

ذوقؔ

اب تو گھبرا کے یہ کہتے ہیں کہ مر جائیں گے
مر کے بھی چین نہ پایا تو کدھر جائیں گے

تم نے ٹھہرائی اگر غیر کے گھر جانے کی
تو ارادے یہاں کچھ اور ٹھہر جائیں گے

ہم نہیں وہ جو کریں خون کا دعویٰ تجھ پر
بلکہ پوچھے گا خدا بھی تو مکر جائیں گے

آگ دوزخ کی بھی ہو جائیگی پانی پانی
جب یہ عاصی عرقِ شرم سے تر جائیں گے

نہیں پائے گا نشاں کوئی ہمارا ہرگز
ہم جہاں سے روشِ تیرِ نظر جائیں گے

ذوقؔ! جو مدرسے کے بگڑے ہوئے ہیں مُلّا
ان کو مے خانے میں لے آؤ، سنور جائیں گے

Mohammed Ibrahim Zauq

Though we say in dismay, we'll end this life,
What shall we do, if death too, fails to bring respite?
If you have set your mind on visiting the rival's place,
We too would have to our plans revise.
I won't sue you for murder, I am not that type,
Even if queried by God, I would straight deny.
Even the infernal fire will shiver with shame,
When we the sinners, soaked in guilt, in the hell arrive.
We'll leave behind us no print, no sign,
Like the shooting glance, from hither we shall hie.
Schooling in the mosque, Zauq, has spoilt the priest,
Bring him to the tavern, he 'uld be all right.

Ab tau ghabra ke yeh kahte hain ke mar jaaenge,
Mar ke bhi chain na paya tau kidhar jaaenge ?
Tum ne thahraai agar ghair ke ghar jaane ki
Tau iraade yahan kuchh aur thahr jaaenge.
Hum nahin woh jo karen khun ka dawa tujh par,
Balke puchhega Khuda bhi tau mukar jaaenge.
Aag dozakh ki bhi ho jaaegi paani, paani,
Jab yeh aasi arq-e-sharm se tar jaaenge.
Nahin paaega nishaan koi hamara hargiz
Hum jahan se rawish-e-teer-e-nazar jaange.
Zauq, jo madarse ke bigare hue hain mullah,
Un ko mai khane main le aao, sanwar jaaenge.

Amir Ahmed Amir Meenai
(1826-1900)

AMIR AHMED AMIR MEENAI
(1826 - 1900)

Amir Meenai was born at Lucknow in 1826. He got his early education from his father, Karm Mohammed Meenai, who was a man of learning and piety. Later, the boy-poet sat at the feet of several other learned preceptors, and acquired a mastery of Urdu, Persian and Arabic, besides a high degree of proficiency in Hindi and Sanskrit. For nearly five years he served in the court of Nawab Wajid Ali Shah, but when, after the revolt of 1857, the Nawab was divested of his power and position, and Lucknow thrown into a state of turmoil, Amir Meenai migrated to Rampur, where he lived a comfortable life under the patronage of Nawab Yousaf Ali Khan, and his successor, Nawab Kalab Ali Khan. It was at Rampur that he spent a greater part of his life (47 years), and it was here that he attained the height of fame as a poet. He was also the poetic mentor of the two nawabs, both of whom were poets in their own right. It was here again that he compiled and published the two parts of his (incomplete) Urdu dictionary called, *Amir-ul-ghaat.* Amir's poetical works are collected under two heads: *Maraat-ul-Ghaaib* and *Sanam Khana-e-Ishq.*

After the death of Nawab Kalab Ali Khan, Ameer was persuaded to go to Hyderabad, where he was enthusiastically received by the Nizam. But he was not destined to live long in Hyderabad. He died in 1900 after a brief, one-month illness.

Amir had an inborn talent for poetry, which he had perfected under the guidance of Muzaffar Ali Asir, a veteran poet and a rigorous mentor. Amir's own erudition and study in literature further enriched his mind and art. Though Amir is a versatile writer, the *ghazal* is his forte. He may be described as a bridge between the two schools of Lucknow and Delhi, for he has blended together the linguistic refinements of the Lucknow school with the sincerity and spontaneity of Zauq and Dagh. This task of synthesizing the two poetic streams could only be accomplished at Rampur, which, after the disruption of cultural life in Delhi and Lucknow, had become the centre of literary activity, bringing together famous poets from both these places. Dagh Dehlvi was then the new trendsetter. Amir was quick and competent to absorb the new influences, and adopt the new mode of Dagh. In fact, both Dagh and Amir Meenai respected each other. Amir called Dagh "the Nightingale of India," and Dagh reciprocated by remembering him in many of his couplets, including the following:

کر گئے رحلت امیر احمد امیر
اب نشاطِ زندگی جاتا رہا

With the death of Amir Ahmed Amir,
Life has lost its charm and zeal.

امیر احمد امیر مینائی

بندہ نوازیوں پہ خدائے کریم تھا
کرتا نہ میں گناہ تو گناہِ عظیم تھا

باتیں بھی کیں خدا نے، دکھایا جمال بھی
واللہ، کیا نصیب جنابِ کلیم تھا

دنیا کی حال اہلِ عدم ہے یہ مختصر
اک دو قدم کا کوچۂ امید و بیم تھا

کرتا میں دردمند طبیبوں سے کیا رجوع!
جس نے دیا تھا درد بڑا وہ حکیم تھا

سامانِ عفو کیا میں کہوں، مختصر ہے یہ
بندہ گناہ گار تھا، خالق کریم تھا

جس دن تھا میں چمن میں ہوا خواہِ گل امیر
نامِ صبا کہیں، نہ نشانِ نسیم تھا

Amir Ahmed Amir Meenai

Gracious God was liberal with doling out His grace benign,
Had I shied away from sin, I would have done a crime.

He held converse with God, also saw His grace unmasked,
How lucky, indeed, was Moses in the olden times.

O dwellers of the realm supreme, such in brief is this world:
A lane a few steps in length, where hope and fear entwine.

What need to consult physicians, considerate and kind?
Was he not a physician great, who caused this ache of mine?

Why detail the grounds of pardon, herein lies the truth:
A sinner was this humble self, God a fount of grace divine.

Whenever in the garden, I thirsted for the rose,
No Zephyrs, no whiff of breeze, there did I find.

Banda nawaazion pe Khuda-e-karim tha,
Karta na main gunaah tau gunaah-e-azim tha.

Baaten bhi kin Khuda ne, dikhaya jamaal bhi,
Wallah! kya nasib janaab-e-Kalim tha.

Duniya ki haal ahl-e-adam, hai yeh mukhtsir,
Ik do qadam ka kucha-e-umeed-o-beem tha.

Karta main dardmand tabibon se kya rajoo,
Jis ne diya tha dard bara woh hakim tha.

Samaan-e-ufw kya mein kahun, mukhtsir hai yeh,
Banda gunaahgaar tha, khaaliq karim tha.

Jis din tha main chaman mein hua khwah-e-gul, Amir,
Naam-e-saba kahin, na nishaan-e-naseem tha.

امیر مینائی

جھونکا ادھر نہ آئے نسیمِ بہار کا
نازک بہت ہے پھول چراغِ مزار کا

پھر بیٹھے بیٹھے وعدۂ وصل اس نے کر لیا
پھر اٹھ کھڑا ہوا وہی روگ انتظار کا

شاخوں سے برگِ گل نہیں جھڑتے ہیں باغ میں
زیور اتر رہا ہے عروسِ بہار کا

ہر گل سے لالہ زار میں یہ پوچھتا ہوں میں
"تو ہی پتہ بتا دے دلِ داغدار کا"

اس پیار سے فشار دیا گورِ تنگ نے
یاد آگیا مزہ مجھے آغوشِ یار کا

ہلتی نہیں ہوا سے چمن میں یہ ڈالیاں
منھ چومتے ہیں پھول عروسِ بہار کا

اٹھتا ہے نزع میں وہ سرہانے سے اے امیرؔ
مٹتا ہے آسرا دلِ امیدوار کا

Amir Meenai

No gust of vernal breeze should blow across this way,
The wick that flickers on the grave is too weak to stay.

Again, a promise to meet me he has made unsought,
The old disease of waiting again on me doth prey.

These are not the floral petals shedding from the trees,
The finery of the spring bride is falling off this way.

I beseech every flower in the poppy grove:
"The whereabouts of my scarred heart, will you tell me, pray?"

The narrow grave enfolded me with such a tender care,
That it brought to mind my friend's warm embrace.

These are not the branches waving in the garden breeze,
The buds and blooms swing and kiss the spring's bridal face.

He is quitting my bedside as death arrives,
I'm being denied my last prop and stay.

Jhonka idhar na aae naseem-e-bahar ka,
Naazuk bahut hai phool chiragh-e-mazaar ka.

Phir baithe baithe waada-e-wasl us ne kar liya,
Phir uth khara hua wohi rog intezaar ka.

Shaakhon se barg-e-gul nahin jharte hain baagh mein,
Zewar utar raha hai aroos-e-bahaar ka.

Har gul se lala zaar mein yeh puchhta hun main,
"Tu hi pata bata de dil-e-daaghdaar ka."

Is payaar se fishaar diya gor-e-tang ne,
Yaad aa gaya maza mujhe aaghosh-e-yaar ka.

Hilti nahin hawa se chaman mein yeh dalian,
Munh choomte hain phool aroos-e-bahar ka.

Uthta hai naza mein woh sarhaane se, ai Amir,
Mit-ta hai aasra dil-e-umeedwaar ka.

امیر مینائی

کہہ رہی ہے حشر میں وہ آنکھ شرمائی ہوئی
ہائے کیسے اس بھری محفل میں رسوائی ہوئی

آئینے میں ہر ادا کو دیکھ کر کہتے ہیں وہ
آج دیکھا چاہیے کس کس کی ہے آئی ہوئی

کہہ تو اے گلچیں اسیرانِ قفس کے واسطے
توڑ لوں دو چار کلیاں میں بھی مرجھائی ہوئی

میں تو رازِ دل چھپاؤں، پر چھپا رہنے بھی دے
جان کی دشمن، یہ ظالم آنکھ للچائی ہوئی

غمزہ و نالہ و ادا سب میں حیا کا ہے لگاؤ
ہائے رے بچپن کہ شوخی بھی ہے شرمائی ہوئی

وصل میں خالی ہوئی اغیار سے محفل تو کیا؟
شرم بھی جائے تو میں جانوں کہ تنہائی ہوئی

گرد اڑی عاشق کی تربت سے تو جھنجھلا کے کہا
"واہ سر چڑھنے لگی پاؤں کی ٹھکرائی ہوئی"

Amir Meenai

So says that embarrassed eye on the Judgement day:
What disgrace I have to face right in public gaze!

Looking in the mirror at her charming face,
"Let us see to-day," she says, "who all will meet their fate."

If you allow, O flower-plucker, I'uld like to pluck,
A few faded buds for the captives in the cage.

Though I try to conceal my secret, but what to do?
My longing eye, this foe to life, me must betray.

Graces, air and guiles — all were coyness-clad,
Even mischief was shyness-tinged, ah, the childhood days!

What, if at the time of union, rivals aren't there,
Unless I'm rid of diffidence, 'tis not a secluded place.

When dust arose from the lover's grave, sharply did he say:
"O, you whom I spurned and kicked, you, to fly in my face!"

Kah rahi hai hashar mein woh aankh sharmaai hui,
Haae kaise is bhari mahfal mein ruswaai hui.

Aaeene mein har ada ko dekh kar kahte hain woh,
Aaj dekha chaaheye kis kis ki hai aai hui.

Kah tu ai gulcheen, aseeraan-e-qafas ke waaste,
Tor lun do chaar kalian main bhi murjhaai hui.

Main tau raaz-e-dil chhipaaun, par chhipa rahne bhi de,
Jaan ki dushman, yeh zaalim aankh lalchaai hui.

Ghamza-o-naaz-o-ada sab mein hai haya ka lagaao,
Haae re bachpan, keh shokhi bhi hai sharmaai hui.

Wasl mein khali hui aghiyaar se mahfal tau kya?
Sharm bhi jaae tau mein jaanun keh tanhaai hui.

Gard uri aashiq ki turbat se tau jhunjala ke kaha,
"Wah sar charhne lagi, paaon ki thukraai hui."

امیرؔ مینائی

تُند مے اور ایسے کمسن کے لیے
ساقیا ہلکی سی لا اِن کے لیے

مجھ سے رخصت ہو مرا عہدِ شباب
یا خدا رکھنا نہ اس دن کے لیے

ہے جوانی خود جوانی کا سنگار
سادگی گہنا ہے اس سِن کے لیے

سب حسیں ہیں زاہدوں کو ناپسند
اب کوئی حور آئیگی ان کے لیے

وصل کا دِن، اور اتنا مختصر
دِن گنے جاتے تھے اس دن کے لیے

ساری دنیا کے ہیں وہ میرے سوا
میں نے دنیا چھوڑ دی جن کے لیے!

لاش پر عبرت یہ کہتی ہے، امیرؔ
"آئے تھے دنیا میں اس دن کے لیے"

Amir Meenai

So strong a wine, for one so young and green,
Get for him O, saqi, something light and lean.

Let me not, O Lord, live to see that day,
When my youth departs, spring deserts the scene.

Youth is in itself an ornament of youth,
Simplicity at this stage brightens up the gleam.

Earthly beauties cut no ice with the priestly clan,
Some houri from heaven will now adorn the scene.

The day of union, so short, so brief!
For this day we counted days and nights umpteen.

He belongs to the world entire, but not, alas, to me,
For whose sake I abandoned the world and all its beings.

This is the moral to be drawn from the corpse, Amir,
We are born on this earth for this final scene.

Tund mai aur aise kamsin ke lieye,
Saqia halki si la in ke lieye.

Mujh se rukhsat ho mira ahd-e-shabab,
Ya khuda rakhna na us din ke lieye.

Hai jawaani khud jawaani ka singaar,
Saadgi gahna hai is sin ke lieye.

Sab haseen hain zaahidon ko naa pasand,
Ab koi hur aaegi unke lieye.

Wasl ka din, aur itna mukhtsir,
Din gine jaate the is din ke lieye.

Saari duniya ke hain woh mere siwa,
Main ne duniya chhor di jin ke lieye.

Laash par ibrat yeh kahti hai, Amir,
"Aae the duniya mein is din ke lieye."

امیر مینائی

ہنس کے فرماتے ہیں وہ، دیکھ کے حالت میری
کیوں تم آسان سمجھتے تھے محبت میری

بعد مرنے کے بھی چھوڑی نہ رفاقت میری!
میری تربت سے لگی بیٹھی ہے حسرت میری

میں نے آغوشِ تصور میں بھی کھینچا تو کہا
پس گئی، پس گئی بے درد نزاکت میری

یار پہلو میں ہے، تنہائی ہے، کہہ دو نکلے
آج کیوں دل میں چھپی بیٹھی ہے حسرت میری

آئینہ صبحِ شبِ وصل جو دیکھا تو کہا
دیکھ ظالم، یہی تھی شام کو صورت میری؟

حُسن اور عشق ہم آغوش نظر آ جاتے!
تری تصویر میں کھنچ جاتی جو حیرت میری

کس ڈھٹائی سے وہ دل چھین کے کہتے ہیں امیرؔ
"وہ مرا گھر ہے، رہے جس میں محبت میری"

Amir Meenai

Looking at my plight, she says with a cunning glee:
You thought it was easy to fall in love with me!

My desire has stood by me even after death,
There she sits glumly glued to my burial seat.

When I hug her tight even in my fancy's lap,
"Ah!" she cries, "My frail self lies crushed, apiece."
'Tis seclusion, my love beside me, what blocks the way?
Why does my desire now develop cold feet?

Looking in the mirror, she said, after the union-night:
"Was this, my shape, O cruel, when we met at eve?"

It would show love and beauty locked in embrace,
If your picture could reflect my yearning unappeased.

Snatching away my heart how boldly she quips:
"The place where my love resides, sure belongs to me."

Hans ke farmaate hain woh, dekh ke haalat meri,
Kyon tum aasaan samajhte the mahabbat meri.

Baad marne ke bhi chhori na rafaaqat meri,
Meri turbat se lagi baithi hai hasrat meri.

Main ne aaghosh-e-tasawur mein bhi kheincha tau kaha,
"Pis gai, pis gai be dard, nazaakat meri."

Yaar pahlu mein hai, tanhaai hai, kahdo nikle,
Aaj kyon dil mein chhipi baithi hai hasrat meri.

Aaeena subah-e-shab-e-wasl jo dekha tau kaha,
"Dekh zaalim, yehi thi shaam ko surat meri?"

Husn aur ishq hum-aaghosh nazar aa jaate,
Teri taswir mein khinch jaati jo hairat meri.

Kis dhitaai se woh dil chheen ke kahte hain, Amir,
"Woh mira ghar hai, rahe jis mein mahabbat meri."

Nawab Mirza Khan Dagh Dehlvi
(1831-1905)

NAWAB MIRZA KHAN DAGH DEHLVI
(1831 - 1905)

Dagh was born in Chandni Chowk, Delhi, on 25 May, 1831. He was only four years old when his father, Nawab Shams-ul-din Khan was sentenced to death for his suspected involvement in the murder of Sir William Fraser, the then Resident of Delhi. Dagh moved from Delhi to Rampur by courtesy of one of his aunts who was a relation of the Nawab of Rampur. Later when Dagh's mother married Mirza Fakhru, son of King Bahadur Shah Zafar, Dagh entered the royal household where he was given the best of education and training, in arts and letters, in horse riding, and in martial arts. He became the poetic disciple of Sheikh Ibrahim Zauq, the king's preceptor, whose expert attention went a long way in digging out and developing his poetic talent. While in Delhi, he had the additional advantage of meeting and seeking the advice of Ghalib, who was also his relation. As a consequence, Dagh soon became a distinguished poet of Delhi, specially notable for the simplicity, naturalness and musicality of his style. Mirza Fakhru died in 1856. Then came the mutiny of 1857 with its attendant terror and turmoil. In the changed circumstances, Dagh was compelled to return to Rampur, where, under the personal care and patronage of the Nawab, he led a comfortable life for nearly 30 years.

After the death of the Nawab of Rampur in 1887, Dagh was left to fend for himself. For several years he wandered from pillar to post in search of livelihood. At last fortune smiled on him and the Nizam of Hyderabad appointed him as the poet of the court and as his poetic mentor on a handsome salary of Rs. 450 per mensem, which was later raised to Rs. 1,000. The Nawab also conferred on him several literary titles including: *Bulbal-e-Hindustan, Dabir-ul-Daula, Fasih-ul-Malik.* This was, by all counts, the most glorious period of his life. Dagh died in Hyderabad of a paralytic stroke, on February 16, 1905.

Dagh's poetic output consists of four *Dewans,* mainly of *ghazals: Gulzar-e-Dagh, Aaftab-e-Dagh, Mahtab-e-Dagh,* and *Yaadgar-e-Dagh.* He also wrote a *masnavi, Faryad-e-Dagh* and a few *qasidas* and *rubaies.* Dagh's distinctive merit as a poet lies in his linguistic felicity, his use of living Urdu idiom, and his mastery of metre and music. He lacks the philosophical mind of Ghalib, the mystic insights of Dard, and the pathos of Mir. But he has all the ingredients of a popular public poet: melody, accessibility, technical virtuosity, and a thorough familiarity with the universal theme of love and romance.

نواب مرزا خاں داغؔ دہلوی

ستم ہی کرنا، جفا ہی کرنا، نگاہِ الفت کبھی نہ کرنا
تمہیں قسم ہے ہمارے سر کی، ہمارے حق میں کمی نہ کرنا

ہماری میّت پہ تم جو آنا، تو چار آنسو بہا کے جانا
ذرا رہے پاسِ آبرو بھی، کہیں ہماری ہنسی نہ کرنا

لیے تو چلتے ہیں حضرتِ دل تمہیں بھی اُس انجمن میں لیکن
ہمارے پہلو میں بیٹھ کر تم ہمیں سے پہلو تہی نہ کرنا

ہوا ہے گر شوق آئینے سے، تو رُخ رہے راستی کی جانب
مثالِ عارض صفائی رکھنا، بہ رنگِ کاکل کجی نہ کرنا

وہ اک ہمارا طریقِ الفت کہ دشمنوں سے بھی مِل کے چلنا
وہ ایک شیوہ ترا ستم گر، کہ دوست سے دوستی نہ کرنا

ہم ایک رستہ گلی کا اُسکی دکھا کے دل کو ہوئے پشیماں
یہ حضرتِ خضر کو جتا دو، کسی کی تم رہ بری نہ کرنا

بُری ہے اے داغؔ رہِ الفت، خدا نہ لے جائے ایسے رستے
جو اپنی تم خیر چاہتے ہو، تو بھول کر دل لگی نہ کرنا

Nawab Mirza Khan Dagh Dehlvi

Be thou atrocious and unkind, deprive me of your gaze benign,
Swear by me you shan't relent, nor ever repine.
If you deign to grace my bier, you should also shed a tear,
Show respect to my mort, mock it not, nor malign.
I'll take you, reverend heart, to the court of love,
Provided you desert me not and somewhere else recline.
If you love to watch the mirror, keep your face straight,
Your heart should be clean as cheeks, not like your locks entwined.
This is my creed of love: I befriend e'en my foes,
This is your approach, O cruel: alien even a friend you find.
I repent showing my heart the way to the lane of love,
Let Khizar beware of this, for guidance leaves regret behind.
The path of love is a dangerous path, may none this path pursue!
If, Dagh, you care for life, never towards love incline.

Sitam hi karna, jafa hi karna, nigaah-e-ulfat kabhi na karna,
Tumhen qasam hai hamare sar ki, hamare haq mein kami na karna.
Hamari maiyat pe tum jo aana, tau chaar aansu baha ke jana,
Zara rahe paas-e-aabroo bhi, kahin hamari hansi na karna.
Lieye tau chalte hain hazrat-e-dil, tumhen bhi us anjuman mein lekin,
Hamare pahlu mein baith kar tum, hamin se pahlu tahi na karna;
Hua hai gar shauq aaeene se, tau rukh rahe raasti ki jaanib,
Masaal-e-aariz safai rakhna, ba-rang-e-kakul kaji na karna.
Woh ik hamara tariq-e-ulfat ke dushmanon se bhi mil ke chalna,
Woh ek shewa tera sitamgar, ke dost se dosti na karna.
Hum ek rasta gali ka uski dikha ke dil ko hue pashemaan,
Yeh hazrat-e-Khizar ko bata do, kisi ki tum rahbari na karna.
Buri hai, ai Dagh, rah-e-ulfat, Khuda na le jaae aise raste,
Jo apni tum khair chahte ho, tau bhool kar dil-lagi na karna.

داغ

خاطر سے یا لحاظ سے میں مان تو گیا
جھوٹی قسم سے آپ کا ایمان تو گیا

دل لے کے مفت کہتے ہیں کچھ کام کا نہیں
الٹی شکایتیں ہوئیں، احسان تو گیا

ڈرتا ہوں دیکھ کر دلِ بے آرزو کو میں
سنسان گھر یہ کیوں نہ ہو، مہمان تو گیا

دیکھا ہے بت کدے میں جو اے شیخ کچھ نہ پوچھ
ایمان کی تو یہ ہے کہ ایمان تو گیا

افشائے رازِ عشق میں گو ذلّتیں ہوئیں
لیکن اسے جتا تو دیا، جان تو گیا

گو نامہ بر سے خوش نہ ہوا پر ہزار شکر
مجھ کو وہ میرے نام سے پہچان تو گیا

ہوش و حواس و تاب و تواں داغؔ جا چکے
اب ہم بھی جانے والے ہیں سامان تو گیا

Dagh Dehlvi

Through coaxing and pleading I was made to yield,
But you too, by forswearing, lost your faith and creed.
Having got my heart gratis, lo, he says: "No use,"
Instead of thanking me, behold, blame on me he heaps.
The desire-deserted heart presents a fearsome sight,
When the guest departs, the house is but bereaved.
Ask me not what all I saw in the idol-house,
In faith, of my zealous faith I was there relieved.
Unveiling my secret heart hurt my self-esteem,
But I did make my point, did explain my need.
Although he wasn't with my courier pleased,
Thank God he knew my name, did pay some heed.
Sense and poise, strength and vigour have left me one and all,
My goods have gone before me, I'm about to leave.

Khaatir se ya lihaaz se main maan tau gaya,
Jhooti qasam se aapka imaan tau gaya.
Dil le ke muft kahte hain kuchh kaam ka nahin,
Ulti shikaiten huin, ahsaan tau gaya.
Darta hun dekh kar dil-e-be-aarzoo ko main,
Sunsaan ghar yeh kyon na ho, mehmaan tau gaya.
Dekha hai but-kade mein jo ai sheikh kuchh na puchh,
Imaan ki tau yeh hai ke imaan tau gaya.
Afshaa-e-raaz-e-ishq mein go zillaten huin,
Lekin use jita tau diya, maan tau gaya.
Go nama bar se khush na hua, par hazaar shukar,
Mujh ko woh mere naam se pahchaan tau gaya.
Hosh-o-hawaas-o-taab-o-tawan, Dagh, jaa chuke,
Ab hum bhi jaane waale hain, samaan tau gaya.

داغ

سازِ یہ کینہ ساز کیا جانیں
ناز والے نیاز کیا جانیں
شمع رو آپ گو ہوئے لیکن
لطفِ سوز و گداز کیا جانیں
کب کسی در کی جبہہ سائی کی
شیخ صاحب نماز کیا جانیں
جو رہِ عشق میں قدم رکھیں
وہ نشیب و فراز کیا جانیں
پوچھئے میکشوں سے لطفِ شراب
یہ مزا پاکباز کیا جانیں
جن کو اپنی خبر نہیں اب تک
وہ مرے دل کا راز کیا جانیں
جو گزرتے ہیں داغؔ پر صدمے
آپ بندہ نواز کیا جانیں

Dagh Dehlvi

Bickering minds repel concord,
Coquetry knows no kindly thought.

Though you own a glowing face,
What know you of a melting heart?

When did the sheikh bend or bow?
The worth of prayer he knoweth not.

Those who choose the path of love,
Are unconcerned with gain or loss.

The drinkers know the taste of wine,
The pious are alien to the draught.

Those who do not know themselves,
Know they aught about my heart?

The shocks and blows that Dagh sustains,
You, my Lord, have tasted not.

Saaz yeh keena saaz kya jaanen,
Naaz waale nayaaz kya jaanen.

Shama-roo aap go hue lekin,
Lutaf-e-soz-o-gudaaz kya jaanen.

Kab kisi dar ki jibba saai ki,
Sheikh sahib namaaz kya jaanen.

Jo rah-e-ishq mein qadam rakhen,
Woh nasheb-o-faraaz kya jaanen.

Puchhieye maikashon se lutaf-e-sharaab,
Yeh maza paakbaaz kya jaanen.

Jin ko apni khabar nahin ab tak,
Woh mere dil ka raaz kya jaanen.

Jo guzarte hain Dagh par sadmein,
Aap banda-nawaaz kya jaanen.

داغؔ

جلوے مری نگاہ میں کون و مکاں کے ہیں
مجھ سے کہاں چھپیں گے وہ ایسے کہاں کے ہیں

کرتے ہیں قتل وہ طلبِ مغفرت کے بعد
جو تھے دعا کے ہاتھ وہی امتحاں کے ہیں

جس دن سے کچھ شریک ہوئی میری مشتِ خاک
اُس روز سے زمیں پہ ستم آسماں کے ہیں

کیسا جواب؟ حضرتِ دل! دیکھئے ذرا
پیغامبر کے ہاتھ میں ٹکڑے زباں کے ہیں

کیا اضطرابِ شوق نے مجھ کو خجل کیا
وُہ پوچھتے ہیں کہیے ارادے کہاں کے ہیں

عاشق تیرے عدم کو گئے کس قدر تباہ
پوچھا ہر ایک نے یہ مسافر کہاں کے ہیں

ہر چند داغؔ ایک ہی عیار ہے مگر
دشمن بھی تو چھٹے ہوئے سارے جہاں کے ہیں

Dagh Dehlvi

The sights of the world at large are sealed within my eyes,
He must belong somewhere on earth, where can he hide?

He first invokes forgiveness, then strikes my head,
The hand raised in prayer, also tests and tries.

Ever since my dust was mixed with the earth below,
The earth is subjected to the tyranny of the skies.

Expect no reply, heart, mark for a while,
Can't you, in the messenger's hand, bits of tongue descry?

Commotion of love entailed embarrassment extreme,
"What are you aiming at?" he asks surprised.

The lovers reached the world beyond in such a wretched plight,
Everyone inquired aghast: "Whence have you arrived?"

Dagh is a clever man, without a peer, no doubt,
His foes, too, are notorious rogues, dreaded worldwide.

Jalwe meri nigah mein kaun-o-makaan ke hain,
Mujh se kahan chhipenge, woh aise kahaan ke hain.

Karte hain qatal woh, talab-e-maghfarat ke baad,
Jo the duaa ke haath, wohi imtehaan ke hain.

Jis din se kuchh sharik hui meri musht-e-khaak,
Us roz se zameen pe sitam aasmaan ke hain.

Kaisa jawaab, hazrat-e-dil, dekheye zaraa,
Paighambar ke haath mein tukre zabaan ke hain.

Kya iztaraab-e-shauq ne mujh ko khajil kiya,
Woh puchhte hain, kaheye, iraade kahaan ke hain.

Aashiq tere adam ko gaye kisqadar tabaah,
Puchha har ek ne yeh musaafir kahan ke hain.

Har chand Dagh ek hi ayyaar hai, magar,
Dushman bhi tau chhate hue saare jahaan ke hain.

داغؔ

سبق ایسا پڑھا دِیا تو نے
دل سے سب کچھ بھُلا دِیا تو نے

لاکھ دینے کا ایک دینا ہے
دلِ بے مُدّعا دِیا تو نے

بے طلب جو مِلا، مِلا مجھکو
بے غرض جو دِیا، دِیا تو نے

کہیں مشتاق سے حجاب ہوا
کہیں پردہ اٹھا دِیا تو نے

مٹ گئے دل سے نقشِ باطل سب
نقشہ اپنا جما دِیا تو نے

مجھ گنہ گار کو جو بخش دیا
تو جہنم کو کیا دِیا تو نے

داغؔ کو کون دینے والا تھا
جو دِیا اے خدا دِیا تو نے

Dagh Dehlvi

What a lesson you have taught!
Everything I have forgot.

'Tis a boon worth a million boons,
This gift of a contented heart.

Whatever you gave, was motive-free,
Whatever I got, got unsought.

Here you hide from the seeker's eye,
There you stand unveiled, unmasked.

All false imprints stand expunged,
So deep have you stamped my heart!

If I, the sinner, can pardoned be,
Who in hell will then be lodged?

Who was there to provide for Dagh?
All I own is the gift of God.

Sabaq aisa parha diya tu ne,
Dil se sab kuchh bhula diya tu ne.

Laakh dene ka ek dena hai,
Dil-e-be mudaa diya tu ne.

Be talab jo mila, mila mujhko,
Be gharaz jo diya, diya tu ne.

Kahin mushtaaq se hijaab hua,
Kahin pardah utha diya tu ne.

Mit gaye dil se naqsh-e-baatil sab,
Naqsha apna jama diya tu ne.

Mujh gunahgaar ko jo bakhsh diya,
Tau jahannum ko kya diya tu ne.

Dagh ko kaun dene wala tha,
Jo diya, ai Khuda, diya tu ne.

داغؔ

کعبے کی ہے ہوس کبھی کوئے بتاں کی ہے
مجھ کو خبر نہیں مری مٹی کہاں کی ہے

کچھ تازگی ہو لذتِ آزار کے لیے
ہر دم مجھے تلاش نئے آسماں کی ہے

حسرت برس رہی ہے میرے مزار سے
کہتے ہیں سب یہ قبر کسی نوجواں کی ہے

قاصد کی گفتگو سے تسلی ہو کس طرح
چھپتی نہیں وہ جو تیری زباں کی ہے

سن کر مرا فسانۂ غم اس نے یہ کہا
ہو جائے جھوٹ سچ، یہی خوبی بیاں کی ہے

کیوں کر نہ آئے خلد سے آدم زمین پر
موزوں وہیں وہ خوب ہے جو شے جہاں کی ہے

اردو ہے جس کا نام ہمیں جانتے ہیں داغؔ
ہندوستاں میں دھوم ہماری زباں کی ہے

Dagh Dehlvi

Sometime I long for Kaaba, sometime for my darling's street,
I do not know where my clay will find its last retreat.

Novelty is a pre-requisite for the thrill of pain,
That's why a new sky is what I always need.

My grave breathes an air of longings unrealised,
People say that someone young lies buried beneath.

How can the messenger's words my doubts allay,
What you yourself had said, couldn't lie concealed.

When he heard my tale of woe, thus did he remark,
To pass a lie as seeming truth marks the art of speech.

Why shouldn't Adam exchange his heaven for the bliss of earth?
On their native soil alone things bloom and breed.

What they call Urdu, Dagh, we alone do know,
Everywhere in Hindustan, our language holds the field.

Kaabe ki hai hawas, kabhi koo-e-butaan ki hai,
Mujh ko khabar nahin meri mitti kahan ki hai.

Kuchh taazgi ho lazzat-e-aazaar ke lieye,
Har dam mujhe talaash naye aasmaan ki hai.

Hasrat baras rahi hai mere mazaar se,
Kahte hain sab yeh qabar kisi naujawaan ki hai.

Qaasid ki gufatgoo se tasalli ho kis tarah,
Chhipti nahin woh jo teri zabaan ki hai.

Sun kar mera fasaana-e-gham us ne yeh kaha,
Ho jaae jhoot such, yehi khubi bayaan ki hai.

Kyon kar na aae khuld se aadam zameen par,
Mauzoon wahin woh khub hai, jo shai jahan ki hai.

Urdu hai jiska naam hameen jante hain, Dagh,
Hindustan mein dhoom hamari zabaan ki hai.

داغ

پھرے راہ سے وہ یہاں آتے آتے
اجل مر رہی تو کہاں آتے آتے

مجھے یاد کرنے سے یہ مدّعا تھا
نکل جائے دم ہچکیاں آتے آتے

نہ جانا کہ دنیا سے جاتا ہے کوئی
بہت دیر کی مہرباں آتے آتے

ابھی سن ہی کیا ہے جو بے باکیاں ہوں
انہیں آئیں گی شوخیاں آتے آتے

چلے آتے ہیں دل میں ارمان لاکھوں
مکاں بھر گیا میہماں آتے آتے

سنانے کے قابل تھی جو بات ان کو
وہی رہ گئی درمیاں آتے آتے

نہیں کھیل اے داغؔ یاروں سے کہہ دو
کہ آتی ہے اردو زباں آتے آتے

Dagh Dehlvi

He has turned back somewhere, coming to this place,
Where do you hide, O death, what makes you wait?

This is why he remembered me, this is what he wished
That I should have passed away, hiccuping all the way.

Didn't you realise, someone was sinking away,
You did come, my kind sir, though came too late.

As yet she is too young to indulge in daring pranks,
She'll learn all these tricks, by and by, one day.

Countless longings come thronging right into my heart,
The house is invaded with the flux of guests today.

The thing that deserved narrating in my tale of woe,
That alone was left unsaid, when I had my say.

'Tis not a child's play, tell your friends, O Dagh,
The task of learning Urdu is uphill all the way.

Phire raah se woh yahaan aate, aate,
Ajal mar rahi tu kahaan aate, aate;

Mujhe yaad karne se yeh mudaa tha,
Nikal jaae dum hichkiyaan aate, aate.

Na jaana ke duniya se jaata hai koi,
Bahut der ki meharbaan aate, aate.

Abhi sin hi kya hai jo be baakiyaan hon,
Unhen aaengi shokhiaan aate, aate.

Chale aate hain dil mein armaan laakhon,
Makaan bhar gaya mehmaan aate, aate.

Sunaane ke qaabil thi jo baat unko,
Wohi rah gayi darmiaan aate, aate.

Nahin khei, ai Dagh, yaaron se kah do,
Ke aati hai Urdu zabaan aate, aate.

Khawaja Altaf Hussain Hali
(1837-1914)

KHWAJA ALTAF HUSSAIN HALI
(1837 - 1914)

Hali occupies a special position in the history of Urdu literature. Though he is not as great a lyricist as Ghalib, Momin, or Mir, he is more versatile than all of them. He is a poet, a critic, a teacher, a reformer and an impressive prose-writer. Circumstances did not permit him to attain formal education in a school or college, yet he had acquired, through sustained self-effort, a perfect command of Urdu, Persian and Arabic, and a good working knowledge of English. As a poet he did not confine himself within the narrow bounds of the *ghazal*, but successfully exploited the other poetic forms such as the *nazm*, the *rubai*, and the elegy. More particularly, he harnessed his poetic abilities to the higher aims of social and moral edification. Art for him was the handmaid to life. His famous long poem, "Musaddas-e-Hali", examines the state of social and moral degradation prevalent in the contemporary Muslim society. His prose treatise, "Mukaddama-e-Shair-o-Shairi"' is a pioneering work of literary criticism. It dwells on the limitations of the traditional *ghazal*, and points to the hollowness of its hackneyed themes and imagery, especially when the form is handled by inferior poets and versifiers. He has also written memorable biographies of Ghalib, Saadi Sheerazi, and Sir Sayed Ahmed Khan, entitled, respectively, "Yaadgar-e-Ghalib", "Hayat-e-Saadi", and "Hayat-e-Javed". His poem "Barkha Rut", describes the beauties of nature in the rainy season; "Hub-e-Watan", underscores the virtues of patriotism; while "Bewa ki Manajaat" focuses on the plight of widows in Indian society. Hali's interests were wide-ranging, and his literary abilities were commensurate with his humanitarian aims.

Both in his poetry and prose, Hali prefers a simple, natural, matter-of-fact style, which makes him easily accessible to all kinds of readers. He has had the privilege of receiving the patronage and guidance of some of the most illustrious men of his age — Mirza Ghalib, Nawab Mustafa Ali Khan Shefta, and Sir Sayed Ahmed Khan — all of whom contributed to the flowering of his genius.

خواجہ الطاف حسین حالیؔ

دردِ دل کو دوا سے کیا مطلب
کیمیا کو طِلا سے کیا مطلب
چشمۂ زندگی ہے ذکرِ جمیل
خضر و آبِ بقا سے کیا مطلب
بادشاہی ہے نفس کی تسخیر
ظِلِّ بالِ ہُما سے کیا مطلب
کام ہے مردمی سے انساں کی
زہد یا اتّقا سے کیا مطلب
ہے اگر رند دامن آلودہ
ہم کو چون وچرا سے کیا مطلب
صوفیٔ شہر باصفا ہے اگر
ہو۔ ہماری بلا سے کیا مطلب
نگہتِ مے پہ غش ہیں جو حالیؔ
ان کو دردِ صفا سے کیا مطلب

Khwaja Altaf Hussain Hali

The ache of heart no remedy knows,
Alchemy doesn't care for gold.

The talk of beauty is the fount of life,
Why look for Khizar, and ambrosial source?

Kingship lies in conquering desire,
The shade of Phoenix is just a hoax.

What matters is the courage of man,
Piety and purity are not his goals.

If the drinker wears a blemished robe,
Why should we grumble, why deplore?

If the Sufi is pure of heart,
It concerns us not, we ignore.

If smell of wine can make them swoon,
Why should they seek the brimful bowl?

Dard-e-dil ko dawa se kya matlib,
Keemiya ko tila se kya matlib.

Chashma-e-zindagi hai zikar-e-jameel,
Khizar-o-aab-o-baqa se kya matlib.

Baadshaahi hai nafs ki taskhir,
Zall-e-baal-e-huma se kya matlib.

Kaam hai mardami se insaan ki,
Zuhd yaa itteqaa se kya matlib.

Hai agar rind daaman-aaluda,
Hum ko chun chira se kya matlib.
Sufi-e-shahr baa-safa hai agar,
Ho, hamari bala se, kya matlib.

Nighat-e-mai pe ghash hain jo Hali,
Unko durd-o-safa se kya matlib.

حالیؔ

ہے یہ تکیہ تری عطاؤں پر
وہی اصرار ہے خطاؤں پر

رہرو و باخبر رہو کہ گمان
رہزنی کا ہے رہنماؤں پر

اُس کے کوچہ میں ہیں وہ بے پر و بال
اُڑتے پھرتے ہیں جو ہواؤں پر

شہسواروں پہ بند ہے جو راہ
وقف ہے یاں برہنہ پاؤں پر

نہیں منعم کو اس کی بُو نہ نصیب
مینہ برستا ہے جو گداؤں پر

نہیں محدود بخششیں تیری
زاہدوں پر نہ پارساؤں پر

حق سے درخواست عفو کی حالیؔ
کیجیے کس منہ سے اِن خطاؤں پر

Altaf Hussain Hali

Assured of Thy infinite grace,
We persist in errant ways.

Beware, O travellers, suspicion grows,
The guides here themselves waylay.

You find them wingless in his street,
Those who always soar and sail.

The paths forbid to the cavalier clans,
Are open to the barefoot race.

The rich are denied even a drop
Of rain that bathes the beggars' face.

Thy favours are not confined
To the pious and priestly race.

How to seek His pardon, Hali,
Submerged in this, o'r sinful state.

Hai yeh takiya teri itaaon par,
Wohi israar hai khataaon par.

Rahrawo baakhabar raho keh gumaan,
Rahzani ka hai rahnamaaon par.

Us ke kucha mein hain woh be par-o-baal,
Urte phirte hain jo hawaaon par.

Shahsawaaron pe band hai jo rah,
Waqf hai yaan barahna paaon par.

Nahin munim ko uski boond nasib,
Meinh barasta hai jo gadaaon par.

Nahin mahdood bakhshishen teri,
Zaahidon par na paarsaaon par.
Haq se darkhwast ufw ki Hali,
Kijeye kis munh se in khataaon par.

حالیؔ

ہے جستجو کہ خوب سے ہے خوب تر کہاں
اب ٹھہرتی ہے دیکھئے جا کر نظر کہاں

یا رب اس اختلاط کا انجام ہو بخیر
تھا اس کو ہم سے ربط مگر اس قدر کہاں

اک عمر چاہیے کہ گوارا ہو نیشِ عشق!
رکھی ہے آج لذّتِ زخمِ جگر کہاں!

ہم جس پہ مر رہے ہیں وہ ہے بات ہی کچھ اور
عالم میں تجھ سے لاکھ سہی تو مگر کہاں

ہوتی نہیں دعا قبول دردِ عشق کی
دل چاہتا نہ ہو تو زباں میں اثر کہاں

حالیؔ نشاطِ نغمہ و مے ڈھونڈتے ہو اب
آئے ہو وقتِ صبح رہے رات بھر کہاں

Altaf Hussain Hali

Something better than the best, this is what I quest,
Let's see my eager eyes, where finally rest.

Would to God this intimacy a happy ending finds,
He did love me before, but not with such a zest.

Getting used to the pangs of love requires a life complete,
The wound of heart is not yet at its painful best.

He for whom I'm dying is a being unique,
There may be millions like you, for you alone I thirst.

The prayer for renouncing love cannot bear fruit,
If the heart doesn't endorse, words lose effect.

Hali, you have come to seek the thrill of lilting song,
Too late in the day you come, where at night you lurked?

Hai justjoo keh khoob se hai khoobtar kahaan,
Ab thahrti hai, dekhieye, jaa kar nazar kahaan.

Yaar is ikhtelaat ka anjaam ho ba-khair,
Tha us ka hum se rabta, magar is qadar kahaan.

Ik umr chaahieye keh gawara ho neesh-e-ishq,
Rakhi hai aaj lazzat-e-zakhm-e-jigar kahaan.

Hum jis peh mar rahe hain woh hai baat hi kuchh aur,
Aalam mein tujh se laakh sahi, tu magar kahaan.

Hoti nahin dua qabool dard-e-ishq ki,
Dil chaahta na ho tau dua mein asr kahaan.

Hali, nishaat-e-naghma wale dhoondte ho ab,
Aae ho waqt-e-subah, rahe raat bhar kahaan.

حالیؔ

دیکھنا ہر طرف نہ مجلس میں
رُخنے نکلیں گے سینکڑوں اس میں
کی نصیحت بُری طرح ناصح
اور اِک بس بِلا دیا بس میں
ہو نہ بینا تو فرق پھر کیا ہے
چشمِ انساں و چشمِ نرگس میں
دین اور فقر تھے کبھی کچھ چیز
اب دھرا کیا ہے، اُس میں اور اس میں
ہو فرشتہ بھی تو نہیں انساں
درد تھوڑا بہت نہ ہو جس میں
جانور۔ آدمی۔ فرشتہ۔ خدا
آدمی کی ہیں سینکڑوں قسمیں
کی ہے خلوت پسند حالیؔ نے
اب نہ دیکھو گے اُس کو مجلس میں

Altaf Hussain Hali

Don't survey the court around,
Faults untold may here be found.

Your sermon, priest, was harsh in tone,
Galling both in sense and sound.

Human eye and the narcissus eye both seem at par,
Unless the human eye perceives truths deep, profound.

Religion and asceticism were once things esteemed,
Both have shed their lustre, both now hollow sound.

Even if he be an angel, he is not a man,
Whose heart is unmoved by others' woes and wounds.

Beast, human, angel, god —
In various forms doth man abound.

Hali has chosen to shun concourse,
At public meets he won't be found.

Dekhna har taraf na majlis mein,
Rukhne niklenge sainkron is mein.

Ki nasihat buri tarah naasih,
Aur ik bis mila diya bis mein.

Ho na beena tau farq phir kya hai,
Chashm-e-insaan-o-chashme-e-nargis mein.

Din aur fuqr the kabhi kuchh cheez,
Ab dhara kya hai us mein aur is mein.

Ho farishta bhi tau nahin insaan,
Dard thora bahut na ho jis mein.

Janwar, aadmi, farishta, Khuda,
Aadmi ki hain sainkron qismen.

Ki hai khilwat pasand Hali ne,
Ab na dekhoge usko majlis mein.

حالی

کل مدّعی کو آپ یہ کیا کیا گماں رہے
بات اُس کی کاٹتے رہے اور ہم زباں رہے

یارانِ تیز گام نے محمل کو جا لیا
ہم محوِ نالۂ جرسِ کارواں رہے

یا کھینچ لائے دیر سے رندوں کو اہلِ وعظ
یا آپ بھی ملازمِ پیرِ مغاں رہے

وصلِ مدام سے بھی ہماری بجھی نہ پیاس
ڈوبے ہم آبِ خضر میں اور نیم جاں رہے

دریا کو اپنی موج کی طغیانیوں سے کام
کشتی کسی کی پار ہو یا درمیاں رہے

حالی کے بعد کوئی نہ ہمدرد پھر ملا
کچھ راز تھے کہ دل میں ہمارے نہاں رہے

Altaf Hussain Hali

Diverse doubts assailed the rival, when, yesterday,
You both concurred with and contradicted his say.

Fleet-footed comrades have caught up with the caravan,
We kept moaning about the receding cavalcade.

The preacher's men will either the drinkers proselyte,
Or stay behind as tavern-keeper's slaves.

Even perpetual union couldn't quench my thirst,
Though I was submerged in nectar, still for life I craved.

The river knows naught else but to swell and surge,
It cares not if you're ruined or rowed across the bay.

No confidant after Hali did I come across,
Some secrets hid in my heart, still lie unveiled.

Kal muddai ko aap par kya kya gumaan rahe,
Baat uski kaat-te rahe, aur hum zabaan rahe.

Yaaraan-e-tez gaam ne mahmal ko jaa liya,
Hum mahw-e-naala-e-jars-e-caarwaan rahe.

Yaa kheinch laae dair se rindon ko ahl-e-waaz,
Yaa aap bhi mulaazim-e-pir-e-mughaan rahe.

Wasl-e-madaam se bhi hamari bujhi na piaas,
Doobe hum aab-e-Khizr mein, aur neem jaan rahe.

Darya ko apni mauj ki tughianion se kaam,
Kishti kisi ki paar ho, yaa darmiaan rahe.

Hali ke baad koi na hamdard phir mila,
Kuchh raaz the keh dil mein hamaare nihaan rahe.

حالؔی

دھوم تھی اپنی پارسائی کی
کی بھی اور کِس سے آشنائی کی

کیوں بڑھاتے ہو اختلاط بہت
ہم کو طاقت نہیں جُدائی کی

مُنھ کہاں تک چھپاؤگے ہم سے
تم کو عادت ہے خود نمائی کی

مِلتے غیروں سے ہو مِلو لیکن
ہم سے باتیں کرو صفائی کی

نہ مِلا کوئی غارتِ ایماں
رہ گئی شرم پارسائی کی

موت کی طرح جس سے ڈرتے ہو
ساعت آپہنچی اُس جدائی کی

زندہ پھرنے کی ہوس حالؔی
انتہا ہے یہ بے حیائی کی

Altaf Hussain Hali

My piety was trumpeted far and wide,
By whom, of all, I got enticed!

Why dost thou grow so intimate?
Severed from you, I can't survive.

You are prone to self-display,
How long can you your visage hide?

Go, meet the rival if you like,
Be frank with me, do not beguile.

None was there to tempt and try,
Thus was saved my virtuous pride.

What I dreaded like death itself,
The time of parting has arrived.

Hali, 'tis the height of shame,
This desire to return aiive.

Dhoom thi apni paarsaai ki,
Ki bhi aur kis se aashnaai ki.

Kyon barhaate ho ikhtlaat bahut,
Hum ko taaqat nahin judaai ki.

Munh kahan tak chhipaaoge hum se,
Tum ko aadat hai khud-numaai ki.

Milte ghairon se ho, milo, lekin,
Hum se baaten karo safai ki.

Na mila koi ghaarat gar-e-imaan,
Rah gai sharam paarsaai ki.

Maut ki tarah jis se darte the,
Saait aa pahunchi us judaai ki.

Zinda phirne ki hawas, Hali,
Inteha hai yeh be hayaai ki.

حالیؔ

جنوں کار فرما ہوا چاہتا ہے
قدم دشت پیما ہوا چاہتا ہے
دمِ گریہ یہ کِس کا تصوّر ہے دل میں
کہ اشکوں سے دریا بہا چاہتا ہے
خط آنے لگے شکوہ آمیز اُن کے
مِلاپ اُن سے گویا ہوا چاہتا ہے
ابھی لینے پائے نہیں دم جہاں میں
اجل کا تقاضا ہوا چاہتا ہے
بہت چین سے دِن گزرتے ہیں حالیؔ
کوئی فتنہ برپا ہوا چاہتا ہے

Altaf Hussain Hali

Madness is about to show in acts,
My feet itch for desert tracts.

Whose thought agitates my breast?
Streams of tears flow unchecked.

His missives are getting plaintive in tone,
Our union sure would take effect.

Even before we find our feet,
Death clamours for our breath.

Unusual calm pervades our life,
It augurs, perhaps, a wild tempest.

Janoon kaar farma hua chaahta hai,
Qadam dasht paima hua chaahta hai.

Dam-e-girya yeh kiska tasawur hai dil mein,
Keh ashkon se darya baha chaahta hai.

Khat aane lage shikwa aamez unke,
Milaap un se goya hua chaahta hai.

Abhi lene paae nahin dam jahan mein,
Ajal ka taqaaza hua chaahta hai.

Bahut chain se din guzarte hain, Hali,
Koi fitna barpa hua chaahta hai.

Akbar Hussain Akbar Allahabadi
(1846-1921)

AKBAR HUSSAIN AKBAR ALLAHABADI
(1846 - 1921)

Akbar was born in 1846 in a respectable family at Bara, near Allahabad. In keeping with the prevalent custom, Akbar received his early education at home at the hands of his father, Sayed Tafazzul Hussain, who was a man of considerable learning. At about the age of 10 Akbar joined the Mission School at Allahabad. He was married at the age of 15 to a girl who was two or three years his senior. It was an unhappy marriage which didn't last long, and Akbar was forced to marry for the second time. He had two sons from each of these two unions. Akbar was an intelligent, persevering boy who always did well in his examinations. With an eye on his future career he studied law, and worked for a while as a practising lawyer. Later he got into government service, and rose to the high rank of a Session Judge. He sought premature retirement for reasons of health, and led a quiet, sequestered life in his old age.

Akbar was a brilliant, ready-witted, affable man, with a marked sense of humour which, incidentally, is also the hallmark of his poetry — be it *ghazal, nazm, rubai, qita.* He treats even the serious themes of love and politics with a touch of humour. He is a social reformer, and his reformist zeal works through the medium of wit and humour. There is hardly any aspect of life which escapes his satirical gaze. A champion of Eastern values, Akbar is specially opposed to a mindless imitation of the Western ways of life, which he found morally and spiritually sterile. In his approach to life and religion, he gives preference, like the mystic saints, to love over reason, to faith over knowledge. In one of his *rubaies,* he stresses his affinity with Spenser the poet, as against Mill the philosopher. He is distinctly original in his style too, for he can use any popular word or phrase of English which can convey his meaning, or increase the humorous impact of his verse. This intermingling of Urdu with English vocabulary was a thing unknown to his predecessors, nor was his practice adopted by the younger generation of writers and poets.

Although Akbar is essentially a lively, optimistic poet, his vision of things got clouded in his later life by his experience of tragedy at home. One of his sons, and a grandson, whom he dearly loved, died young. This caused him great shock and despair. Consequently towards the end of his life he got considerably subdued, and became increasingly pensive and religious. He died in 1921 at the age of 75.

اکبر حسین اکبر الہ آبادی

یہ موجودہ طریقے راہیِ ملکِ عدم ہونگے
نئی تہذیب ہوگی اور نئے ساماں بہم ہونگے
نئے عنواں سے زینت دکھائیں گے حسیں اپنی
نہ ایسا پیچ زُلفوں میں، نہ گیسو میں یہ خم ہونگے
نہ خاتونوں میں رہ جائیگی پردے کی یہ پابندی
نہ گھونگھٹ اس طرح سے حاجبِ روئے صنم ہونگے
خبر دیتی ہے تحریکِ ہوا تبدیلِ موسم کی
کِھلیں گے اور ہی گُل، زمزمے بُلبُل کے کم ہونگے
بہت ہوں گے مغنّی نغمۂ تقلیدِ یورپ کے
مگر بے جوڑ ہوں گے اس لیے بے تال و سم ہونگے
گزشتہ عظمتوں کے تذکرے بھی رہ نہ جائینگے
کتابوں ہی میں دفن افسانۂ جاہ و حشم ہونگے
تمہیں اس انقلابِ دہر کا کیا غم ہے اے اکبرؔ
بہت نزدیک ہیں وُہ دِن نہ تم ہوگے نہ ہم ہونگے

Akbar Hussain Akbar Allahabadi

The current ways of life will soon depart from earth,
New culture, new modes of life will now take their birth.

The beauty will adore itself in a new style,
The coiling locks and curling hair will now fall in dearth.

The women will discard the robes that confine and bind,
No longer the beauteous mein behind the veil shall lurk.

The wind that blows indicates the birth of seasons new,
New flowers will bloom on earth, nightingales forget their mirth.

Imitators of Western music will reign supreme,
Their songs will be out of tune, a cacophonous burst.

Past glories will find a mention nowhere on earth,
Glorious tales of name and fame inside the books will rust.

But why are you perturbed, Akbar, about the changing times?
You and I will cease to be, and mingle with the dust.

Yeh maujooda tareeqe raahieye mulk-e-adam honge,
Nai tahzib hogi aur nai saamaan baham honge.

Naye unwan se zeenat dikhainge huseen apni,
Na aisa pech zulfon mein, na gaisu mein yeh kham honge.

Na khaatoonon mein rah jaaegi parde ki yeh paabandi,
Na ghungat istarah se haajib-e-roo-e-sanam honge.

Khabar deti hai tahrik-e-hawa tabdil-e-mausam ki,
Khileinge aur hi gul, zamzame bulbul ke kam honge.

Bahut honge mughanni naghma-e-taqlid-e-Europe ke,
Magar be jor honge, islieye be-tal-o-sum honge.

Guzashta azmaton ke tazkare bhi rah na jaaenge,
Kitaabon mein hi dafan afsaana-e-jaah-o-hasham honge.

Tumhen is inqalaab-e-dahar ka kya gham hai, ai Akbar,
Bahut nazdik hain woh din, na tum hoge, na hum honge.

اکبر الٰہ آبادی

کہاں وہ اب لُطفِ باہمی ہے، محبتوں میں بہت کمی ہے
چلی ہے کیسی ہوا الٰہی کہ ہر طبیعت میں برہمی ہے
مری وفا میں ہے کیا تزلزل، مری اطاعت میں کیا کمی ہے
یہ کیوں نگاہیں پھری ہیں مجھ سے، مزاج میں کیوں یہ برہمی ہے
وہی ہے فضلِ خدا سے اب تک ترقّیِ کارِ حُسن و الفت
نہ وہ ہیں مشقِ ستم میں قاصر، نہ خونِ دِل کی یہاں کمی ہے
عجیب جلوے ہیں ہوش دُشمن کہ وہم کے بھی قدم رُکے ہیں
عجیب منظر ہیں حیرت افزا، نظر جہاں تھی وہیں تھمی ہے
نہ کوئی تکریمِ باہمی ہے، نہ پیار باقی ہے اب دِلوں میں
یہ صرف تحریر میں "ڈیر سر" ہے یا "جناب مکرمی" ہے
کہاں کے مسلم، کہاں کے ہندو بھُلائی ہیں سب نے اگلی رسمیں
عقیدے سب کے ہیں تین تیرہ، نہ گیارہویں ہے، نہ اشٹمی ہے
اگرچہ میں رندِ محترم ہوں مگر اسے شیخ سے نہ پوچھو
کہ اُن کے آگے تو اس زمانے میں ساری دنیا جہنمی ہے

Akbar Allahabadi

Gone the joy of shared regard, genuine love is fading fast,
What a wind has swept the land, every heart is deep distraught.

Has my love suffered decline, does my faith seem to flag?
Why art thou indifferent grown, why dost thou thus cut me short?

Love and beauty, God be thanked, haven't deflected from their path,
Copious flows the lovers' blood, relentless are the beauty's darts.

Wondrous sights that rob the sense, and all doubts dispel!
Bewildering scenes that stun the eyes and make us stare, aghast!

Mutual regard is long deceased, hearts are shorn of love,
"Dear Sir", or "Reverend Sir", are now reserved for letter-cards.

Neither Hindus nor Muslims respect traditional rites,
Their beliefs are awry gone, they don't observe the feasts and fasts.

Although I'm a veteran drinker, but don't ask the Sheikh,
Since to him the world entire is the devil's bosom-pal.

Kahan woh ab lutf-e-baahmi hai, mahabbton mein bahut kami hai,
Chali hai kaisi hawa Ilahi, keh har tabiat mein barhami hai.

Meri wafa mein hai kya tazalzal, meri itaait mein kya kami hai?
Yeh kyon nigaahen phirri hain mujh se, mizaaj mein kyon barhami hai?

Wohi hai fazal-e-Khuda se ab tak, taraqqi-e-kaar-e-husn-o-ulfat,
Na woh hain mashq-e-sitam mein qaasir, na khoon-e-dil ki yahan kami hai.

Ajib jalwe hain hosh dushman, keh waham ke bhi qadam ruke hain,
Ajib manzir hain hairat afza, nazar jahan thi wahin thami hai.

Na koi takrim-e-baahmi hai, na pyaar baaqi hai ab dilon mein,
Yeh sirf tahrir mein "dear sir" hai, yaa "janaab-e-mukarrmi" hai.

Kahan ke Muslim, kahan ke Hindu, bhulaai hain sab ne agli rasmen,
Aqide sab ke hain tin terah, na gayarwin hai, na ashtmi hai.

Agarche main rind-e-muhtram hun, magar ise Sheikh se na puchho,
Ke un ke aage tau is zamaane mein saari duniya jahannmi hai.

اکبرؔ الٰہ آبادی

دنیا میں ہوں، دنیا کا طلب گار نہیں ہوں
بازار سے گزرا ہوں، خریدار نہیں ہوں

زندہ ہوں مگر زیست کی لذت نہیں باقی
ہر چند کہ ہوں ہوش میں، ہشیار نہیں ہوں

اس خانۂ ہستی سے گزر جاؤں گا بے لوث
سایہ ہوں فقط، نقش بہ دیوار نہیں ہوں

وہ گُل ہوں، خزاں نے جسے برباد کیا ہے
الجھوں کسی دامن سے، میں وہ خار نہیں ہوں

یارب مجھے محفوظ رکھ اُس بُت کے ستم سے
میں اُس کی عنایت کا طلبگار نہیں ہوں

گو دعوئِ تقویٰ نہیں درگاہِ خدا میں
بُت جس سے ہوں خوش ایسا گنہگار نہیں ہوں

افسردگی وضعف کی کچھ حد نہیں اکبرؔ
کافر کے مقابل میں بھی دیں دار نہیں ہوں

Akbar Allahabadi

Though I live in the world, for the world I don't care,
I'm passing through the mart with no intent to buy its ware.

I am alive, but for me life has lost its zest,
Though I keep my wits intact, I lack the wit to do or dare.

I'll quit the stage of life untainted, untouched,
Not even a painted picture, I'm a shadow bare.

I'm a flower burnt and blighted by the autumn's blast,
Not a thorn that would hook the skirts of people everywhere.

Save, O God, from the tyranny of that dear despot,
I do not seek his favours, nor for his kindness care.

Though I can't protest my piety at the bar of God,
I'm not such a sinner for whom my love would care.

Weariness and depression have crossed all confines,
Poorer than the atheists, is the faith I share.

Duniya mein hun, duniya ka talabgaar nahin hun,
Bazaar se guzra hun, kharidaar nahin hun.

Zinda hun magar zeest ki lazzat nahin baaqi,
Har chand keh hun hosh mein, hushiar nahin hun.

Is khana-e-hasti se guzar jaaunga be-laus,
Saaya hun faqt, naqsh-ba-deewar nahin hun.

Woh gul hun khazaan ne jise barbaad kiya hai,
Uljhun kisi daaman se, main woh khaar nahin hun.

Yaarab mujhe mahfooz rakh us but ke sitam se,
Main uski inaait ka talabgaar nahin hun.

Go daawa-e-taqwa nahin dargaah-e-Khuda mein,
But jis se hon khush aisa gunahgaar nahin hun.

Afsurdagi-o-zauf ki kuchh had nahin, Akbar,
Kaafir ke muqaabil mein bhi deendar nahin hun.

اکبر الٰہ آبادی

ہر قدم کہتا ہے تو آیا ہے جانے کے لیے
منزلِ ہستی نہیں ہے دِل لگانے کے لیے

کیا مجھے خوش آئے یہ حیرت سرائے بے ثبات
ہوش اُڑنے کے لیے ہے جان جانے کے لیے

خُوب امیدیں بندھیں لیکن ہوئیں حرماں نصیب
بدلیاں اُٹھیں مگر بجلی گرانے کے لیے

سائنس کی ترکیب پر مٹی کو پیار آ ہی گیا
خود ہوئی قید اُس کو سینے سے لگانے کے لیے

جب کہا میں نے بھلا دو غیر کو، ہنس کر کہا
یاد پھر مجھ کو دِلانا بھول جانے کے لئے

مجھ کو خوش آتی ہے مستی، شیخ جی کو فربہی
میں ہوں پینے کے لیے اور وہ ہیں کھانے کیلیے

سُر کہاں کے، ساز کیسا، کیسی بزمِ سامعیں
جوشِ دِل کافی ہے، اکبرؔ تان اُڑانے کے لیے

Akbar Allahabadi

Every step doth proclaim: "Here we come to go,
The world is not the place to engage our heart and soul."

How can this transit camp satisfy our heart,
Where we must lose our wits, where our life must go.

Many a hope sprightly rose, but sank down depressed,
Many a cloud formed itself, but turned to lightning stroke.

The dust at last compassionate grew towards the sinking heart,
It got itself imprisoned to hold it in its fold.

When I said, "You should the rival clean forget,"
"Remind me please," he quipped, "when I recall that foe."

Rapture is my favourite state, obesity the Sheikh's,
He loves to hog and hog, I to quaff the bowl.

What's a tune, or timbrel, what an audience rapt?
Enough is the fire of heart to make us sing and soar.

Har qadam kahta hai: tu aaya hai jaane ke lieye,
Manzil-e-hasti nahin hai dil lagaane ke lieye.

Kya mujhe khush aaey yeh hairat saraey be-sabaat,
Hosh urne ke lieye hai, jaan jaane ke lieye.

Khub ummeedein bandhi, lekin hueen hirmaan nasib,
Badliaan uthin magar bijli giraane ke lieye.

Saans ki tarkib par mitti ko payaar aa hi gaya,
Khud hui qaid usko seene se lagaane ke lieye.

Jab kaha main ne bhula do ghair ko, hans kar kaha:
Yaad phir mujh ko dilana bhul jaane ke lieye.

Mujh ko khush aai hai masti, Sheikh ko farbahi,
Main hun peene ki lieye, aur woh hain khane ke lieye.

Sur kahan ke, saaz kaisa, kaisi bazm-e-saamaeen,
Josh-e-dil kaafi hai, Akbar, taan uraane ke lieye.

اکبرؔ الٰہ آبادی

فلسفی کو بحث کے اندر خُدا مِلتا نہیں
ڈور کو سُلجھا رہا ہے اور سرا مِلتا نہیں

معرفت خالِق کی عالم میں بہت دشوار ہے
شہرِ تن میں جب کہ خود اپنا پتہ ملتا نہیں

غافلوں کے لطف کو کافی ہے دنیاوی خوشی
عاقلوں کو بے غمِ عقبیٰ مزا ملتا نہیں

کشتیِ دِل کی الٰہی بحرِ ہستی میں ہو خیر
ناخُدا ملتے ہیں لیکن باخُدا مِلتا نہیں

زندگانی کا مزا ملتا تھا جن کی بزم میں
اُن کی قبروں کا بھی اب مجھ کو پتا مِلتا نہیں

صرف ظاہر ہو گیا سرمایۂ زیب و صفا
کیا تعجب ہے جو باطن باصفا مِلتا نہیں

پختہ طبعوں پر حوادث کا نہیں ہوتا اثر
کوہساروں میں نشانِ نقشِ پا مِلتا نہیں

Akbar Allahabadi

The philosopher fails to find God in his subtle debates,
While he unravels the knot, the end eludes his gaze.

Realisation of God on earth is an arduous task,
Unless you can know thyself deep in the body's cage.

The sluggards are quite content with mundane delights,
The wise cannot but strive for the ultimate.

God save the boat of heart in the sea of life,
An oarsman is easy to find, but not a man of faith.

We can't even trace the graves of o'r former mates,
Whose presence was the joy of life, the assembly's central grace.

All cosmetic art is spent on decking up the face,
No wonder, of inward charm there's not a trace.

Strong minds are left unruffled by the blows of fate,
Footsteps cannot leave their mark on the mountain face.

Falsafi ko bahs ke andar Khuda milta nahin,
Dor ko suljha raha hai, aur sira milta nahin.

Maarfat khaaliq ki aalam mein bahut dushwaar hai,
Shahr-e-tan mein jabkeh khud apna pata milta nahin.

Ghaafilon ke lutaf ko kaafi hai duniyaawi khushi,
Aaqlon ko be gham-e-uqwa maza milta nahin.

Kashti-e-dil ki, Illahi, bahr-e-hasti mein ho khair,
Naakhuda milte hain, lekin baa-khuda milta nahin.

Zindgaani ka maza milta tha jinki bazm mein,
Un ki qabron ka bhi ab mijhko pata milta nahin.

Sarf-e-zaahir ho gaya sarmaaya-e-zeb-o-safa,
Kya taajjub hai keh baatin baa safa milta nahin.

Pukhta-tabbon par hawaadis ka nahin hota asar,
Kohsaaron mein nishaan-e-naqsh-e-pa milta nahin.

اکبر الٰہ آبادی

رنگِ شراب سے مری نیت بدل گئی
واعظ کی باتیں رہ گئیں ساقی کی چل گئی

تیار تھے نماز پہ ہم، سُن کے ذکرِ حُور
جلوہ بُتوں کا دیکھ کے نیّت بدل گئی

مچھلی نے ڈھیل پائی ہے، لُقمے پہ شاد ہے
صیّاد مطمئن ہے کہ کانٹا نِگل گئی

چمکا ترا جمال جو محفل میں وقتِ شام
پروانہ بے قرار ہوا، شمع جل گئی

عقبیٰ کی باز پُرس کا جاتا رہا خیال
دنیا کی لذتوں میں طبیعت بہل گئی

حسرت بہت ترقیِ دُختر کی تھی اُنھیں
پردہ جو اُٹھ گیا تو وہ آخر نکل گئی

Akbar Allahabadi

The sight of the purple wine made me change my mind,
The preacher's word remained unheard, saqi's word was law divine.

I was all set for prayers, when someone mentioned the 'hurs',
The sight of fairy belles unsettled my mind.

The fish takes it easy, relishing the morsel sweet,
Thinking it has swallowed the bait, the hunter feels so fine.

As your beauty glimmered and glowed at the evening meet,
The candle burnt itself alive, the moth did restless whine.

I clean forgot the reckoning day that lay in wait,
Pleasures of the world so engrossed my mind.

The progress of his daughter was his cherished dream,
As the veil uplifted, the dream peaked and pined.

Rang-e-sharaab se meri neeat badal gai,
Waaiz ki baaten rah gaien, saqi ki chal gai.

Tayyaar the namaaz pe hum, sun ke zikr-e-hur,
Jalwa buton ka dekh ke neeat badal gai.

Machhli ne dhil paai hai, luqme pe shaad hai,
Sayyaad mutmain hai keh kaanta nigal gai.

Chamka tira jamaal jo mahfal mein waqt-e-shaam,
Parwana be-qaraar hua, shama jal gai.

Uqwa ki baaz purs ka jaata rha khayaal,
Duniya ki lazzaton mein tabiat bahl gai.

Hasrat bahut taraqqi-e-dukhtar ki thi unhen,
Purdah jo uth gaya, tau woh aakhir nikal gai.

اکبرؔ الٰہ آبادی

ہنگامہ ہے کیوں برپا تھوڑی سی جو پی لی ہے
ڈاکہ تو نہیں ڈالا، چوری تو نہیں کی ہے
نا تجربہ کاری سے واعظ کی یہ باتیں ہیں
اِس رنگ کو کیا جانے پوچھو تو کبھی پی ہے
اِس مے سے نہیں مطلب دل جس سے ہے بیگانہ
مقصود ہے اِس مے سے دل ہی میں جو کھنچتی ہے
واں دِل میں کہ صدمے دو، یاں جی میں کہ سب سہہ لو
اُن کا بھی عجب دل ہے۔ میرا بھی عجب دِل ہے
ہر ذرّہ چمکتا ہے انوارِ الٰہی سے
ہر سانس یہ کہتی ہے، ہم ہیں تو خدا بھی ہے
سورج میں لگے دھبّہ، فطرت کے کرشمے ہیں
بُت ہم کو کہیں کافر، اللہ کی مرضی ہے

Akbar Allahabadi

If I've drunk a little, why this furore?
I haven't robbed anyone, nor forced open a door.

Inexperience is the cause of the priest's uproar,
Has he known this state at all, has he seen the bowl?

I'm not concerned with wine which the heart detests,
The wine distilled within the heart, is what my heart adores.

There he says: "Deliver the blows," here I say, "Endure,"
What a queer heart he hath, what a heart I hold!

Every grain owes its glow to the light divine,
Every breath that we breathe, His presence underscores.

A blot staining the sun's face! mysterious are the nature's ways,
The idols questioning my faith! Thy will, O God, shall hold!

Hangaama hai kyon barpa, thori si jo pi li hai,
Daka tau nahin dala, chori tau nahin ki hai.

Naa tajurbakaari se waaiz ki yeh baaten hain,
Is rang ko kya jaane, puchho tau kabhi pi hai.

Is mai se nahin matlib dil jis se hai begaana,
Maqsud hai us mai se dil hi mein jo khinchti hai.

Waan dil mein ke sadme do, yaan ji mein ke sab sah lo,
Un ka bhi ajab dil hai, mera bhi ajab dil hai.

Har zarra chamakta hai anwaar-e-Illahi se,
Har saans yeh kahti hai, hum hain tau Khuda bhi hai.

Suraj mein lage dhabba, fitrat ke karishme hain,
But hum ko kahen kaafir, Allah ki marzi hai!

Ali Mohammed Shad Azimabadi
(1846-1927)

ALI MOHAMMED SHAD AZIMABADI
(1846 - 1927)

Shad is counted among the illustrious poets of the *ghazal* who have made a notable contribution to the growth and enrichment of this poetic form. He liberated the *ghazal* from the superficial elegance produced by the linguistic acrobatics of the Lucknow school, and infused into it a spirit of genuine passion and poetry. He was a friend and contemporary of such eminent writers and reformers as Sir Sayyed Ahmed Khan, Shibli, Hali, Akbar, Iqbal, Amir Meenai, Dagh and Hasrat Mohani, all of whom recognise his worth as man and poet.

Shad was born in 1846 at Azimabad (Patna) in the house of his maternal grandparents. He belonged to a rich and respectable family, but because of his carefree, unworldly nature, he paid little attention to preserving, much less multiplying, his material assets. Consequently, in old age he had to pass through a period of economic difficulty.

Shad was a whole-time poet, with an inborn gift for poetry. Early in his boyhood he had acquired a thorough grounding in Urdu, Persian and Arabic, which he had learnt from famous local teachers and scholars. He received poetic instruction from a number of masters, including, finally, Shah Ulfat Hussain Faryaad, who may be called his poetic preceptor. Shad was a versatile poet whose poetic output included, in addition to *ghazals, rubaies, masnavis, qasidas* and *marsias,* as also prose stories. His poetic works have been published in five volumes. In spite of this, Shad felt deeply dissatisfied with the sort of response given to his poetry. In a number of verses he advises his son not to adopt poetry as his exclusive vocation. This kind of discontent is perhaps the lot of all sensitive men of letters. Nevertheless, Shad is now given due recognition, and his *ghazals* are included in the syllabi of schools and colleges. A selection of his rubaies also finds a place of pride in the present author's book: *Masterpieces of Urdu Rubaiyat*, (Sterling Publishers, Delhi).

Shad's poetry makes an appeal both to the connoisseur and the commoner. This is because he gives us deep thoughts in simple, natural language. Though he generally deals with the traditional and universal themes of love and mysticism, these themes are charged with deep philosophical insights, conveyed through meaningful metaphors.

Shad died in 1927 at the age of eighty-one.

علی محمد شاد عظیم آبادی

مصیبت جس سے زائل ہو، وہی سامان کر دیگا
نہ گھبرانا خدا سب مشکلیں آسان کر دیگا

خوشی سے مشکلوں کا سامنا کر، منھ نہ پھیر اے دل
ترے عقدوں کا حل، ترا یہی اوسان کر دیگا

بشر پر منحصر کیا، تذکرہ اس کا تو ہے ناحق
یہ عشقِ ذو فنوں، حیواں کو بھی انسان کر دیگا

تری روپوشیاں اے حسن کب بیکار جائینگی
یہی پردہ عیاں عالم میں تیری شان کر دیگا

دِلا گھبرا رہا ہے کیوں، غنیمت ہے کہ عشق آیا
ترے اے میزباں، سب کام یہ مہمان کر دیگا

کوئی گر سلطنت بھی دے تجھے ہرگز نہ لے اے دل
سُبک ہر طرح سے تجھ کو غیر کا احسان کر دیگا

یقیں کر لے کہ خود وہ جلوہ گر پردے میں ہیں ورنہ
یہی ظالم گماں تیرا تجھے حیران کر دیگا

Ali Mohammed Shad Azimabadi

He'll create conditions that will your troubles dissolve,
Rest assured, God will all your problems solve;
Face your trials with a smile, shrink not, O heart,
Your conduct will, no doubt, all your riddles resolve.
Why talk of man alone, why debate his single case?
Even a beast, at the touch of love, into a man evolves.
The veil on your face, O Beauty, will not fruitless lie,
Because of it your glory will round the world revolve.
Why feel upset, my heart, rejoice! Love has come,
This guest will surely your errands discharge.
Even if offered a kingdom spurn it, O heart,
You'll feel burdened for ever for the debt involved.
You must believe that God Himself reigns behind the veil,
Or else, your doubting self will keep you ever distraught.

Museebat jis se zaayal ho, wohi samaan kar dega,
Na ghabrana Khuda sub mushkilen aasaan kar dega.
Khushi se mushkilon ka saamna kar, munh na pher, ai dil,
Tire uqdon ka hal, tera yehi ausaan kar dega.
Bashar par munhasar kya, tazkara iska tau hai naahaq,
Yeh ishq-e-zu fatun, haiwan ko bhi insaan kar dega.
Tiri rooposhian, ai husn, kab bekaar jaaengi,
Yehi pardah ayaan aalam mein teri shan kar dega.
Dila ghabra raha hai kyon, ghanimat hai ke ishq aaya,
Tire, ai mezbaan, sub kaam yeh mehmaan kar dega.
Koi gar saltanat bhi de tujhe, hargiz na le, ai dil,
Subak har tarah se tujhko ghair ka ahsaan kar dega.
Yaqin kar le khud woh jalwagar parde mein hai, warna,
Yehi zaalim gumaan tera tujhe hairan kar dega.

شادؔ

اسیرِ جسم ہوں . میعادِ قید لامعلوم
یہ کس گناہ کی پاداش ہے خُدا معلوم

تری گلی بھی مجھے یوں تو کھینچتی ہے بہت
دراصل ہے مری مٹی کہاں کی کیا معلوم

سفر ضرور ہے اور عذر کی مجال نہیں
مزا تو یہ ہے نہ منزل نہ راستہ معلوم

دعا کروں نہ کروں سوچ ہے یہی کہ تجھے
دُعا سے پہلے مرے دل کا مُدعا معلوم

سُنی حکایتِ ہستی تو درمیاں سے سُنی
نہ ابتدا کی خبر ہے نہ انتہا معلوم

کچھ اپنے پاؤں کی ہمت بھی چاہیے اے پیر
یہی نہیں تو مددگاریِ عصا معلوم

طلب کریں بھی تو کیا شے طلب کریں اے شادؔ
ہمیں کو آپ نہیں اپنا مُدعا معلوم

Shad Azimabadi

I'm the prisoner of the body, the term of sentence is unknown,
God alone knows the sin which I thus atone.
Your street, too, no doubt, fascinates my heart,
But who knows where my dust is destined to be sown.
Imperative is the voyage of life, no way to escape,
The beauty is, both path and goal are to us unknown.
Do I need to pray or not, I feel perplexed,
Ere even I ope my lips, my thought to Thee is known.
We only heard the tale of life somewhere in-between,
Nor the beginning, nor the end to us was intoned.
Old man, your feet must some strength possess,
Trust not your walking stick can take you far, alone.
Even if I ask a boon, what should, Shad, it be?
I know not what my heart really wants to own.

Aseer-e-jism hun, maiyaad-e-qaid laa maalum,
Yeh kis gunah ki padaash hai, Khuda maalum.
Tiri gali bhi mujhe yun tau kheenchti hai bahut,
Dar asaal hai meri mitti kahan ki, kya maalum.
Safar zarur hai, aur uzar ki majaal nahin,
Maza tau yeh hai na manzil, na raasta maalum.
Dua karun na karun soch hai yehi ke tujhe,
Dua se pehle mere dil ka muddaa maalum.
Suni hikaayat-e-hasti tau darmian se suni,
Na ibtada ki khabar, na inteha maalum.
Kuchh apne paaon ki himmat bhi chaahieye, ai pir,
Yehi nahin tau madadgaari-e-asa maalum.
Talab karen bhi tau kya shai talab karen, ai Shad,
Hameen ko aap nahin apna muddaa maalum.

شاد

ڈھونڈوگے اگر ملکوں ملکوں، ملنے کے نہیں نایاب ہیں ہم
تعبیر ہے جس کی حسرت وغم، اے ہم نفسو وہ خواب ہیں ہم

میں حیرت وحسرت کا مارا خاموش کھڑا ہوں ساحل پر
دریائے محبّت کہتا ہے، آ، کچھ بھی نہیں پایاب ہیں ہم

اے دردِ محبت کچھ تو ہی بتا، اب تک یہ معمہ حل نہ ہوا
ہم میں ہے دلِ بیتاب نہاں، یا آپ دلِ بیتاب ہیں ہم

لاکھوں ہی مسافر چلتے ہیں منزل پہ پہنچتے ہیں دو ایک
اے اہلِ زمانہ قدر کرو، نایاب نہ ہوں، کم یاب ہیں ہم

مرغانِ قفس کو پھولوں نے اے شادؔ یہ کہلا بھیجا ہے
آجاؤ جو تم کو آنا ہو، ایسے میں ابھی شاداب ہیں ہم

Shad Azimabadi

Search for us throughout the world, us you cannot find,
A dream premonishing regret and grief, such is our kind.
Stunned and silent on the shore, wistfully I gaze,
The river of love gives the call: "Come, I'm easy to find."
O, ache of love, tell me, pray, I can't resolve the riddle,
Am I the restless heart myself, or is the heart in me confined?
Countless travellers start from home, a few attain the goal,
O folks, give us due respect, though not unique, we're rare in kind.
The flowers have sent a message to the birds encaged:
Come sharp, if you feel inclined, lest our youth declines.

Dhoondoge agar mulkon, mulkon, milne ke nahin, naayaab hain hum,
Taabir hai jiski hasrat-o-ghum, ai hum nafso, woh khwab hain hum.
Main hairat-o-hasrat ka mara khamosh khara hun saahil par,
Darya-e-mahabbat kahta hai, aa kuchh bhi nahin, paayaab hain hum.
Ai dard-e-mahabbat, kuchh tu hi bata, ab tak yeh muimma hal na hua,
Hum mein hai dil-e-betaab nihaan, yaa aap dil-e-betaab hain hum?
Laakhon hi mussafir chalte hain, manzil pe pauhnchte hain do ek,
Ai ahl-e-zamana, qadar karo, naayaab na hon, kam yaab hain hum.
Murghaan-e-qafas ko phoolon ne ai Shad ye kahla bheja hai,
Aa jaao jo tum ko aana ho, aise mein abhi shadab hain hum.

شاد

سر پہ کلاہِ کج دھرے زلفِ دراز خم بہ خم
آہوئے چشم ہے غضب، ترکِ نگاہ ہے ستم

چاند سے مُنھ پہ خال دو، ایک ذقن پہ رُخ پہ ایک
اس سے خرابیٔ عرب، اس سے تباہیٔ عجم

وہ خمِ گیسوئے دراز، دامِ خیالِ عاشقاں
ہوگئے بے طرح شکار، اب نہ رہے کہیں کے ہم

عشوۂ دل گداز وہ، ذبح کرے جو بے چھری
ناز وہ دشمنِ وفا، رحم کی جس کو ہے قسم

دل جو بڑا رفیق تھا، وہ تو ہے دستِ غیر میں
رہ گئی ایک زندگی، وہ کہیں آرزو سے کم

نالۂ آتشیں و آہ، چشمِ تر و غبارِ دل
آتش و آب و خاک و باد، ایک جگہ ہوئے بہم

طولِ کلامِ بے محل، شاد اگرچہ عیب ہے
لکھتے کچھ اور حالِ دل، حیف کہ رُک گیا قلم

Shad Azimabadi

Tilted cap adorns the head, curl on curl the locks unfurl,
The deer-like eyes cast a spell, the glances deadly darts do hurl.
The moon-like face two moles displays, one on cheek, one on chin,
This heralding Ajam's doom, that of the Arab world.
Those serpentining tresses, dragnet of the lover's thoughts,
Where can I find refuge, caught in their deadly whirl?
That enthralling coquetry, it can slay without a sword,
Those faith-destroying graces, by compassion never swirled.
The heart which was my bosom pal, now lies with someone else,
Life alone is left behind, but who now cares for life and world.
Sighs and the burning wails, tearful eye and mouldering heart,
Earth and air, fire and water, all together lie encurled.
Undue stretching of a tale is, Shad, a fault albeit,
I'uld lengthen out my tale, my pen alas, its flag has furled.

Sar pe kulah-e-kaj dhare, zulf-e-daraaz kham ba kham,
Aahoo-e-chashm hai ghazab, tark-e-nigah hai sitam.
Chaand se munh pe khaal do, ek zaqan pe, rukh pe ek,
Is se kharabi-Arab, us se tabaahi-e-Ajam.
Woh kham-e-gaisu-e-daraaz, daam-e-khayal-e-aashiqan,
Ho gaye be tarah shikar, ab na rahe kahin ke hum.
Ushwa-e-dil gudaz woh, zibah kare jo be chhuri,
Naz woh dushman-e-wafa, raham ki jisko hai qasam.
Dil jo bara rafiq tha, woh tau hai dast-e-ghair mein,
Rah gai ek zindagi, woh kahin aarzoo se kum.
Naala-e-aatshin-o-aah, chashm-e-tar-o-ghubar-e-dil,
Aatish-o-aab-o-khak-o-baad, ek jagah hue baham.
Tul-e-kalaam-e-be mahal, Shad agarche aib hai,
Likhte kuchh aur haal-e-dil, haif ke ruk gaya qalam.

شاد

اے شبِ غم ہم ہیں اور باتیں دلِ ناکام سے
سوتے ہیں نامِ خدا، سب اپنے گھر آرام سے
جاگنے والوں پہ کیا گزری وہ جانیں کیا بھلا
سو رہے ہیں جا کے بستر پر جو اپنے شام سے
جیتے جی ہم تو غمِ فردا کی دھن میں مر گئے
کچھ وہی اچھے ہیں جو واقف نہیں انجام سے
نالہ کرنے کے لیے بھی طبعِ خوش درکار ہے
کیا بتاؤں دل ہٹا جاتا ہے کیوں اس کام سے
دیکھتے ہو مے کدے میں مے کشو ساقی بغیر
کس غضب کی بے کسی پیدا ہے شکلِ جام سے
رات دن پیتے ہیں بھر بھر کر مئے عشرت کے جام
کچھ وہی اچھے ہیں نا واقف ہیں جو انجام سے
اسم کو اپنے مسمّیٰ سے ہے لازم کچھ لگاؤ
شادؔ آخر کس طرح خوش ہوں میں اپنے نام سے

Shad Azimabadi

O fearsome night, here am I closeted with my worthless heart,
All else, in the name of God, lie in beds, sleeping fast.
What know they of the fate of those who spend sleepless nights,
They who doze off to sleep every eve without a thought.
Worrying about the morrow has drained my life away,
Blessed are they who care not about with their final lot.
You require a genial mood even to raise a wail,
I cannot say why my heart is allergic to this task.
Mark, O drinkers, the tavern's plight, bereft of saqi's grace,
A state of utter helplessness drowns the cup and flask.
Day and night they quaff the cups, brimming with joyous wine,
Blessed are they who care not about their final lot.
A name must have something to do with its sense and root,
How can my name please me, O Shad, after all!

Ai shab-e-gham, hum hain aur baaten dil-e-nakaam se,
Sote hain naam-e-Khuda, sub apne ghar aaram se.
Jaagne waalon pe kya guzri woh jaanen kya bhala,
So rahe hain ja ke bistar par jo apne sham se.
Jeete ji hum tau gham-e-farda ki dhun mein mar gaye,
Kuchh wohi achhe hain jo waaqif nahin anjaam se.
Naala karne ke lieye bhi taba-e-khush darkaar hai,
Kya bataaun dil hata jaata hai kyon is kaam se.
Dekhte ho maikade mein maikasho saaqi baghair,
Kis qism ki bekasi paida hai shakl-e-jaam se.
Raat din peete hain bhar bhar kar mai-e-ishrat ke jaam,
Kuchh wohi achhe hain na waaqif hain jo anjaam se.
Ism ko apne musammi se hai laazim kuchh lagaao,
Shad aakhir kis tarah khush hun main apne naam se.

شاد

کالی کالی آنکھیں ہیں۔ گوری گوری رنگت ہے
لمبے لمبے گیسو ہیں، اور بھولی بھولی صورت ہے
آڑی آڑی چتون ہے، اور ٹیڑھے ٹیڑھے ابرو ہیں
نیچی نیچی نظریں ہیں اور کچھ کچھ دل میں الفت ہے
رہ رہ کر گھبراتا ہے۔ دل شام سے اُمڈا آتا ہے
تازہ تازہ عشق ہوا ہے دھیمی دھیمی وحشت ہے
حسن کی خوبی جو کچھ کہئے عیب چھپانا ہے ورنہ
جھوٹے جھوٹے وعدوں میں کچھ ایسی ویسی ذلت ہے
بھر بھر آئیں دل نہ بھلا، کس طرح سے شاد ان شعروں پر
سچی سچی باتیں ہیں اور پوری پوری حالت ہے

Shad Azimabadi

The eyes are black and beautiful, complexion fair and sweet,
Long and loose hang the locks, the face innocence breathes.
The brow is broad and winsome, eyebrows arched and sharp,
The heart feels the stirrings of love, the looks downward creep.
Restlessness assails the heart which longs, since eve, to weep,
Love is in its nascent form, in gentle waves the madness leaps.
You may extol the virtues of beauty, you may suppress its faults,
The false promises that it makes, somewhat its worth decrease.
Why shouldn't your lyrics, Shad, touch our heart and soul?
They describe the facts of life, and sketch the life complete.

Kaali kaali aankhen hain, gori gori rangat hai,
Lambe lambe gaisu hain, aur bholi bholi surat hai.
Aari aari chitwan hai, aur terhe terhe abru hain,
Neechi neechi nazren hain, aur kuchh kuchh dil mein ulfat hai.
Rah rah kar ghabrata hai, dil shaam se umda aata hai,
Taaza taaza ishq hua hai, dhimi dhimi wahshat hai.
Husn ki khubi jo kuchh kahieye, aib chhupana hai warna,
Jhute jhute waadon mein kuchh aisi waisi zillat hai.
Bhar bhar aayen dil na bhala, kis tarah se, Shad, in sheron par,
Sachchi sachchi baaten hain, aur puri puri haalat hai.

شادؔ

کیوں اے فلک جو ہم سے جوانی جُدا ہوئی
اِک خود بخود جو دِل میں خوشی تھی وہ کیا ہوئی

گستاخ بلبلوں سے بھی بڑھ کر صبا ہوئی
کُچھ جُھک کر گوشِ گُل میں کہا اور ہوا ہوئی

مایوس دِل نے ایک نہ مانی امید کی
کہہ سُن کے یہ غریب بھی حق سے ادا ہوئی

دنیا کا فکر، موت کا ڈر، آبرو کا دھیان
دو دِن کی زندگی مرے حق میں بلا ہوئی

موتی تمہارے کان کے تھرّا رہے ہیں کیوں
فریاد کس غریب کی گوش آشنا ہوئی

برسا جو ابرِ رحمتِ خالق بروزِ حشر
سبزہ کی طرح پھر مری نشو و نما ہوئی

بیماریوں سے چھُٹ گئے اے شادؔ حشر تک
قُربان اس علاج کے، اچھی دوا ہوئی

Shad Azimabadi

When, O heavens, from my life, youth did depart,
Why with it, my inner joy, suddenly got dissolved?
More impudent than nightingale the breeze turned to be,
It whispered something to the rose, and vanished from the spot.
The despairing heart heeded not the pleas and prayers of hope,
Having said a word or two, it felt its debts discharged.
Thought of the world, fear of death, concern for self-esteem,
The two-day span of life for me proved a narrow pass.
Why the jewels in your ears thus quiver and quake,
Which helpless heart with its plaint has stirred your ears at last?
When God sent His gracious rain on the day of doom,
All at once I was revived, like the freshening grass.
At one stroke I got rid of all the ills of life,
Kudos to your healing art, what a magic it has wrought!

Kyon ai falak jo hum se jawani juda hui,
Ik khud bakhud jo dil mein khushi thi woh kya hui?
Gustaakh bulbulon se bhi barh kar saba hui,
Kuchh jhuk ke gosh-e-gul mein kaha aur hawa hui.
Maayoos dil ne ek na maani umeed ki,
Kah sun ke yeh gharib bhi haq se ada hui.
Duniya ka fikar, maut ka dar, aabroo ka dhyan,
Do din ki zindagi mere haq mein bala hui.
Moti tumhare kaan ke tharra rahe hain kyon,
Faryaad kis gharib ki gosh aashna hui?
Barsa jo abr-e-rahmat-e-khaaliq baroz-e-hashar,
Sabza ki tarah phir miri nashw-o-numa hui.
Beemarion se chhut gaye, ai Shad, hashar tak,
Qurbaan is ilaaj ke, achhi dawa hui.

Shaukat Ali Khan Fani Badayuni
(1879-1941)

SHAUKAT ALI KHAN FANI BADAYUNI
(1879 - 1941)

Shaukat Ali Khan Fani was born in Islam Nagar, a small town in Badayun district, Uttar Pradesh. His father, Mohammed Shujaat Ali Khan was a police inspector. After doing his B.A. from Bareilly College, Bareilly, Fani studied law at Aligarh, and obtained an LL.B. degree. He practised law at Lucknow, Agra, Bareilly and Aligarh, but with no great success. This is because Fani was temperamentally a poet, least interested in legalistic hair-splitting. Spurred by his poetic instinct, he had started writing verse at the young age of eleven. He wrote his poetry at first under the pen-names of "Shaukat", and later adopted "Fani" as his poetic name. Like many of his illustrious predecessors, Fani also went to Hyderabad where he was patronised by Maharaj Kishan Parshad. He also worked as a headmaster in a government school. Despite all this, Fani had to struggle against financial and physical problems in his later life. He died in Hyderabad in 1941, a sad, lonely man, feeling out of place in the far-off land of Deccan. The following couplet aptly describes his state of alienation:

فانیؔ ہم تو جیتے جی وہ میت ہیں بے گور و کفن
غربت جس کو راس نہ آئی اور وطن بھی چھوٹ گیا

Fani, I'm a living corpse, untombed, undraped,
Unwelcome in the alien land, exiled from home and hearth.

Fani is exclusively a poet of the *ghazal*. His poetry is deeply subjective and lyrical. Though his subjects include love, beauty and mystic thought, he is essentially a master of melancholia. His favourite theme is the theme of loss, despair and death, and his favourite tune is a haunting wail of regret and loneliness. In this respect he may be called a descendant of Mir Taqi Mir, but he has a distinctively individual style. His poems are a transcript of his personal life and experience, and his style is modern, urbane and insightful. His poetical works are available under two collections: *Baqiaat-e-Fani,* and *Arfaniaat-e-Faani.*

شوکت علی خاں فانیؔ بدایونی

شوق سے ناکامی کی بدولت کوچۂ دِل ہی چھوٹ گیا
ساری امیدیں ٹوٹ گئیں دِل بیٹھ گیا جی چھوٹ گیا

فصلِ گل آئی یا اجل آئی کیوں درِ زنداں کھلتا ہے
کیا کوئی وحشی اور آپہنچا یا کوئی قیدی چھوٹ گیا

لیجے کیا دامن کی خبر اور دستِ جنوں کو کیا کہیے
اپنے ہی ہاتھ سے دِل کا دامن مدّت گزری چھوٹ گیا

منزلِ عشق پہ تنہا پہنچے کوئی تمنّا ساتھ نہ تھی
تھک تھک کر اسی راہ میں آخر اِک اِک ساتھی چھوٹ گیا

فانیؔ ہم تو جیتے جی وُہ میت ہیں بے گور و کفن
غربت جس کو راس نہ آئی اور وطن بھی چھوٹ گیا

Shaukat Ali Khan Fani Badayuni

Frustration-foiled, all desires quit the lane of heart,
Depression drowned my mind and soul, hope stood dissolved.

Who has arrived, spring or death? Why do they open the prison gate?
Has a manic made to the cage, or a prisoner jumped the wall?

How to inquire about my hem, or talk about my frantic hand?
Long past I lost control of the reins of my heart.

Alone I reached the goal of love, denuded of desire,
Every comrade fell en route, worn out at last.

Fani, I'm a living corpse, untombed, undraped,
Unwanted in the alien land, exiled from home and hearth.

Shauq se naakaami ki badaulat kucha-e-dil hi chhoot gaya,
Saari ummeedein toot gayien, dil baith gaya, ji chhoot gaya.

Fasal-e-gul aai, yaa ajal aai, kyon dar-e-zindaan khulta hai,
Kya koi wahshi aur aa pahuncha yaa koi qaidi chhoot gaya?

Lijieye kya daaman ki khabar aur dast-e-janoon ko kya kaheye?
Apne he haath se dil ka daaman muddat guzri choot gaya.

Manzil-e-ishq pe tanha pahunche, koi tamanna saath na thi,
Thak thak kar is raah mein aakhir ik ik saathi chhoot gaya.

Fani hum tau jeete ji woh mayyat hain be gor-e-kafan,
Ghurbat jisko raas na aai aur watan bhi chhoot gaya.

فانیؔ

اِک معمّہ ہے سمجھنے کا نہ سمجھانے کا
زندگی کاہے کو ہے، خواب ہے دیوانے کا

مختصر قصۂ غم یہ ہے، کہ دِل رکھتا ہوں
رازِ کونین، خلاصہ ہے اس افسانے کا

زندگی بھی تو پشیماں ہے یہاں لا کے مجھے
ڈھونڈتی ہے کوئی حِیلہ، مرے مرجانے کا

تم نے دیکھا ہے کبھی گھر کو بدلتے ہوئے رنگ
آؤ، دیکھو نہ تماشا مرے غم خانے کا

اب اسے دار پہ لے جا کے سلا دے ساقی
یوں بہکنا نہیں اچھا ترے مستانے کا

دِل سے پہنچی تو ہیں آنکھوں میں لہو کی بوندیں
سلسلہ شیشے سے مِلتا تو ہے پیمانے کا

ہڈیاں ہیں کئی، لپٹی ہوئی زنجیروں میں
لیے جاتے ہیں جنازہ ترے دیوانے کا

ہر نفس عمرِ گزشتہ کی ہے میّت فانیؔ
زندگی نام ہے مَر مَر کے جئے جانے کا

Fani Badayuni

Life is but a riddle, puzzling in extreme,
Why call it life at all? 'tis a madman's dream.

This, in brief, is the tale of grief — I possess a heart,
The secret of the world at large — defines my central theme.

Even life regrets the act of bringing me to being,
It's looking for some excuse to snuff out my beam.

Have you ever seen a house reflecting different hues?
Come, see my chamber dark with its shifting scenes.

Take him to the gallows, saqi, put him there to sleep,
Let not your maddened lover meander and scream.

Drops of blood have reached the eyes proceeding from the heart,
The cup and flask have met at last, so to me doth seem.

A bunch of bones in manacles bound!
There goes your lover's coffin for its last requiem.

Every breath sings the dirge of the life deceased,
Living in the midst of death — explains the life's theme.

Ik muimma hai samajhne ka na samjhaane ka,
Zindagi kaahe ko hai, khwaab hai diwaane ka.

Mukhtsar qissa-e-ghum yeh hai, ke dil rakhta hun,
Raaz-e-kaunin, khulaasa hai is afasaane ka.

Zindagi bhi tau pashemaan hai yahaan laa ke mujhko,
Dhoondti hai koi heela, mire mar jaane ka.

Tum ne dekha hai kabhi ghar ko badalte hue rang,
Aao, dekho na tamaasha mire ghum khaane ka.

Ab ise daar pe le jaa ke sula de saqi,
Yun bahkana nahin achha tire diwaane ka.

Dil se pahunchi tau hain aankhon mein lahu ki boondein,
Silsala sheehse se milta tau hai paimaane ka.

Haddiaan hain kai, lipti hui zanjeeron mein,
Lieye jaate hain janaaza tire diwaane ka.

Har nafs umr-e-guzashta ki hai mayyat, Fani,
Zindagi naam hai mar mar ke jieye jaane ka.

فانیؔ

یہ کس قیامت کی بیکسی ہے، نہ میں ہی اپنا نہ یار میرا
نہ خاطرِ بے قرار میری، نہ دیدۂ اشک بار میرا

نشانِ تربت عیاں نہیں ہے، "نہیں"، کہ باقی نشاں نہیں ہے
مزار میرا کہاں نہیں ہے، کہیں نہیں ہے مزار میرا

وصال تیرا، خیال تیرا، جو ہو تو کیونکر، نہ ہو تو کیونکر
نہ تجھ پہ کچھ اختیار میرا، نہ دِل پہ کچھ اختیار میرا

نگاہِ دِل دوز کی دہائی ۔ جمالِ جاں سوز کی دہائی
رہِ محبّت میں غم نے لُوٹا شکیب و صبر و قرار میرا

مَیں دردِ فرقت سے جاں بلب ہوں، تمہیں یقینِ وفا نہیں ہے
مجھے نہیں اعتبار اپنا، تمہیں نہیں اعتبار میرا

قدم نکال، اب تو گھر سے باہر جو دم بھی سینے سے سہل نکلے
دِکھا نہ اب انتظار اپنا، لحد کو ہے انتظار میرا

سُنا ہے اُٹھا ہے اِک بگولہ، جلو میں کچھ آندھیوں کو لے کر
طوافِ دشتِ جنوں کو شاید، گیا ہے فانی غبار میرا

Fani Badayuni

What a terrible helplessness, I can neither own myself, nor on him rely,
The restless heart is not my own, nor my streaming eyes.

No visible trace of my grave, traceless yet is not my grave,
Everywhere is my grave, nowhere is my grave in sight.

Your union, your thought, how to achieve, how to dissolve?
Nor on you, nor on my heart any claim have I.

Oh, the heart-piercing glance, oh, the beauty deadly cute!
Travails of love have robbed me of peace, content and pride.

I'm dying of separation, you doubt my love and faith,
I mistrust my own self, you my trust belie.

Step out of your home so that I may have an easy end,
Keep me not in waiting now, the grave for me in waiting lies.

A whirlwind has risen, they say, winged with the mighty gale,
Maybe, my frantic dust is eddying about in the wilds.

Yeh kis qayaamat ki be-kasi hai, na main hi apna, ne yaar mera,
Na khaatir-e-be qaraar meri, na deeda-e-ashkbaar mera.

Nishaan-e-turbat ayaan nahin hai, nahin, ke baqi nishaan nahin hai,
Mazaar mera kahaan nahin hai, kahin nahin hai mazaar mera.

Wisaal tera, khayaal tera, jo ho tau kyonkar, na ho tau kyonkar,
Na tujh pe kuchh ikhtiaar mera, na dil pe kuchh ikhtiaar mera.

Nigaah-e-dildoz ki duhaai, jamaal-e-jaansoz ki duhaai,
Rah-e-mahabbat mein ghum ne loota, shakeb-o-sabar-o-qaraar mera.

Main dard-e-furqat se jaan-ba-lab hun, tumhen yaqeen-e-wafa nahin hai,
Mujhe nahin aitbaar apna, tumhen nahin aitbaar mera.

Qadam nikaal ab tau ghar se bahar, jo dam bhi seene se sahal nikle,
Dikha na ab intezaar apna, lahd ko hai intezaar mera.

Suna hai utha hai ik bagoola, jilau mein kuchh aandhion ko le kar,
Tawaaf-e-dasht-e-janoon ko shaaid, gaya hai, Fani, ghubaar mera.

فانی

لطف و کرم کے پُتلے ہو، اب قہر و ستم کا نام نہیں
دِل پہ خُدا کی مار، کہ پھر بھی چین نہیں آرام نہیں

جتنے مُنھ ہیں اُتنی باتیں، دِل کا پتہ کیا خاک ملے
جس نے دِل کی چوری کی ہے، ایک اُسی کا نام نہیں

رُک کے جو سانسیں آئیں گئیں، مانا کہ وہ آہیں تھیں لیکن
آپ نے تیور کیوں بدلے، آہوں میں کسی کا نام نہیں

عِشق کے آزاری بھی کہیں، مرنے سے جی جاتے ہیں
لے، یہ تسلّی رہنے دے، اے موت ترا یہ کام نہیں

کب سے پڑی ہیں دل میں، تیرے ذکر کی ساری راہیں بند
برسیں گزری، اس بستی میں، رسمِ سلام و پیام نہیں

دل ہی پہ اپنا بس نہیں چلتا، ان کی شکایت کیا کیجیے
آپ ہم اپنے دشمن ٹھہرے، دوست پہ کچھ الزام نہیں

دِل سے کِسی کی آنکھوں تک کچھ راز کی باتیں پہنچی ہیں
آنکھ سے دِل تک آیا ہو، ایسا تو کوئی پیغام نہیں

نزع میں فانی تو نے یہ کِس کا چُپکے چُپکے نام لیا
کیوں، او کافر، تیری زباں پر اب بھی خدا کا نام نہیں

Fani Badayuni

You are the very soul of grace, no tyranny, no rage,
Curse of God upon this heart, 'tis still restless, dismayed.

As many tongues, as many tales, how the hell one finds the heart,
When his name alone is missing who has my heart waylaid.

The faltering breaths that I breathed, let's accept, were sighs indeed,
Why do you change your colour, sighs cannot insinuate.

Can martyrs of love acquire a new lease of life?
Don't beguile me, O death, this is not your trade.

All doors of mutual converse have long remained closed,
The land of heart has long missed the greetings' kindly grace.

When I can't command my heart, of him I shan't complain,
I'm a foe to myself, I shouldn't fault my mate.

Some secrets of the heart have reached someone's eyes,
A message from the eyes to the heart, is what I now await.

In your dying moments, Fani, whose name do you repeat?
Why can't you, O faithless, God's name iterate?

Lutaf-o-karam ke putle ho, ab qahr-o-sitam ka naam nahin,
Dil pe Khuda ki maar, ke phir bhi chain nahin, aaraam nahin.

Jitne munh hain, utni baaten, dil ka pata kya khaak mile,
Jis ne dil ki chori ki hai, ek usi ka naam nahin.

Ruk ke jo saansen aaein, gayein, maana keh woh aahen thee, lekin,
Aap ne tewar kyon badle, aahon mein kisi ka naam nahin.

Ishq ke aazaari bhi kahin, mar jaane se ji jaate hain,
Le, yeh tasalli rahne de, ai maut, tera yeh kaam nahin.

Kab se pari hain dil mein tere zikar ki saari raahen band,
Barsen guzrin, is basti mein, rasm-e-salaam-o-payaam nahin.

Dil hi peh apna bas nahin chalta, un ki shikaayat kya kijeye,
Aap hum apne dushman thahre, dost pe kuchh ilzaam nahin.

Dil se kisi ki aankhon tak kuchh raaz ki baaten pahunchi hain,
Aankh se dil tak aaya ho, aisa tau koi paighaam nahin.

Nazah mein Fani tu ne yeh kis ka chupke, chupke naam liya?
Kyon O kaafir, teri zabaan par ab bhi Khuda ka naam nahin.

فانیؔ

دُنیا مِری بلا جانے، مہنگی ہے یا سستی ہے
موت مِلے تو مُفت نہ لوں ہستی کی کیا ہستی ہے

آبادی بھی دیکھی ہے، ویرانے بھی دیکھے ہیں
جو اُجڑے اور پھر نہ بسے، دِل وُہ نرالی بستی ہے

عجزِ گناہ کے دم تک ہیں عصمتِ کامل کے جلوے
پستی ہے تو بلندی ہے، رازِ بلندی پستی ہے

جان سی شَے بِک جاتی ہے ایک نظر کے بدلے میں
آگے مرضی گاہک کی، اِن داموں تو سستی ہے

جگ سونا ہے تیرے بغیر، آنکھوں کا کیا حال ہوا
جب بھی دُنیا بستی تھی، اب بھی دُنیا بَستی ہے

آنسو تھے سو خُشک ہوئے، جی ہے کہ اُمڈا آتا ہے
دِل پہ گھٹا سی چھائی ہے کھلتی ہے نہ برستی ہے

دِل کا اُجڑنا سہل سہی، بسنا سہل نہیں ظالم
بستی بسنا کھیل نہیں، بستے بستے بستی ہے

فانیؔ جس میں آنسو کیا، دل کے لہو کا کال نہ تھا
ہائے! وُہ آنکھ اب پانی کی دو بوندوں کو ترستی ہے

Fani Badayuni

Whether the world is dear or cheap, what the hell care I?
I reject even death gratis, who cares for life?

I've seen the bustling towns, I've seen the wilds,
The city of heart, once ravaged, ever desolate lies.

The grovelling guilt is the cause of virtue's towering sights,
The height exists because of depth, in depth the height resides.

Even a thing like life is selling for a mere glance,
The rest depends on the buyer, the thing is cheaply priced.

The world is barren without your presence, behold my eye's piteous plight,
Then too the world did prosper, now too the world doth thrive.

Tears have dried at the source, the heart is welling forth,
It is overcast with clouds, which neither burst nor fly.

'Tis easy to ravage the heart, not so easy to habilitate,
No child's play to people a place, slowly doth it come alive.

The eyes which once rained down blood instead of simple tears,
Yearn in vain to shed a drop, what a sad plight!

Duniya meri bala jaane, mahngi hai yaa sasti hai,
Maut mile tau muft na lun, hasti ki kya hasti hai.

Aabaadi bhi dekhi hai, weeraane bhi dekhe hain,
Jo ujre aur phir na base, dil woh niraali basti hai.

Ijz-e-gunaah ke dum tak hain, ismat-e-kaamal ke jalwe,
Pasti hai tau balandi hai, raaz-e-balandi pasti hai.

Jaan si shai bik jaati hai ek nazar ke badle mein,
Aage marzi gaahak ki, in daamon tau sasti hai.

Jag soona hai tere baghair, aankhon ka kya haal hua,
Jab bhi duniya basti thi, ab bhi duniya basti hai.

Aansu the so khushk hue, ji hai ke umda aataa hai,
Dil peh ghatta si chhaai hai, khulti hai na barasti hai.

Dil ka ujarna sahal sahi, basna sahal nahin zaalim,
Basti basna khel nahin, baste baste basti hai.

Fani jis mein annsu kya, dil ke lahu ka kaal na tha,
Haaei! woh aankh ab paani ki do boondon ko tarsti hai.

فانیؔ

مر کے ٹوٹا ہے کبھی سلسلۂ قیدِ حیات
مگر اتنا ہے کہ زنجیر بدل جاتی ہے

اثرِ عشق تغافل بھی ہے، بیداد بھی ہے
وُہی تقصیر ہے، تعزیر بدل جاتی ہے

کہتے کہتے مرا افسانہ گلہ ہوتا ہے
دیکھتے دیکھتے تدبیر بدل جاتی ہے

روز ہے دردِ محبت کا نرالا انداز
روز دِل میں تری تصویر بدل جاتی ہے

گھر میں رہتا ہے، ترے دم سے اُجالا ہی کچھ اور
مہ و خورشید کی تنویر بدل جاتی ہے

غم نصیبوں میں ہے فانیؔ غمِ دُنیا ہو کہ عِشق
دِل کی تقدیر سے تدبیر بدل جاتی ہے

Fani Badayuni

When can death terminate the captivity of life?
Different fetters, albeit, will our limits decide.

Tyranny and indifference, love can both entail,
The same fault can be differently chastised.

My tale becomes a plaint when dwelt at length,
Fate changes its aspects before my very eyes.

Each day the ache of love a new style displays,
Each day your picture presents a new profile.

The house acquires a special glow from your radiant being,
The sun and moon begin to emit a preternatural light.

Sorrow is my destiny, be it of love or life,
Plans come a cropper when Fate turns hostile.

Mar ke toota hai kabhi silsala-e-qaid-e-hayaat?
Magar itna hai keh zanjeer badal jaati hai.

Asr-e-ishq taghaaful bhi hai, bedaad bhi hai,
Wohi taqsir hai, taazir badal jaati hai.

Kahte kahte mira afsaana gila hota hai,
Dekhte dekhte tadbir badal jaati hai.

Roz hai dard-e-mahabbat ka nirala andaaz,
Roz dil mein tiri tasvir badal jaati hai.

Ghar mein rahta hai tire dam se ujaala hi kuchh aur,
Mah-o-khurshid ki tanvir badal jaati hai.

Ghum naseebon mein hai, Fani, ghum-e-duniya ho ke ishq,
Dil ki taqdir se tadbir badal jaati hai.

فانیؔ

عشق نے دِل میں جگہ کی تو قضا بھی آئی
درد دُنیا میں جب آیا تو دوا بھی آئی

دِل کی ہستی سے کیا عشق نے آگاہ مجھے
دِل جب آیا تو دھڑکنے کی صدا بھی آئی

صدقے اُتریں گے اسیرانِ قفس چھُوٹے ہیں
بجلیاں لے کے نشیمن پہ گھٹا بھی آئی

ہاں نہ تھا بابِ اثر بند مگر کیا کہئے
آہ پہنچی تھی، کہ دُشمن کی دُعا بھی آئی

آپ سوچا ہی کئے اُس سے مِلوں یا نہ مِلوں
موت مشتاق کو مٹّی میں مِلا بھی آئی

لو، مسیحا نے بھی، اللہ نے بھی یاد کیا
آج بیمار کو ہچکی بھی، قضا بھی آئی

دیکھ یہ جادۂ ہستی ہے سنبھل کر فانیؔ
پیچھے پیچھے وہ دبے پاؤں قضا بھی آئی

Fani Badayuni

When love sprang in the heart, death too leapt to sight,
When pain emerged in the world, potion too arrived.

Love made me conscious of the entity of my heart,
The beat became audible, when the heart got enticed.

Caged birds have gained freedom, tributes galore will flow,
Clouds charged with lightning round the nests fly.

It isn't that the effect had gone, but, what to say,
As my sighs scaled the skies, the enemy's prayers broke their might.

You were still debating, to meet or not to meet,
Death, in the meanwhile, ended your lover's strife.

Lo, I'm remembered both by my Messiah and God,
Hiccup and the call of death, hand-in-hand arrive.

Fani, this is the road of life, be careful, beware,
Death too is chasing you, on tiptoe, on the sly.

Ishq ne dil mein jagah ki tau qaza bhi aai,
Dard duniya mein jab aaya tau dawa bhi aai.

Dil ki hasti se kiya ishq ne aagah mujhe,
Dil jab aaya tau dharkne ki sada bhi aai.

Sadqe utrenge, aseeraan-e-qafas chhoote hain,
Bijliaan le ke nasheman pe ghata bhi aai.

Haan na tha baab-e-asr band, magar kya kahieye?
Aah pahunchi thi keh dushman ki dua bhi aai.
Aap socha hi kieye, us se milun, yaa na milun,
Maut mushtaaq ko mitti mein mila bhi aai.

Lo, masiha ne bhi, Allah ne bhi yaad kiya,
Aaj bimaar ko hichki bhi, qaza bhi aai.

Dekh yeh jaada-e-hasti hai, sambhal kar, Fani,
Peechhe peechhe woh dabe paaon qaza bhi aai.

Brij Narain Chakbast
(1882-1926)

BRIJ NARAIN CHAKBAST
(1882 - 1926)

Chakbast's ancestors hailed from Kashmir and had settled in Delhi, U.P., and Bihar in 15th century A.D. His father, Udit Narain Chakbast, was born at Lucknow in, probably, 1843. Brij Narain was born at Faizabad in 1882. After the death of his father in 1887 the family shifted to Lucknow. It was here that the boy-poet received his education which included, apart from a thorough grounding in Urdu and Persian, an LL.B. degree also. Chakbast married in 1905, but lost his wife and first child in 1906. He married again in 1907, and settled down as a practising lawyer at Lucknow. He was also actively involved in social and political affairs, and was an ardent champion of the Home Rule. He lived for only 44 years and died of a paralytic stroke in 1926.

Chakbast is primarily a poet of the *nazm.* He began his poetic career with a *nazm* in 1894, and ended, in 1925, with a *nazm* again. His famous poems are: *Khak-e-Hind, Ramayan ka Ek Scene, Nala-e-Dard,* and *Nala-e-Yaas.* He also wrote a *masnavi* entitled: *Gulzar-e-Naseem,* and a play named: *Kamla.* He wrote no more than 50 *ghazals,* but most of them are remarkable for the beauty of their thought and the lucidity and urbanity of his style. Much of his verse is didactic, patriotic and aphoristic. He uses impressive, Persianised diction in the manner of Ghalib and Aatish, by whose poetry he was deeply influenced. Chakbast is among the few early Urdu poets who had the benefit of a university degree. He is also distinctive for not having used his "takhallus", his poetic name, in the conclusions of his *ghazals* — which perhaps shows the humility and modesty of his temperament.

برج نارائن چکبست

دردِ دِل ، پاسِ وفا ، جذبۂ ایماں ہونا
آدمیّت ہے یہی اور یہی انساں ہونا

نو گرفتارِ بلا طرزِ فغاں کیا جانیں
کوئی ناشاد سِکھا دے انہیں نالاں ہونا

رہ کے دُنیا میں ہے یُوں ترکِ ہوس کی کوشش
جِس طرح اپنے ہی سائے سے گریزاں ہونا

زندگی کیا ہے عناصر میں ظہورِ ترتیب
موت کیا ہے انھی اجزا کا پریشاں ہونا

دِل اسیری میں بھی آزاد ہے آزادوں کا
ولولوں کے لیے ممکن نہیں زنداں ہونا

گُل کو پامال نہ کر لعل و گوہر کے مالک
ہے اِسے طرّۂ دستارِ غریباں ہونا

ہے مرا ضبطِ جنوں جوشِ جنوں سے بڑھ کر
ننگ ہے میرے لیے چاکِ گریباں ہونا

Brij Narain Chakbast

Fidelity, compassion, abiding faith,
These comprise humanity, these a man do make.

What know they of the mode of wailing, these neo-victims of faith,
Let someone used to sorrow, teach them plaintive lays.

The attempt to shed desire, living amidst the world,
Is the attempt to run away from one's own shade.

What is life but elements orderly arranged,
What is death but elements diffused, disarrayed.

The free at heart cannot ever be encaged,
Who can suppress the passions that within us rage?

Trample not the rose, O man of pelf and pride,
Some humble headgear 'tis supposed to decorate.

Self-control is better far than frenzy uncontrolled,
A torn collar is to me a mark of disgrace.

Dard-e-dil, paas-e-wafa, jazba-e-imaan hona,
Aadmeeat hai yehi, aur yehi insaan hona.

Nau gariftaar-e-bala tarz-e-fughaan kya jaanen,
Koi naashaad sikha de inhen naalaan hona.

Rah ke duniya mein yun tark-e-hawas ki koshish,
Jis tarah apne hi saae se gurezaan hona.

Zindagi kya hai, anaasir mein zahur-e-tartib,
Maut kya hai inhi ijza ka pareshaan hona.

Dil aseeri mein bhi aazaad hai aazaadon ka,
Walwalon ke lieye mumkin nahin zindaan hona.
Gul ko paamaal na kar, laal-o-guhar ke maalik,
Hai ise turrah-e-dastaar-e-ghareebaan hona.

Hai mera zabt-e-janoon josh-e-janoon se barh kar,
Nang hai mere lieye chaak garebaan hona.

چکبست

فنا کا ہوش آنا زندگی کا دردِ سر جانا
اجل کیا ہے خمارِ بادۂ ہستی اُتر جانا

عزیزانِ وطن کو غنچہ و برگ و ثمر جانا
خدا کو باغباں اور قوم کو ہم نے شجر جانا

عروسِ جاں نیا پیراہنِ ہستی بدلتی ہے
فقط تمہید آنے کی ہے دُنیا سے گزر جانا

مصیبت میں بشر کے جوہرِ مردانہ کھلتے ہیں
مبارک بزدلوں کو گردشِ قسمت سے ڈر جانا

کرشمہ یہ بھی ہے اے بے خبر! افلاسِ قومی کا
تلاشِ رزق میں اہلِ ہُنر کا در بدر جانا

وہ سودا زندگی کا ہے کہ غم انساں سہتا ہے
نہیں تو ہے بہت آساں اس جینے سے مر جانا

چمن زارِ محبت میں اُسی نے باغبانی کی
کہ جس نے اپنی محنت ہی کو محنت کا ثمر جانا

Brij Narain Chakbast

Mortality gives the clarion call, life's fretful stir resolves,
What is death? — the wine of life, diluted and dissolved!

We treat the younger folks as buds, leaves and fruits,
To us the nation is a tree, and God, the gardener of us all.

The bridal soul adorns herself in ever newer robes,
Our going hence prelude our sure recall.

Adversity digs out the bravest part of man,
Welcome are the craven hearts to dread the fortune's darts.

This too is a mark of shame that in search of bread,
The talent has to suffer exile, and look for alien marts.

Such is the lure of life that man can swallow ills,
Or else, 'tis easier to die, than live the way we art.

He alone is a gardener true in the field of love,
Who knows that love's labour is its own reward.

Fana ka hosh aanaa, zindagi ka dard-e-sar jaana,
Ajal kya hai, khumaar-e-baadaa-e-hasti utar jaana.

Azizaan-e-watan ko ghuncha-o-barg-o-samar jaana,
Khuda ko baghbaan aur qaum ko hum ne shajar jaana.

Aroos-e-jaan naya parahan-e-hasti badalti hai,
Faqt tamheed aane ki hai duniya se guzar jaana.

Museebat mein bashar ke jauhar-e-mardaana khilte hain,
Mubaarik buzdilon ko gardish-e-qismat se dar jaana.

Karishma yeh bhi hai, ai be-khabar, iflaas-e-qaumi ka,
Talaash-e-rizq mein ahl-e-hunar ka dar-ba-dar jaana.

Woh sauda zindagi ka hai, ke ghum insaan sahta hai,
Nahin tau hai bahut aasaan is jeene se mar jaana.
Chaman zaar-e-muhabbat mein usi ne baghbaani ki,
Ke jis ne apni mehnat ko hi mehnat ka samar jaana.

چکبست

اُڑا کر صحنِ گلشن سے، مٹا کر آشیاں میرا
مرے سائے کے پیچھے پھر رہا ہے باغباں میرا

مرے احباب پیش آتے ہیں مجھ سے بے وفائی سے
وفاداری میں شاید کر رہے ہیں امتحاں میرا

تہ و بالا کیا ہے گردشِ اعمال نے مجھکو
نہ دُشمن ہے زمیں میری، نہ دُشمن آسماں میرا

صفائے قلب سے، اللہ رے، انساں کی عظمت
فرشتے چومتے ہیں آکے سنگِ آستاں میرا

یہ ماتم ہے مصوّر اُٹھ گیا گلزارِ قدرت کا
ہر اِک طائر، ہر اِک برگِ چمن ہے نوحہ خواں میرا

سفر میں زندگی کے سو گیا ہوں تھک کے منزل پر
اجل کے نام سے بدنام ہے خوابِ گراں میرا

اسیری میں زُباں سے میری سُن کے رازِ آزادی
گریباں پھاڑ کر سر دُھن رہا ہے پاسباں میرا

الٰہی خیر ہو کیا سرگزشتِ دِل سُنائے گا
لرزتا ہے مِری آنکھوں میں کیوں اشکِ رواں میرا

Brij Narain Chakbast

Having made me flee the garden, having ruined my nest,
My gardener is after my shadow, this is now his quest.

My friends treat me in a cold, unkindly way,
Perhaps 'tis my loyalty which they want to test.

The whirlwind of my own deeds has unsettled my being,
Neither the earth, nor the sky, is against me set.

How, my God! the pure-in-heart are with the glory crowned!
Angels descend from heaven to kiss my threshold's dust.

The painter of the charms of nature, is alas, no more.
Every leaf and every bird thus bewails my death.

Fatigued by the rigours of travel, I fell asleep at journey's end,
My deep sleep is mis-named as the spell of death.

When in prison I expound the freedom's secret sense,
The excited watch tears his shirt, wildly wags his head.

Help, O God, I know not what tale it will divulge,
A tremulous droplet in my eye would not let me rest.

Ura kar sehn-e-gulshan se, mita kar aashian mera,
Mere saaye ke peechhe phir raha hai baagbaan mera.

Mire ahbaab pesh aate hain mujh se be-wafaai se,
Wafadaari mein shaaid kar rahe hain imtehaan mera.

Tah-o-bala kiya hai gardish-e-aamaal ne mujh ko,
Na dushman hai zameen meri, na dushman aasmaan mera.

Safa-e-qalab se, Allah re, insaan ki azmat,
Farishte choomte hain aa ke sang-e-aastaan mera.

Yeh maatam hai musawwar uth gaya gulzaar-e-qudrat ka,
Har ik taair, har ik barg-e-chaman hai noha khwaan mera.

Safar mein zindagi ke so gaya hun thak ke manzil par,
Ajal ke naam se badnaam hai khwaab-e-giraan mera.

Aseeri mein zabaan se meri sun ke raaz-e-aazadi,
Garebaan phaar kar sar dhun raha hai, paasban mera.

Ilahi khair ho, kya surguzasht-e-dil sunaaega,
Larzta hai miri aankhon mein kyon ashk-e-rawan mera.

چکبست

مِری بے خودی ہے وُہ بے خودی کہ خودی کا وہم و گماں نہیں
یہ سرورِ ساغرِ مے نہیں، یہ خمارِ خوابِ گراں نہیں

جو ظہورِ عالمِ ذات ہے، یہ فقط ہجومِ صفات ہے
ہے جہاں کا اور وجود کیا، جو طلسمِ وہم و گماں نہیں

یہ حیاتِ عالمِ خواب ہے، نہ عذاب ہے نہ ثواب ہے
وُہ کفر و دیں میں خراب ہے جسے علمِ رازِ نہاں نہیں

وُہ ہے سب جگہ جو کرو نظر، وُہ کہیں نہیں جو ہو بے بصر
مجھے آج تک نہ ہوئی خبر وُہ کہاں ہے اور کہاں نہیں

نہ وُہ خُم میں بادہ کا جوش ہے، نہ وُہ حسنِ جلوہ فروش ہے
نہ کِسی کو رات کا ہوش ہے، وُہ شب کو سحر کا سماں نہیں

یہ زمیں پہ جِن کا تھا دبدبہ کہ بلند عرش پہ نام تھا
اُنہیں یوُں فلک نے مٹا دیا کہ مزار کا بھی نشاں نہیں

Brij Narain Chakbast

Such is my state transcendent, sense of self is utterly lost,
'Tis not the thrill of wine, nor the result of dreaming fast.
The world apparent to our sight is congregation of sound and sight,
This pageant of earth and sky is nothing but illusion vast.
Life is but a state of sleep, neither good, nor bad,
Those who do not see the truth, by faith and doubt are tossed.
He is everywhere if you discern, nowhere, to the unconcerned,
Till-to-day I couldn't find, where He lives, where doth not.
The cup no more pulsates with wine, nor beauty glows with former shine,
None is bothered about the night, which has lost its nascent gloss.
Those who ruled the earth with might, and set their standards in the sky,
Are swept away by the tide of time, even their graves are utterly lost.

Meri be-khudi hai woh be-khudi, ke khudi ka wahm-o-gumaan nahin,
Yeh saroor-e-saaghir-e-mai nahin, yeh khumaar-e-khwaab-e-giraan nahin.
Jo zahoor-e-aalam-e-zaat hai, yeh faqt hajum-e-sifaat hai,
Hai jahaan ka aur wajood kya, jo talism-e-wahm-o-gumaan nahin.
Yeh hayaat aalam-e-khwaab hai, na azaab hai, na sawaab hai,
Woh kufr-o-deen mein kharaab hai, jise ilm-e-raaz-e-nihaan nahin.
Woh hai sab jagah jo karo nazar, woh kahin nahin jo ho be basar,
Mujhe aaj tak na hui khabar, woh kahan hai aur kahaan nahin.
Na woh khum mein baada ka josh hai, na woh husn-e-jalwa farosh hai,
Na kisi ko raat ka hosh hai, woh shab ko sahar ka samaan nahin.
Yeh zameen pe jin ka tha dabdada, ke buland arsh pe naam tha,
Unhen yun falak ne mita diya, ke mazaar ka bhi nishaan nahin.

چکبست

دِل ہی بجھا ہوا ہو تو لطفِ بہار کیا
ساقی ہے کیا، شراب کیا، سبزہ زار کیا
یہ دِل کی تازگی ہے وُہ دِل کی فسردگی
اس گلشنِ جہاں کی خزاں کیا بہار کیا
دیکھا سرورِ بادۂ ہستی کا خاتمہ
اب دیکھیں رنگ لائے اجل کا خمار کیا
دُنیا سے لے چلا جو تو حسرتوں کا بوجھ
کافی نہیں ہے سر پہ گُناہوں کا بار کیا
بعدِ فنا فضول ہے نام و نشاں کی فکر
جب ہم نہیں رہے تو رہے گا مزار کیا
اعمال کا طلسم ہے نیرنگِ زندگی
تقدیر کیا ہے، گردشِ لیل و نہار کیا
انساں کے بغض و جہل سے دُنیا تباہ ہے
طوفاں اُٹھا رہا ہے، مشتِ غبار کیا

Brij Narain Chakbast

Can spring give delight, if you feel depressed?
Beauty, wine or verdure, nothing can impress.

One is the buoyancy of heart, the other deep despair,
These define spring and fall, if not, what else?

We have seen the wine of life drained to the lees,
What hues, now let's see, the wine of death reflects.

Why dost thou carry along dreams unfulfilled?
Aren't you with the weight of sins already depressed?

Futile it is to worry about posthumous name and fame,
When we are dead, can our tombs resist the kiss of death?

Life owes its wondrous charm to the strength of deeds,
The whirling wheels of Time and Fate leave it unimpressed.

Human folly and spite have brought the world to ruin,
What a havoc doth it raise — a handful of dust!

Dil hi bujha hua ho tau lutaf-e-bahaar kya
Saqi hai kya, sharaab kya, subza zaar kya?

Yeh dil ki taazgi hai, woh dil ki fasurdagi,
Is gulshan-e-jahan ki khazaan kya, bahaar kya?

Dekha saroor-e-baada-e-hasti ka khaatma,
Ab dekhen rang laaye ajal ka khumaar kya!

Duniya se le chala jo tu hasraton ka bojh,
Kafi nahin hai sar pe gunaahon ka baar kya?

Baad-e-fana fazul hai naam-o-nishan ki fikar,
Jab hum nahin rahe tau rahega mazaar kya?

Aamaal ka talism hai nairang-e-zindagi,
Taqdir kya hai, gardish-e-lail-o-nihaar kya?

Insaan ke bughz-o-jihal se duniya tabaah hai,
Toofan utha raha hai, musht-e-ghubaar kya?

Asghar Hussain Asghar Gondvi
(1884-1936)

ASGHAR HUSSAIN ASGHAR GONDVI
(1884 - 1936)

Asghar was born at Gonda (U.P.). His father, Taffazul Hussain, was an ordinary clerk, a man of modest means who couldn't afford to educate his son in a good school or college. Consequently, Asghar studied only up to the 8th class, but he attained through self-effort a complete mastery of Urdu, Persian and Arabic, besides achieving proficiency in English. It is said that in his early youth Asghar led a life of sensuous abandon, but later, under the influence of Sayed Abdul Ghani Kazmi, a religious saint and mystic, he turned a new leaf and led a life of piety and self-control. He had a great love of literature, religion and philosophy, more specially, the philosophy of the Sufi saints. Like Jigar, Asghar too traded in spectacles for sometime to earn his living. Later he worked in the railway engineering department, followed by a short stint at the India Press at Allahabad. He died of a paralytic stroke in 1936.

Asghar is a specialist of the *ghazal.* His poetic works are available under two volumes: *Nishat-e-Rooh* and *Sarud-e-Zindagi.* The central theme of his poetry is love, not earthly and material, but mystic and transcendental. He expresses his feelings with consummate artistry, using the imagery of romantic poetry, so that he can be enjoyed at both the secular and spiritual levels. According to him life is a perpetual quest, an eternal search for the fount of love and beauty, and all objects of this earth are engaged in the pursuit of this one aim. Reason and analytical probing cannot take us to the source of light and love. What we need is a spirit of self-surrender and a sense of humility. Then alone can we rise above the apparent confusion of creeds and realise that one Truth for which the whole creation is striving.

In his impressive, Persianised style, Asghar seems to have been influenced by Ghalib, while in his emphasis on the greatness of man, and the value of struggle, he reminds us of Iqbal, who too, we may recall, gives utmost importance to the virtues of love, faith and action.

اصغر حسین اصغر گونڈوی

پھر میں نظر آیا، نہ تماشا نظر آیا
جب تُو نظر آیا مجھے تنہا نظر آیا

اللہ رے دیوانگیِ شوق کا عالم
اک رقص میں ہر ذرّۂ صحرا نظر آیا

اُٹھے عجب انداز سے وُہ جوشِ غضب میں
چڑھتا ہوا اِک حسن کا دریا نظر آیا

کِس درجہ ترا حُسن بھی آشوبِ جہاں ہے
جِس ذرّے کو دیکھا وُہ تڑپتا نظر آیا

اب خُود ترا جلوہ جو دِکھا دے، وُہ دِکھا دے
یہ دیدۂ بینا تو تماشا نظر آیا

تھا لطفِ جنوں دیدۂ خوں نابہ فشاں سے
پھولوں سے بھرا دامنِ صحرا نظر آیا

Asghar Hussain Asghar Gondvi

I could neither see myself, nor the surrounding scene,
When I caught a glimpse of Thee, Thou alone wert seen.
Ah, the state of frenzied faith, mark, O, my God!
Every grain of desert sand to vault and dance did seem.
How he rose in a menacing way, stirred by a rage sublime,
Like the beauty's river in spate, with a dazzling sheen.
Thy beauty is a tempest wild for the world at large,
Not a grain did I find but was restless seen.
Thy sight alone, if at all, something might reveal,
This eye, deemed discerning, ineffectual doth seem.
Ecstatic bliss resides in the blood-dripping eyes,
Flower-bedecked seems to me the entire desert scene.

Phir main nazar aaya, na tamasha nazar aaya,
Jab tu nazar aaya mujhe, tanha nazar aaya.
Allah re deewangi-e-shauq ka aalam,
Ik raqs mein har zarra-e-sahra nazar aaya.
Uthe ajab andaaz se woh josh-e-ghazab mein,
Charhta hua ik husn ka darya nazar aaya.
Kis darja tera husn bhi aashob-e-jahan hai,
Jis zarre ko dekha woh tarapta nazar aaya.
Ab khud tera jalwa jo dikha de, woh dikha de,
Yeh deeda-e-beena tau tamasha nazar aaya.
Tha lutaf-e-janoon deeda-e-khoonnaaba fishaan se,
Phoolon se bhara daaman-e-sahra nazar aaya.

اصغر گونڈوی

سرگرمِ تجلّی ہو، اے جلوۂ جانانہ!
اُڑ جائے دھواں بن کر کعبہ ہو کہ بُت خانہ
یہ دین وُہ دُنیا ہے، یہ کعبہ وُہ بُت خانہ
اِک اور قدم بڑھ کر اے ہمّتِ مردانہ
اب تک نہیں دیکھا ہے کیا اُس رُخِ خنداں کو؟
اِک تارِ شعاعی سے اُلجھا ہے جو پروانہ
زاہد کو تعجب ہے، صوفی کو تحیّر ہے
صد رشکِ طریقت ہے، اِک لغزشِ مستانہ
اِک قطرۂ شبنم پر خورشید ہے عکس آرا
یہ نیستی و ہستی، افسانہ ہے افسانہ
انداز ہے جذب اس میں سب شمعِ شبستاں کے
اِک حُسن کی دُنیا ہے خاکسترِ پروانہ

Asghar Gondvi

Manifest Thy glorious form, Thy beloved face unveil,
Let the mosque and shrine smoke-like exhale.
This is faith, that's heresy, this mosque, that shrine,
O courage invincible, go beyond their pale.
It hasn't seen perhaps that smile-scattering face,
Why should the moth, otherwise, to the ray be nailed?
The saint stands stunned, the mystic mystified,
Better far than their creed, is the love's staggering gait.
A droplet of dew with reflected sun ablaze!
The talk of life and death sounds a fairy tale.
It has absorbed the grace of the assembly lamp,
The ashes of the moth the beauty's world impale.

Sar garm-e-tajalli ho, ai jalwa-e-janaanan,
Ur jaae dhuan ban kar, kaaba ho ke butkhana;
Yeh deen, woh duniya hai, yeh Kaaba, woh butkhana,
Ik aur qadam barh kar, ai himmat-e-mardaana.
Ab tak nahin dekha hai, kya us rukh-e-khandaan ko,
Ik taar-e-shuaai se uljha hai jo parwaana.
Zaahid ko taajjub hai, Sufi ko tahayyur hai,
Sud rashk-e-tariqat hai, ik laghzish-e-mastana.
Ik qatra-e-shabnam par khurshid hai aks aara,
Yeh nesti-o-hasti, afsana hai, afsana.
Andaaz hain jazab ismen sub shama-e-shabastaan ke,
Ik husn ki duniya hai khaakastar-e-parwaana.

اصغر گونڈوی

آلامِ روزگار کو آساں بنا دیا
جو غم ہوا اُسے غمِ جاناں بنا دیا

ہیں کامیابِ دید بھی محرومِ دید بھی
جلوؤں کے اژدہام نے حیراں بنا دیا

یوں مسکرائے جان سی کلیوں میں پڑ گئی
یُوں لب کشا ہوئے کہ گلستاں بنا دیا

کچھ شورشوں کی نذر ہُوا خُونِ عاشقاں
کچھ جم کے رہ گیا، اسے حرماں بنا دیا

کچھ آگ دی ہوس میں تو تعمیرِ عشق کی
جب خاک کر دیا، اسے عرفاں بنا دیا

کہتے ہیں اِک فریبِ مسلسل ہے زندگی
اس کو بھی وقفِ حسرت و حرماں بنا دیا

اِس کاروبارِ حُسن کو مستوں سے پوچھئے
جِسکو فریبِ ہوش نے عصیاں بنا دیا

Asghar Gondvi

I have simplified the sorrows of life, all griefs disarmed,
Grief of love has subsumed grief of every form.
Both success and failure have crowned my quest,
The multitudinous sights have left me dazed and charmed.
When she gave a smile, the buds woke to life,
When she opened her lips, a garden sprang to form.
The lovers' blood was partly used in raising loud alarms,
Partly it got congealed, so despair was formed.
Lust refined in fire, gives birth to love,
When reduced to cinders, mystic gleam is born.
Life, they say, is a mirage, persistent and prolonged,
Yet we spend this life weeping night and morn.
Only the maddened hearts know the beauty's charm,
Miscalled a sin by wisdom misinformed.

Aalaam-e-rozgaar ko aasan bana diya,
Jo ghum hua use ghum-e-janaan bana diya;
Main kaamyaab-e-deed bhi, mehroom-e-deed bhi,
Jalwon ke azhdahaam ne hairan bana diya.
Yun muskaraey jaan si kalion mein par gai,
Yun lab kusha hue ke gulistaan bana diya.
Kuchh shorishon ki nazar hua khoon-e-aashiqaan,
Kuchh jum ke rah gaya, use hirmaan bana diya.
Kuchh aag di hawas mein tau taameer-e-ishq ki,
Jab khaak kar diya use irfaan bana diya.
Kahte hain ik fareb-e-musalsal hai zindagi,
Usko bhi waqf-e-hasrat-o-hirman bana diya.
Is kaarobaar-e-husn ko maston se puchhieye,
Jisko fareb-e-hosh ne isiaan bana diya.

اصغرؔ گونڈوی

میخانۂ ازل میں، جہانِ خراب میں
ٹھہرا گیا نہ ایک جگہ اضطراب میں

اُس رُخ پہ ہے نظر، کبھی جامِ شراب میں
آیا کہاں سے نُورِ شبِ ماہتاب میں

اقلیمِ جاں میں ایک طلاطم مچا دیا
یُوں دیکھیے تو کچھ نہیں تارِ رباب میں

اے کاش میں حقیقتِ ہستی نہ جانتا
اب لطفِ خواب بھی نہیں احساسِ خواب میں

میری ندائے درد پہ کوئی صدا نہیں
بکھرا دیے ہیں کچھ مہ و انجم جواب میں

اب کون تشنگانِ حقیقت سے یہ کہے
ہے زندگی کا راز تلاشِ سراب میں

اصغرؔ غزل میں چاہیے وُہ موجِ زندگی
جو حُسن ہے بُتوں میں جو مستی شراب میں

Asghar Gondvi

Nor in the tavern celestial, nor in the worldly heath,
Could I rest contented, restlessness besieged.
Now I gaze at her face, now at the cup of wine,
How has the moonlit night such a glow achieved!
To think of it, the lute strings so innocuous seem,
A tempest within the heart they can yet unleash.
I wish I hadn't known the truth about this life,
To recognise the dream, is to rob it of its gleam.
My anguished cry, elicited no reply,
Some response through moon and stars, though, I did receive.
Who should tell the Reality-seekers such a bare truth?
Life is but chasing mirages that for aye recede.
The *ghazal,* Asghar, in effect, should pulsate with life,
As belles bubble with beauty, wine with rapture seethes.

Maikhana-e-azal mein, jahan-e-kharaab mein,
Thahra gaya na ek jagah izteraab mein.
Us rukh pe hai nazar, kabhi jam-e-sharaab mein,
Aaya kahan se nur shab-e-maahtaab mein?
Aqleem-e-jaan mein ek talatum macha diya,
Yun dekhieye tau kuchh nahin taar-e-rubaab mein.
Ai kash, main haqiqat-e-hasti na janta
Ab lutaf-e-khwaab bhi nahin ahsas-e-khwaab mein.
Meri nida-e-dard pe koi sada nahin,
Bikhra dieye hain kuchh mah-o-anjum jawaab mein.
Ab kaun tishangaan-e-haqiqat se ye kahe,
Hai zindagi ka raaz talash-e-saraab mein.
Asghar, ghazal mein chaahieye woh mauj-e-zindagi,
Jo husn hai buton mein, jo masti sharaab mein.

اصغر گونڈوی

کیا کہئے جاں نوازیِ پیکانِ یار کو
سیراب کر دیا دلِ منّت گذار کو

جوشِ شباب و تشنۂ صہبا، ہجومِ شوق
تعبیر یوں بھی کرتے ہیں فصلِ بہار کو

ہر ذرّہ آئینہ ہے کسی کے جمال کا
یوہیں نہ جانئے مرے مُشتِ غبار کو

تھی بوئے دوست موجِ نسیمِ سحر کے ساتھ
یہ اور لے اُڑی مِری مُشتِ غبار کو

کچھ اور ہی فضا دلِ بے مُدّعا کی ہے
دیکھا ہے روزِ وصل و شبِ انتظار کو

اصغرؔ نشاطِ روح کا اِک کھِل گیا چمن
جُنبش ہوئی جو خامۂ رنگیں نگار کو

Asghar Gondvi

Her life-reviving darts all praise defy,
My grateful heart stands richly gratified.
Blooming youth, boundless love, and rapturous wine,
This is how sometime the spring may be described.
Every grain is a mirror reflecting someone's grace,
The worth of this handful of dust you mustn't minimise.
The fragrance of my friend too was mixed with the breeze,
It was this that to my dust wings did provide.
The desireless heart stands in a class apart,
The state of union, and of waiting, I have both tried!
The garden of my soul's delight, Asghar, come to bloom,
When on the page my magic pen I plied.

Kya kahieye jaan nawaazi-e-paikaan-e-yaar ko,
Sairaab kar diya dil-e-mannat gudaaz ko.
Josh-e-shabab-o-nasha-e-sahba, hajum-e-shauq,
Taabir yun bhi karte hain fasl-e-bahaar ko;
Har zarra aaeena hai kisi ke jamal ka,
Yunhi na jaaneye mere musht-e-ghubaar ko.
Thi boo-e-dost mauj-e-naseem-e-sahar ke saath,
Yeh aur le uri meri musht-e-ghubaar ko.
Kuchh aur hi faza dil-e-be mudaa ki hai,
Dekha hai roz-e-wasal-o shab-e-intezaar ko.
Asghar nishat-e-rooh ka ik khil gaya chaman,
Jumbish hui jo khama-e-rangeen nigar ko.

اصغر گونڈوی

یہ عشق نے دیکھا ہے، یہ عقل سے پنہاں ہے
قطرہ میں سمندر ہے، ذرّہ میں بیاباں ہے

ہے عشق کہ محشر میں یوں مست و خراماں ہے
دوزخ بگریباں ہے، فردوس بداماں ہے

ہے عشق کی شورش سے رعنائی اور زیبائی
جو خون اچھلتا ہے، وہ رنگِ گلستاں ہے

پھر گرمِ نوازش ہے ضو مہرِ درخشاں کی
پھر قطرۂ شبنم میں ہنگامۂ طوفاں ہے

سو بار ترا دامن ہاتھوں میں مرے آیا
جب آنکھ کھلی دیکھا اپنا ہی گریباں ہے

اِک شورشِ بے حاصل، اِک آتشِ بے پروا
آتشکدۂ دل میں اب کفر نہ ایماں ہے

اصغرؔ سے ملے لیکن اصغرؔ کو نہیں دیکھا
اشعار میں سنتے ہیں کچھ کچھ وہ نمایاں ہے

Asghar Gondvi

Reason knows it not, to love 'tis revealed,
A drop contains the ocean, a grain desert conceals.
'Tis love that struts in pride on the day of doom,
Hell tugging his tunic, heaven twitching his heels.
All beauty and grace derive from love divine,
The garden owes its bloom to the blood that boils and wheels,
Once again the radiant sun throws an amorous glance,
The stirrings of a storm within again the dew-drop feels.
Many a time I had thought I had caught your hem,
It was, alas, my own collar which my hand had seized.
A turmoil unprofitable, a fire unconfined,
Nor faith nor heresy doth my heart conceal.
Albeit we've met Asghar, him we haven't seen,
In his verse, we hear, he somewhat stands revealed.

Yeh ishq ne dekha hai, yeh aqal se pinhan hai,
Qatra mein samundar hai, zarra mein beeabaan hai.
Hai ishq ke mahshar mein yun mast-o-khiraman hai,
Dozakh bagarebaan hai, firdos badamaan hai.
Hai ishq ki shorish se raanai-o-zebaai,
Jo khoon uchhalta hai, woh rang-e-gulistan hai.
Phir garm-e-nawazish hai, zau mehar-e-darakhshan ki,
Phir qatra-e-shabnam mein hangaama-e-tufaan hai.
Sau baar tera daaman haathon mein mere aaya,
Jab aankh khuli, dekha, apna hi garebaan hai.
Ik shorish-e-be haasil, ik aatish-e-be parwah,
Aatishkadah-e-dil mein ab kufar na imaan hai.
Asghar se mile lekin Asghar ko nahin dekha
Ashaar mein sunte hain kuchh kuchh woh numaayan hai.

اصغرؔ گونڈوی

اسرارِ عشق ہے دِلِ مُضطر لیے ہوئے
قطرہ ہے بے قرار سمندر لیے ہوئے

موجِ نسیمِ صبح کے قربان جایئے
آئی ہے بُوئے زُلفِ معنبر لیے ہوئے

کیا مستیاں چمن میں ہیں جوشِ بہار سے
ہر شاخِ گل ہے ہاتھ میں ساغر لیے ہوئے

پہلی نظر بھی آپ کی اُف کس بلا کی تھی
ہم آج تک وہ چوٹ ہیں دِل پر لیے ہوئے

تصویر ہے کھنچی ہوئی نازو نیاز کی
میں سر جھکائے اور وُہ خنجر لیے ہوئے

میں کیا کہوں، کہاں ہے محبّت، کہاں نہیں
رگ رگ میں دوڑی پھرتی ہے نشتر لیے ہوئے

اصغرؔ حریمِ عشق میں ہستی ہی جُرم ہے
رکھنا کبھی نہ پاؤں یہاں سر لیے ہوئے

Asghar Gondvi

Secrets of love lie concealed within the restless heart,
A little drop doth confine a surging sea at large.
Praise be to the morning breeze and its gentle waves,
Here it comes laden with the fragrance of her locks.
Behold the garden's riotous mood, inspired by spring,
Every floral branch doth flaunt a goblet fully charged.
How deadly, ah me! was your maiden glance,
The wound caused by your dart rankles in my heart.
A perfect picture it presents of submission and pride,
I stand with downcast head, he with a dagger sharp.
I cannot say precisely where love within me bides,
I find it coursing through my veins like a piercing dart.
Entering the love's lane alive is nothing but a sin,
Better not approach this place with a head at all.

Asrar-e-ishq hai dil-e-muztir lieye hue,
Qatra hai be-qarar samundar lieye hue.
Mauj-e-naseem-e-subah ke qurban jaaieye,
Aai hai boo-e-zulf-e-muambar lieye hue.
Kya mastiaan chaman mein hain josh-e-bahaar se,
Har shakh-e-gul hai haath mein saaghar lieye hue.
Pahli nazar bhi aapki, uf, kis bala ki thi,
Hum aaj tak woh chot hain dil par lieye hue.
Tasvir hai khinchi hui naaz-o-niaz ki,
Main sar jhukai aur woh khanjar lieye hue.
Main kya kahun kahan hai mahabbat kahan nahin,
Rag rag mein dauri phirti hai nishtar lieye hue.
Asghar harim-e-ishq mein hasti hi jurm hai,
Rakhna kabhi na paaon yahaan sar lieye hue.

اصغر گونڈوی

عِشق کی فطرت ازل سے حسن کی منزل میں ہے
قیس بھی محمل میں ہے، لیلیٰ اگر محمل میں ہے

جُستجو ہے زندگی، ذوقِ طلب ہے زندگی
زندگی کا راز لیکن دوریِٔ منزل میں ہے

لالہ و گل تم نہیں ہو، ماہ و انجم تم نہیں
رنگِ محفل بن کے لیکن کون اس محفل میں ہے

اس چمن میں آگ برسے گی کہ آئے گی بہار
اِک لہو کی بوند کیوں ہنگامہ آرا دِل میں ہے

اُٹھ رہی ہے مٹ رہی ہے موجِ دریائے وجود
اور کچھ ذوق طلب میں ہے نہ کچھ منزل میں ہے

طور پر لہرا کے جس نے پھونک ڈالا طور کو
اِک شرارِ برق بن کر میرے آب و گِل میں ہے

اصغرِ افسردہ ہے محرومِ موجِ زندگی
تو نوائے رُوح پرور بن کے کِس محفل میں ہے

Asghar Gondvi

Love, since the world began, in Beauty finds its goal,
If Laila rides atop the camel, there too bides Qais's soul.
Life is but a long quest, a name for ceaseless zest,
The secret of life resides in chasing distant goals.
You are not the rose or tulip, nor the moon nor star,
Who then informs the world and everywhere doth roll?
Will the garden be set ablaze, or with flowers decked?
A drop of blood in my heart is restive beyond control.
The wave of the river of life now ebbs, now flows,
Nothing else our quest implies, nor our search for goal.
That which had burnt the Mount with its dazzling flame,
Turned to a lightning spark, imbues my heart and soul.
Asghar, the down-hearted, is now despaired of life,
O for Thy thrilling voice, that may stir the soul!

Ishq ki fitrat azal se husn ki manzil mein hai,
Qais bhi mehmal mein hai, Laila agar mehmaal mein hai.
Justjoo hai zindagi, zauq-e-talab hai zindagi,
Zindagi ka raaz lekin doori-e-manzil mein hai.
Lala-o-gul tum nahin ho, maah-o-anjum tum nahin,
Rang-e-mehfil ban ke lekin kaun is mehfil mein hai?
Is chaman mein aag barsegi ke aaegi bahaar,
Ik lahu ki boond kyon hangaama aara dil mein hai?
Uth rahi hai, mit rahi hai mauj-e-dariya-e-wajud,
Aur kuchh zauq-e-talab mein na kuchh manzil mein hai.
Tur pe lahra ke jis ne phoonk dala Tur ko,
Ik sharara-e-barq ban kar mere aab-o-gil mein hai.
Asghar-e-afsurda hai mehroom-e-mauj-e-zindagi,
Tu nawai rooh parwar ban ke kis mehfil mein hai.

Ali Sikander Jigar Moradabadi
(1893-1960)

ALI SIKANDER JIGAR MORADABADI
(1893 - 1960)

Jigar Moradabadi was born at Banaras in 1893. His father Maulvi Ali Nazr, was a poet with a published *Dewan* to his credit. Jigar may thus be said to have inherited his poetic taste, which, however, he developed with assiduous care, under the influence of four poetic mentors: Dagh Dehlvi, Hyat Bakhsh Rasa, Ameer Ullah Tasleem, and, above all, Asghar Gondvi, who was also the poet's friend and counsellor in personal and marital affairs.

Jigar's formal education did not go beyond matriculation. In fact, he did not attach much importance to erudition derived from books, and believed, with Alexander Pope, that "proper study of mankind is man." Jigar travelled extensively in India, first in connection with his business of selling spectacles, then as a famous poet, much sought-after at *mushairas* all over the country. In his own lifetime he was certainly the most popular poet, by virtue of, not only his intrinsic merit as a poet, but also the melodious voice with which he used to recite his poems.

Jigar was primarily, one may say, purely, a poet of the *ghazal.* He was a poet of love, beauty and wine, but he treated these themes in his own distinctive way, for he had a rich, personal experience in all these fields. He fell in love as a young man with a courtesan (Waheedan of Bijnor), who later became his wife. It was perhaps in the association of this woman that Jigar was initiated into drinking, which eventually became an addiction. His second marriage with Asghar Gondvi's sister-in-law ended in divorce because his wife and her relations could not put up with the poet's bacchanalian ways. When he remarried after an interlude of divorce, he was asked, as a condition of marriage, to give up drinking, which restriction, we are told, he willy-nilly accepted. It is this first-hand experience of wine, women and love that lends an element of individuality to his poetry. Like Mir Taqi Mir, Jigar is a poet of unfulfilled love, but he can find a cause of joy in the very experience of love. There is, as such, an element of buoyancy and mystic ecstasy even in situations which are generally deemed sorrowful. This is evident from lines like: *"Hijar ki shab aur itni roshan!"* (The night of severance, and so bright!)

Jigar's poetic works include: *Dagh-e-Jigar, Shola-e-Tur,* and *Aatish-e-Gul.* In recognition of his poetic excellence Jigar was awarded Padma Vibhushan by the Government of India, and an honorary doctorate by Aligarh University. Jigar died at Gonda (U.P.) in 1960.

علی سکندر جگرؔ مُرادآبادی

کوئی یہ کہہ دے گلشن گلشن
لاکھ بلائیں ایک نشیمن
پھُول کھلے ہیں گلشن گلشن
لیکن اپنا اپنا دامن
عشق ہے پیارے کھیل نہیں ہے
عشق ہے کارِ شیشہ و آہن
آج نہ جانے راز یہ کیا ہے
ہجر کی شب اور اتنی روشن
عمریں بیتیں، صدیاں گزریں
ہے وہی اب تک عقل کا بچپن
تُو نے سلجھ کر گیسوئے جاناں
اور بڑھا دی دِل کی اُلجھن
کانٹوں کا بھی حق ہے پیارے
کون چھڑائے اپنا دامن
چلتی پھرتی چھاؤں ہے پیارے
کس کا صحرا، کیسا گلشن

Ali Sikander Jigar Moradabadi

All through the gardens, let it be proclaimed:
Nest is best, bliss or bane.
Gardens smile with plenteous bloom,
But you'll get what is ordained.
It's love, my dear, not a child's play,
Iron and crystal clash together in this deadly game.
The night of severance, and so bright!
I know not, why? I can't explain.
Centuries have passed, ages elapsed,
Infantile as ever, doth reason remain.
By straightening out your locks, my love,
You have embroiled my heart in chains.
Who would disengage his hem?
The thorns too have a rightful claim.
The world is but a shifting shade,
Grove or desert - all of same.

Koi yeh kah de gulshan gulshan,
Laakh balaain, ek nasheman.
Phool khile hain gulshan gulshan,
Lekin apna, apna daaman.
Ishq hai pearey, khel nahin hai,
Ishq hai kaar-e-sheesha-o-aahan.
Aaj na jaane raaz yeh kya hai?
Hijar ki shab, aur itni roshan.
Umren beetin, sadiyaan guzrin,
Hai wohi ab tak aqal ka bachpan.
Tu ne sulajh kar, gaisu-e-jaanaan,
Aur barha di dil ki uljhan.
Kaanton ka bhi haq hai, pearey,
Kaun chhuraaey apna daaman!
Chalti phirti chhaaon hai, pearey,
Kiska sahra, kaisa gulshan.

جگر مراد آبادی

عشقِ لا محدود جب تک رہنما ہوتا نہیں
زندگی سے زندگی کا حق ادا ہوتا نہیں

بیکراں ہوتا نہیں، بے انتہا ہوتا نہیں
قطرہ جب تک بڑھ کے قلزم آشنا ہوتا نہیں

زندگی اک حادثہ ہے اور ایسا حادثہ
موت سے بھی ختم جس کا سلسلہ ہوتا نہیں

درد سے معمور ہوتی جا رہی ہے کائنات
اک دلِ انساں مگر درد آشنا ہوتا نہیں

اس مقامِ قرب تک اب عشق پہنچا ہے جہاں
دیدہ و دل کا بھی اکثر واسطہ ہوتا نہیں

اللہ اللہ یہ کمالِ ارتباطِ حُسن و عشق
فاصلے ہوں لاکھ دل سے دل جُدا ہوتا نہیں

وقت آتا ہے اک ایسا بھی سرِ بزمِ جمال
سامنے ہوتے ہیں وہ اور سامنا ہوتا نہیں

کیا قیامت ہے کہ اِس دورِ ترقی میں جگرؔ
آدمی سے آدمی کا حق ادا ہوتا نہیں

Jigar Moradabadi

Unless life be guided by love unconfined,
It can't redeem the pledge made to Life divine.

Unless the drop merges into the mighty sea,
It cannot feel the surge, nor soar beyond its kind.

Life is an accident of such a wondrous kind,
Even death cannot this process undermine.

The universe is getting surcharged with pain,
Yet the human heart remains unfeeling, unkind.

At such a stage of closeness has love arrived,
Even heart and eyes of little use it finds.

What a strong bond, ah God, love and beauty binds!
You may set them leagues apart, the hearts remain combined.

Sometimes we reach such a stage in the path of love,
Though we stand face to face, we can't unlock our minds.

How very tragic, Jigar, in this progressive age,
Man cannot act the role assigned to human kind.

Ishq-e-laa mahdood jab tak rahnuma hota nahin,
Zindagi se zindagi ka haq ada hota nahin.

Bekaraan hota nahin, be intehaa hota nahin,
Qatra jab tak barh ke qulzam aashna hota nahin.

Zindagi-ik-haadsa hai, aur aisa haadsa,
Maut se bhi khatam jiska silsila hota nahin.

Dard se maamoor hoti jaa rahi hai kaaeynaat,
Ik dil-e-insaan magar dard aashna hota nahin.

Is maqaam-e-qurb tak ab ishq pahuncha hai jahan,
Deeda-o-dil ka bhi aksar waasta hota nahin.
Allah Allah, yeh kamaal-e-irtabaat-e-husn-o-ishq,
Faasle hon laakh dil se dil juda hota nahin.

Waqt aataa hai ik aisa bhi sar-e-bazm-e-jamaal,
Saamne hote hain woh aur saamna hota nahin.

Kya qayaamat hai ke is daur-e-taraqqi mein, Jigar,
Aadmi se aadmi ka haq ada hota nahin.

جگر مرادآبادی

یہ مے خانہ ہے بزمِ جم نہیں ہے
یہاں کوئی کسی سے کم نہیں ہے

شکستِ دِل شکستِ غم نہیں ہے
مجھے اتنا سہارا کم نہیں ہے

ذرا سا دِل ہے لیکن کم نہیں ہے
اس میں کون سا عالم نہیں ہے

نہ جا شانِ تغافل پر کہ اے دوست
مقامِ التجا بھی کم نہیں ہے

تو پھر کیا ہے اگر یہ حُسنِ فطرت
مآلِ لغزشِ آدم نہیں ہے

کہاں کا حُسن اگر اُٹھ جائے پردہ
حقیقت کیا؟ اگر مبہم نہیں ہے

ارے او شکوہ سنجِ عمرِ فانی
یہ فانی زندگی بھی کم نہیں ہے

کہیں ایثارِ غم جاتا ہے ضائع
چمن شاداب ہے شبنم نہیں ہے

Jigar Moradabadi

'Tis a tavern, not a royal resort,
None is a vassal, none a lord.

The heart's defeat is not sorrow's fall,
This is enough to prop my heart.

The heart though small is yet so vast,
Countless states herein consort.

Be not indifference-proud, O friend,
Places galore to kneel and fall.

What else are these beauteous forms,
If not the result of Adam's fall?

Can beauty stay when the veil is gone,
Reality is but mystery garbed.

O ye, complainant of the transient life,
This transient life is not so short.

Sacrificial pains are never in vain,
The garden blooms, dews depart.

Yeh mai khana hai, bazm-e-jam nahin hai,
Yahan koi kisi se kam nahin hai.

Shikast-e-dil shikast-e-ghum nahin hai,
Mujhe itna sahaara kam nahin hai.

Zara sa dil hai lekin kam nahin hai,
Is mein kaun saa aalam nahin hai.

Na jaa shaan-e-taghaaful par ke ai dost,
Maqaam-e-iltejaa bhi kam nahin hai.
Tau phir kya hai agar yeh husn-e-fitrat,
Maal-e-laghzash-e-aadam nahin hai.

Kahan ka husn agar uth jaae pardah,
Haqiqat kya agar mubham nahin hai.

Arey O, shikwa — sanj-e-umr-e-fani,
Yeh fani zindagi bhi kam nahin hai.

Kahin isaar-e-ghum jaata hai zaayaa,
Chaman shadaab hai, shabnam nahin hai.

جگر مرادآبادی

سب ہی اندازِ حسن پیارے ہیں
ہم مگر سادگی کے مارے ہیں

اُس کی راتوں کا انتقام نہ پوچھ
جس نے ہنس ہنس کے دن گزارے ہیں

لالہ و گُل کو تجھ سے کیا نسبت
نامکمل سے استعارے ہیں

شبِ فرقت بھی جگمگا اُٹھی
اشکِ غم ہیں کہ ماہ پارے ہیں

آتشِ عشق وُہ جہنم ہے
جس میں فردوس کے نظارے ہیں

وُہ ہمیں ہیں کہ جن کے ہاتھوں نے
گیسوئے زندگی سنوارے ہیں

حُسن کی بے نیازیوں پہ نہ جا
بے اشارے بھی کچھ اشارے ہیں

Jigar Moradabadi

Dear to us, no doubt, is beauty's every grace,
But we fall specially for a simple, artless face.

Ask me not how vengeful turn out his nights,
Who in sunny splendour has spent his days.

How can tulip and rose be compared with you?
Weak are these metaphors to illustrate your grace.

The night of separation, too, has come aglow,
Are these the tears of sorrow, or bits of moon ablaze?

The fire of love is such a hell,
The sights of heaven which displays.

We are the ones whose dexterous hands,
The locks of life, have trimmed and shaped.

Beauty's indifference is but a pose,
She drops no hints, yet insinuates.

Sab hi andaaz-e-husn pearey hain,
Hum magar saadgi ke maare hain.

Uski raaton ka inteqaam na puchh,
Jis ne hans hans ke din guzaare hain.

Laal-o-gul ko tujh se kya nisbat,
Na mukammal se istaare hain.

Shab-e-furqat bhi jagmaga uthi,
Ashk-e-ghum hain ke maah paare hain.

Aatish-e-ishq woh jahannum hai,
Jis mein firdaus ke nazzaare hain.

Woh hameen hain ke jin ke haathon ne,
Gaisu-e-zindagi sanware hain.

Husn ki be nayaazion pe mat jaa,
Be ishaare bhi kuchh ishaare hain.

جگر مرادآبادی

یہ صحن و روِش، یہ لالہ و گل، ہونے دو جو ویراں ہوتے ہیں
تخریبِ جنوں کے پردے میں تعمیر کے ساماں ہوتے ہیں
منڈلاتے ہوئے جب ہر جانب طوفاں ہی طوفاں ہوتے ہیں
دیوانے کچھ آگے بڑھتے ہیں اور دست و گریباں ہوتے ہیں
رندوں نے جو چھیڑا زاہد کو، ساقی نے کہا کس طنز سے آج
اوروں کی وہ عظمت کیا جانیں کم ظرف جو انساں ہوتے ہیں
تو خوش ہے کہ تجھکو حاصل ہیں، میں خوش ہوں کہ مرے حصے میں نہیں
وُہ کام جو آساں ہوتے ہیں، وہ جلوے جو ارزاں ہوتے ہیں
آسودۂِ ساحل تو ہے مگر، شاید یہ تجھے معلوم نہیں
ساحل سے بھی موجیں اٹھتی ہیں، خاموش بھی طوفاں ہوتے ہیں
یہ خون جو ہے مظلوموں کا ضائع تو نہ جائے گا لیکن
کتنے وہ مبارک قطرے ہیں جو صرفِ بہاراں ہوتے ہیں
جو حق کی خاطر جیتے ہیں، مرنے سے کہیں ڈرتے ہیں جگر
جب وقتِ شہادت آتا ہے، دِل سینوں میں رقصاں ہوتے ہیں

Jigar Moradabadi

Let these blooming gardens fade, if they must, and fall,
Behind the veil of devastation lies the constructive hand of God.

When storms gathering in the sky threaten the earth on every side,
Some manic souls give the lead and ride the storm rough-shod.

When the revellers teased the priest, the saqi archly quipped:
"How can the petty minds the soul of goodness spot?"

You delight that you possess them, I'm happy I do not own,
The tasks which are easy to do, the sights cheaply bought.

Squatting safely on the shore, you, mayhap, are not aware,
The shore too may breed the storm, the silence could be tempest-tossed.

The blood of the oppressed folk would not go in vain,
How lucky, yet, are the drops which fertilise the crops!

Those who are pledged to truth, are not afraid to die,
Hearing the call for sacrifice, their hearts begin to throb.

Yeh sehan-o-rawish, yeh laala-o-gul, hone do jo weeran hote hain,
Takhrib-e-janoon ke parde mein taamir ke saamaan hote hain.

Mandlaate hue jab har jaanib toofaan hi toofaan hote hain,
Dewaane kuchh aage barhte hain aur dast-o-garebaan hote hain.

Rindon ne jo chhera zaahid ko, saqi ne kaha kis tanaz se aaj,
Auron ki woh azmat kya jaane, kam zarf jo insaan hote hain.
Tu khush hai ke tujh ko haasil hain, main khush hun ke mere hisse mein nahin,
Woh kaam jo aasaan hote hain, woh jalwe jo arzaan hote hain.

Aasuda-e-saahil tu hai magar, shayaad yeh tujhe maalum nahin,
Saahil se bhi maujain uthti hain, khaamosh bhi toofaan hote hain.

Yeh khun jo hai mazloomon ka, zaaya tau na jaaeyga lekin,
Kitne woh mubarik qatre hain jo sarf-e-bahaaraan hote hain.

Jo haq ki khaatir jeete hain, marne se kahin darte hain Jigar,
Jab waqt-e-shahadat aataa hai, dil seenon mein raqsaan hote hain.

جگر مراد آبادی

کسی صورت نمودِ سوزِ پنہانی نہیں جاتی
بجھا جاتا ہے دِل، چہرے کی تابانی نہیں جاتی

نہیں جاتی کہاں تک فکرِ انسانی نہیں جاتی
مگر اپنی حقیقت آپ پہچانی نہیں جاتی

صداقت ہو تو دِل سینوں سے کھنچنے لگتے ہیں واعظ
حقیقت خود کو منوا لیتی ہے مانی نہیں جاتی

بلندی چاہئے انسان کی فطرت میں پوشیدہ
کوئی ہو بھیس لیکن شانِ سلطانی نہیں جاتی

جسے رونق ترے قدموں نے دیکر چھین لی رونق
وُہ لاکھ آباد ہو اُس گھر کی ویرانی نہیں جاتی

محبت میں اک ایسا وقت بھی دِل پر گزرتا ہے
کہ آنسو خشک ہو جاتے ہیں طغیانی نہیں جاتی

جگر وہ بھی ز سرتاپا محبت ہی محبت ہیں
مگر اُن کی محبت صاف پہچانی نہیں جاتی

Jigar Moradabadi

Inner fire cannot but shine in the face,
Though the heart flickers, the face retains its grace.

Boundless is the human mind in its depth and reach,
Yet, our own selves we cannot evaluate.

If you are a man of truth, you can conquer hearts,
Truth makes its own defence, without advocates.

What you need is the spark hid within the soul,
Imperial grace shows itself despite your outward state.

The house first graced by you, and then deprived of grace,
Despite every effort, remains desolate.

Lovers have to pass through such a time of life,
When tears dry up at the fount, floods won't abate.

Even my beloved, Jigar, breathes love, from top to toe,
But she doesn't show her love in her looks or face.

Kisi soorat namood-e-soz-e-pinhaani nahin jaati,
Bujha jaata hai dil, chehre ki taabaani nahin jaati.

Nahin jaati kahan tak fikr-e-insaani nahin jaati,
Magar apni haqiqat aap pahchaani nahin jaati.

Sadaqat ho tau dil seenon se khinchne lagte hain, waaiz,
Haqiqat khud ko manwa leti hai, maani nahin jaati.
Bulandi chaahieye insaan ki fitrat mein poshida,
Koi ho bhes lekin shaan-e-sultaani nahin jaati.

Jise raunaq tere qadmon ne de kar chheen li raunaq,
Woh laakh aabaad ho, us ghar ki weeraani nahin jaati.

Mahabbat mein ik aisa waqt bhi dil par guzarta hai,
Ke aansu khushk ho jaate hain, tughyaani nahin jaati.

Jigar woh bhi za sar taa paa mahabbat hi mahabbat hain,
Magar unki mahabbat saaf pahchaani nahin jaati.

جگر مرادآبادی

دُنیا کے ستم یاد نہ اپنی ہی وفا یاد
اب مجھ کو نہیں کچھ بھی محبت کے سوا یاد

چھیڑا تھا جسے پہلے پہل تیری نظر نے
اب تک ہے وُہ اِک نغمۂ بے ساز و صدا یاد

جب کوئی حسین ہوتا ہے سرگرمِ نوازش
اُس وقت وُہ کچھ اور بھی آتے ہیں سِوا یاد

کیا جانئے کیا ہو گیا اربابِ جنوں کو
مرنے کی ادا یاد نہ جینے کی ادا یاد

مُدّت ہوئی اِک حادثۂ عِشق کو لیکن
اب تک ہے ترے دِل کے دھڑکنے کی صدا یاد

میں ترکِ رہ و رسمِ جنوں کر ہی چُکا تھا
کیوں آ گئی ایسے میں تِری لغزشِ پا یاد

کیا لطف کہ مَیں اپنا پتہ آپ بتاؤں
کیجئے کوئی بھولی ہوئی خاص اپنی ادا یاد

Jigar Moradabadi

I don't remember the world's excesses, nor my proven faith,
My mind recalls nothing but love, with its attendant grace.

The song awakened in my soul by your maiden glance,
That song sans word or sound, still reverberates.

When some beauty bestows on me a kindly, loving glance,
Then I miss her all the more, and pine for bygone days.

I know not what has gone wrong with my manic mates,
To live in style, or die in grace, is beyond their humdrum tastes.

The accident of love had occurred long, long ago,
Yet I hear within my soul your heart pulsate.

I had well-nigh broken with the love's frantic ways,
Why had I to recall, ah me! your staggering gait.

What fun, if I myself disclose my place and name,
Some peculiar forgotten grace, pray recapitulate.

Duniya ke sitam yaad, na apni hi wafa yaad,
Ab mujhko nahin kuchh bhi mahabbat ke siwa yaad.

Chhera tha jise pehle pehal teri nazar ne,
Ab tak hai woh ik naghma-e-be-saaz-o-sada yaad.

Jab koi haseen hota hai sar garm-e-niwazish,
Uswaqt woh kuchh aur bhi aate hain siwa yaad.

Kya jaaneye kya ho gaya arbaab-e-janoon ko,
Marne ki ada yaad, na jeene ki ada yaad.

Muddat hui ik haadsa-e-ishq ko lekin,
Ab tak hai tere dil ke dharkne ki sada yaad.

Main tark-e-rah-o-rasm-e-janoon kar hi chuka tha,
Kyon aagai aise mein tiri laghzash-e-paa yaad.

Kya lutaf ke main apna pata aap bataaun,
Keejieye koi bhuli hui khas apni ada yaad.

جگرؔ مرادآبادی

اگر نہ زہرہ جبینوں کے درمیاں گزرے
تو پھر یہ کیسے کٹے زندگی کہاں گزرے

مجھے یہ وہم رہا مدّتوں کہ جرأتِ شوق
کہیں نہ خاطرِ معصوم پر گراں گزرے

جنوں کے سخت مراحل بھی تری یاد کے ساتھ
حسین حسین نظر آئے جواں جواں گزرے

ہجومِ جلوہ میں پروازِ شوق کیا کہنا
کہ جیسے روح ستاروں کے درمیاں گزرے

خطا معاف زمانے سے بدگماں ہو کر
تری وفا پہ بھی کیا کیا ہمیں گماں گزرے

خلوص جس میں ہو شامل وہ دورِ عشق و ہوس
نہ رائگاں کبھی گزرا نہ رائگاں گزرے

اسی کو کہتے ہیں جنت اسی کو دوزخ بھی
وہ زندگی جو حسینوں کے درمیاں گزرے

بہت حسین سہی، صحبتیں گلوں کی مگر
وہ زندگی ہے جو کانٹوں کے درمیاں گزرے

Jigar Moradabadi

If we do not live o'r life, 'mid sparkling brows and eyes,
How can then we live at all, where can then we find respite?

For long did I misconstrue that my bold demands
Might shock her innocence, hurt her heart fragile.

Even the crucial stage of frenzy, aided by your thoughts,
Shone like vignettes of beauty, young and buoyant hied.

The flight of love mid wondrous heights cannot be described,
As if the soul upward soars, shooting through the starry skies.

Disenchanted with the world (will you please forgive!)
I began to doubt your love though tested and tried.

Any phase of love or lust, provided it is sincerity based,
Never has it gone in waste, never will it wasted lie.

Herein lies heaven concealed, here in too the hell,
Life spent in beauty's court, a mixed fare provides.

Life lived in the lap of flowers presents, no-doubt, a pleasant sight,
But to live amid the thorns is the real test of life.

Agar na zohra-jabeenon ke darmiaan guzre,
Tau phir yeh kaise kate zindagi, kahan guzre?

Mujhe yeh wahm raha muddaton ke jurrat-e-shauq,
Kahin na khatir-e-maasum par giraan guzre.

Janoon ke sakht maraahal bhi teri yaad ke saath,
Haseen haseen nazar aae, jawaan jawaan guzre.

Hajum-e-jalwa mein parwaaz-e-shauq kya kahna,
Ke jaise rooh sitaaron ke darmiaan guzre.

Khata maaf zamaane se bad gumaan ho kar,
Teri wafa pe bhi kya kya hamen gumaan guzre.

Khaloos jis mein ho shaamil woh daur-e-ishq-o-hawas,
Na raaigaan kabhi guzra, na raaigaan guzre.

Isi ko kahte hain jannat, isi ko dozakh bhi,
Woh zindagi jo haseenon ke darmiaan guzre.

Bahut haseen sahi, suhbaten gulon ki magar,
Woh zindagi hai jo kaanton ke darmiaan guzre.

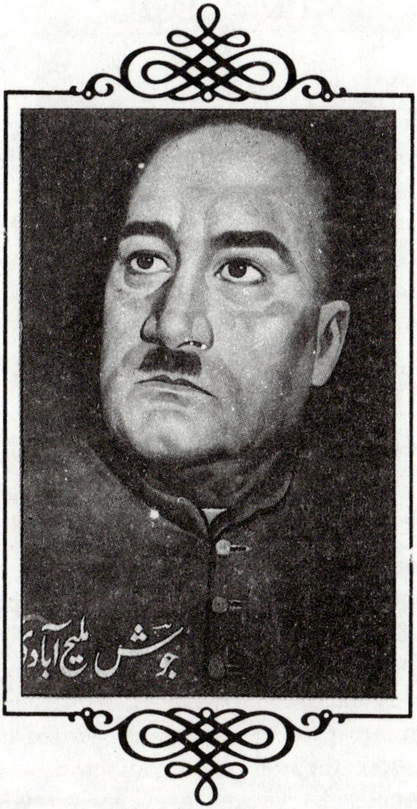

Shabir Hasan Josh Malihabadi
(1898-1982)

SHABIR HASAN JOSH MALIHABADI
(1898 - 1982)

Josh Malihabadi was a poet, patriot, and a public figure whose poetry enthused the hearts of millions of people in the pre-Independence days. A friend of the poor and the dispossessed, and a tireless crusader for freedom, Josh exploited to the full the resources of his poetic genius for spreading the message of social and political revolution. In one of his famous couplets he has thus defined his mission as a poet:

کام ہے میرا تغیّر، نام ہے میرا شباب
میرا نعرہ انقلاب و انقلاب و انقلاب

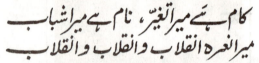

I'm youth embodied, revolution is my aim,
"Change, change, and change," is my sole refrain.

Josh has written *ghazals, rubaies,* and *nazms* — all in abundance, but he is essentially a poet of the *nazm,* and a specialist of the *rubai.* He had a facile pen and could compose fairly long poems just at one sitting. Some of his famous poems such as, *Kissan, Baghawat, Bhooka Hindustan, Husan aur Mazdoori, Zawaal-e-Jahanbani, Zaeefa,* are fine specimens of spirited and inspiring verse, written with compassion and conviction, and a matching artistic competence. His *ghazals* are charged with the same passion and power which characterise his *nazms.* A master craftsman and a wizard of words, Josh overwhelms his readers with the sheer force of linguistic opulence and emotional power. He may not be a profound thinker, but he is a firebrand poet capable of mesmerising his audience with his verbal fusillades and poetic eloquence. In his ready command of word and rhyme, and in his passionate fight against cant and oppression, Josh reminds us of Lord Byron, the great romantic radical and rebel. In addition, Josh possesses a remarkable gift for describing natural scenes with precision and loving artistry.

Josh was born in Lucknow in December 1898. He inherited his poetic taste from his forebears; for his father, grandfather, and great grandfather, all were poets of acknowledged merit. He received his schooling at Lucknow, Agra, and Aligarh, and studied up to Senior Cambridge. Due to the death of his father, Bashir Ahmed Khan, in 1916, Josh was debarred from the benefit of college education. He was greatly influenced by Dr. Rabindranath Tagore, whom he met during his sojourn at Calcutta in 1921. He then went to Hyderabad and worked for a few years in Osmania University, supervising translation work. However, he spent the best part of his life in Delhi, where he stayed from 1934 till after Independence, with a short stint at Poona and Bombay, where he wrote songs and lyrics for the cinema. He was appointed editor of the Urdu magazine, *Aajkal,* and was honoured with Padma Vibhushan by the Government of India. Some of his famous publications include: *Shola-o-Shabnam, Harf-o-Hikayat, Janoon-o-Hikmat, Aayaat-o-Naghmaat,* and *Sumbal-o-Salaasal.*

In 1956, Josh migrated to Pakistan, where, in the fag-end of his life he felt sadly alone and alienated. Pakistanis called him a "Kafir," while Indians considered him a traitor to the country of his birth. His prose miscellany, "Yaadon ki Baaraat," is a memorial to his past, and contains impressive sketches of several eminent figures such as Jawaharlal Nehru, Sarojini Naidu, and Firaq Gorakhpuri.

Josh died on 22 February, 1982.

جوش ملیح آبادی

مِلا جو موقع تو روک دونگا جلال روزِ حساب تیرا
پڑھوں گا رحمت کا وہ قصیدہ کہ ہنس پڑیگا عتاب تیرا

یہی تو ہیں دو ستون محکم، انھی پہ قایم ہے نظمِ عالم
یہی تو ہے رازِ خلدِ آدم، نگاہِ میری شباب تیرا

صبا تصدق تیرے نفس پر، چمن ترے پیرہن پہ قرباں
شمیم دوشیزگی میں کیسا بسا ہوا ہے شباب تیرا

تمام محفل کے روبرو گو، اُٹھائی نظریں مِلائی آنکھیں
سمجھ سکا ایک بھی نہ لیکن، سوال میرا جواب تیرا

ہزار شاخیں ادا سے لچکیں، ہوا نہ تیرا سا لوچ پیدا
شفق نے کتنے ہی رنگ بدلے، مِلا نہ رنگِ شباب تیرا

ادھر مِرا دِل تڑپ رہا ہے تری جوانی کی جستجو میں
اُدھر مِرے دِل کی آرزو میں مچل رہا ہے شباب تیرا

کرے گی دونوں کا چاک پردہ، رہے گا دونوں کو کرکے رُسوا
شورشِ ذوقِ دید میری، یہ اہتمام حجاب تیرا

جڑیں پہاڑوں کی ٹوٹ جاتیں، فلک تو کیا عرش کانپ اُٹھتا
اگر مَیں دِل پر نہ روک لیتا، تمام روزِ شباب تیرا

Shabir Hasan Josh Malihabadi

Given a chance, on Judgment day, I'll quell your rage,
Your wrath would change to laugh, so shall I hymn your praise.

These two are the sturdy pillars, these sustain the world,
The secret too of Adam's Eden: your youth, my gaze.

The breeze is envious of your breath, garden adores your robes,
Your budding youth breathes an air of nascent virgin grace.

We raised our eyes, exchanged glances, right in public view,
Yet none could make out what I asked, or what reply you gave.

A hundred hues the sky did don, none approached your bloom,
The waving branches tried and tried, none could match your grace.

Here my heart is restless grown thirsting for your youth,
There your youth twists and turns, and for my heart craves.

These two will betray our hearts, expose us both to shame:
My unabashed desire, your persistent veil.

Hills would have got uprooted, heavens would have quailed,
If my heart had not stemmed the tide of your youth in spate.

Mila jo mauqa tau rok doonga jalal roz-e-hisaab tera,
Parhunga rahmat ka woh qasida, ke hans parega itaab tera.

Yehi tau hain do satoon-e-muhkam, inhi pe qaayam hai nazm-e-aalam,
Yehi tau hai raaz-e-khuld-e-Adam, nigaah meri, shabab tera.

Saba tasadduq tere nafs par, chaman tere parahan pe qurbaan,
Shamim-e-dosheezgi mein kaisa basa hua hai shabab tera.

Tamaam mahfal ke roo-ba-roo go, uthaai nazren, milaai aankhen,
Samajh saka ek bhi na lekin, sawal mera, jawab tera.

Hazaar shaakhen ada se lachkin, hua na tera sa loch paida,
Shafq ne kitne hi rang badle, Mila na rang-e-shabab tera.

Idhar mera dil tarap raha hai teri jawani ki justjoo mein,
Udhar mere dil ki arzoo mein machal raha hai shabab tera.

Karegi donon ka chaak purdah, rahega donon ko karke ruswa,
Shorish-e-zauq-e-deed meri, yeh ihtemaam-e-hijaab tera.

Jaren paharon ki toot jaatin, falak tau kya arsh kaanp uthta,
Agar main dil par na rok leta, tamaam zor-e-shabab tera.

جوشؔ ملیح آبادی

ارض و سما کو ساغر و پیمانہ کر دیا
رِندوں نے کائنات کو مے خانہ کر دیا

اے حُسن داد دے کہ تمنّائے عشق نے
تیری حیا کو عشوۂ تُرکانہ کر دیا

قُرباں تُرے کہ اِک نگۂ التفات نے
دِل کی جھجک کو جرأتِ رندانہ کر دیا

کچُھ روز تو نازشِ فرزانگی رہی
آخر ہجومِ عقل نے دیوانہ کر دیا

صد شکر درسِ حکمتِ ناحق شناس کو
ہم نے رہینِ نعرۂ مستانہ کر دیا

دُنیا نے ہر فسانہ "حقیقت" بنا دیا
ہم نے حقیقتوں کو بھی "افسانہ" کر دیا

آواز دو کہ جنسِ دو عالم کو جوشؔ نے
قربانِ یک تبسّمِ جانانہ کر دیا

Josh Malihabadi

The earth and sky have been turned into the cup and flask,
The drinkers treat the universe like a tavern vast.

O beauty, be grateful to our deep desire,
Like a Turkish glance, your coy looks now dart.

A single, gracious glance from you, bless ye, my God!
To my timorous heart a reckless courage imparts.

The nascent reason was at first received with applause,
The flood of wisdom it entailed has drowned o'r sense at last.

The wisdom worldly-wise, which deeper truths denies,
Thank God, we've dissolved in wild hallelujahs.

The world converted every tale into a fact of life,
We treated even the facts as tales of distant past.

Josh has sold both the worlds, let it be proclaimed,
A smile from his darling sweet was all the price he asked.

Arz-o-sama ko saaghar-e-paimaana kar diya,
Rindon ne kaainaat ko maikhaana kar diya.

Ai husn daad de ke tamanna-e-ishq ne,
Teri haya ko ushwa-e-turkaana kar diya.

Qurbaan tire keh ik nigah-e-iltafaat ne,
Dil ki jhijak ko jurrat-e-rindaana kar diya.

Kuchh roz tau naazish-e-farzaanagi rahi,
Aakhir hajum-e-aqal ne diwana kar diya.

Sud shukr dars-e-hikmat-e-naa haq shanaas ko,
Hum ne raheen-e-naara-e-mastaana kar diya.

Duniya ne har fasana haqiqat bana diya,
Hum ne haqiqat ko bhi afsana kar diya.

Aawaaz do ke jins-e-do aalam ko Josh ne,
Qurbaan-e-yak tabassum-e-janaana kar diya.

جوشؔ ملیح آبادی

اے شخص! اگر جوشؔ کو تو ڈھونڈنا چاہے
وُہ پچھلے پہر حلقۂ عرفاں میں مِلے گا
اور صبح کو وہ ناظرِ نظارۂ قدرت
طرفِ چمن و صحنِ بیاباں میں مِلے گا
اور دِن کو وُہ سرگشتۂ اسرار و معانی
شہرِ ہُنر و کوئے ادیباں میں ملے گا
اور شام کو وُہ مردِ خُدا رندِ خرابات
رحمت کدۂ بادہ فروشاں میں مِلے گا
اور رات کو وُہ خلوتیِٔ کاکُل و رُخسار
بزمِ طرب و کوچۂ خوباں میں ملے گا
اور ہوگا کوئی جبر تو وُہ بندۂ مجبور
مُردے کی طرح خانۂ ویراں میں مِلے گا

Josh Malihabadi

O man, if you're looking for Josh, him you'll find,
In the small hours among the mystic kind.

At dawn you'll find this man, this lover of natural sights,
Surveying the gardens, or barrens unconfined.

This seeker of sense and essence at daytime can be seen,
At centres of art and learning studiously inclined.

At dusk, this man of God, who loves to drink and booze,
Can be met at taverns, overflowing with wine.

This wooer of cheeks and curls can at night be found,
Hunting in the lane of love, sensuously reclined.

And if tyranny strikes somewhere, this helpless man,
Can be found at the ravaged site, stunned in sense and mind.

Ai shakhs, agar Josh ko tu dhoondhna chaahe,
Woh pichhle pahr halqa-e-irfaan mein milega.

Aur subah ko woh naazir-e-nazzaara-e-qudrat,
Tarf-e-chaman-o-sehan-e-bayabaan mein milega.

Aur din ko woh sar gashta-e-asraar-o-maani,
Shahr-e-hunar-o-koo-e-adbiaan mein milega.

Aur shaam ko woh mard-e-khudawand-e-kharabaat,
Rahmat kadah-e-baada faroshaan mein milega.

Aur raat ko woh khilwati-e-kaakul-o-rukhsaar,
Bazm-e-tarb-o-kucha-e-khubaan mein milega.

Aur hoga koi jabar tau woh banda-e-majboor,
Murde ki tarah khana-e-weeraan mein milega.

جوشؔ ملیح آبادی

فکر ہی ٹھہری تو دِل کو فکرِ خُوباں کیوں نہ ہو؟
خاک ہونا ہے تو خاکِ کوئے جاناں کیوں نہ ہو؟

زیست ہے جب مستقل آوارہ گردی ہی کا نام
عقل والو! پھر طوافِ کوئے جاناں کیوں نہ ہو؟

مستیوں سے جب نہیں مستوریوں میں بھی نجات
دِل کھلے بندوں غریقِ بحرِ عصیاں کیوں نہ ہو؟

اِک نہ اِک ہنگامے پر موقوف ہے جب زندگی
میکدے میں رند رقصاں و غزلخواں کیوں نہ ہو؟

جب خوش و ناخوش کسی کے ہاتھ میں دینا ہے ہاتھ
ہمنشیں! پھر بیعتِ جامِ زرافشاں ہی کیوں نہ ہو؟

جب بشر کی دسترس سے دور ہے "حبل المتین"
دستِ وحشت میں پھر اک کافر کا داماں کیوں نہ ہو؟

اِک نہ اِک رفعت کے آگے سجدہ لازم ہے تو پھر
آدمی محوِ سجودِ سروِ خُوباں کیوں نہ ہو؟

اِک نہ اِک ظلمت سے جب وابستہ رہنا ہے تو جوشؔ
زندگی پر سایۂ زلفِ پریشاں کیوں نہ ہو؟

Josh Malihabadi

Why not think of the darling sweet, if think we must?
Why not choose the street of love, if we have to roll in dust?

Why not saunter, o ye wise, in the lane of love,
If life be another name for endless wanderlust.

When even o'r secret selves are not immune to passion's surge,
Why not then plunge headlong in the sea of sins accurst?

When life owes its liveliness to some tumultuous roar,
Why shouldn't the revellers be with song and dance aburst?

When we have to put our hand in someone else's hand,
Why not hold the golden cup and give it all the trust?

When the hand of Lord divine lies beyond our reach,
Why shouldn't the frenzied hand tug at some infidel's skirt?

When we have to kneel before someone high and grand,
Why not choose that cypress-shape, and give her deep respect?

When to live in darkness is writ in man's fate,
Why can't her sable locks provide us with a shady crest?

Fikar hi thahri tau dil ko fikar-e-khubaan kyon na ho,
Khaak hona hai tau khaak-e-koo-e-jaanaan kyon na ho?

Zeest hai jab mustqil aawaara gardi hi ka naam,
Aqal walo, phir tawaaf-e-koo-e-jaanan kyon na ho?

Mastion se jab nahin mastoorion mein bhi nijaat,
Dil khule bandon ghariq-e-bahr-e-isiaan kyon na ho?

Ik na ik hangaame par mauqoof hai jab zindagi,
Humnasheen, phir bait-e-jaam-e-zar fishaan hi kyon na ho?

Jab bashar ki dastras se door hai "habal-ul-mateen",
Dast-e-wahshat mein phir ik kaafir ka daamaan kyon na ho?

Ik na ik rifat ke aage sijda laazim hai tau phir,
Aadmi mahw-e-sajood-e-sarw-e-khubaan kyon na ho?

Ik na ik zulmat se jab waabasta rahna hai tau Josh,
Zindagi par saaya-e-zulf-e-pareshaan kyon na ho?

جوشؔ ملیح آبادی

نقشِ خیالِ دل سے مٹایا نہیں ہنوز
بے درد میں نے تجھ کو بھلایا نہیں ہنوز

تیری ہی زلفِ ناز کا اب تک اسیر ہوں
یعنی کسی کے دام میں آیا نہیں ہنوز

یادش بخیر جس پہ کبھی تھی تری نظر
وہ دِل کسی سے میں نے لگایا نہیں ہنوز

محرابِ جاں میں تو نے جلایا تھا خود جسے
سینے کا وہ چراغ بجھایا نہیں ہنوز

بے ہوش ہو کے جلد تجھے ہوش آگیا
میں بد نصیب ہوش میں آیا نہیں ہنوز

تو کاروبارِ شوق میں تنہا نہیں رہا
میرا کسی نے ہات بٹایا نہیں ہنوز

گردن کو آج بھی تری باہوں کی یاد ہے
یہ منتوں کا طوق بڑھایا نہیں ہنوز

مرکر بھی آئے گی یہ صدا قبرِ جوشؔ سے
بے درد میں نے تجھ کو بھلایا نہیں ہنوز

Josh Malihabadi

Your memory from my mind I haven't yet erased,
I haven't forgotten you, O unkind, ingrate!

I'm still a captive of your coiling locks,
In other words, I haven't been by someone else encaged.

Bless ye, the heart that was the centre of your gaze,
That heart I haven't yet elsewhere engaged.

That lamp that you had lighted in my heart's alcove,
That lamp is still aflame, undimmed, unhazed.

You had soon come to, after you had swooned,
I, the unfortunate, am still lost and dazed.

You had no dearth of partners in the game of love,
I'm still companionless in this amorous race.

My neck remembers still your enfolding arms,
I haven't till today a new yoke embraced.

You'll hear these words even from my grave,
"I haven't forgotten you, O unkind, ingrate!"

Naqshe-khayaal dil se mitaaya nahin hanooz,
Be dard main ne tujh ko bhulaya nahin hanooz.

Teri hi zulf-e-naaz ka ab tak aseer hun,
Yaani kisi ke daam mein aaya nahin hanooz.
Yaadish ba-khair jis pe kabhi thi teri nazar,
Woh dil kisi se main ne lagaaya nahin hanooz.

Mehraab-e-jaan mein tu ne jalaya tha khud jise,
Seene ka woh chiragh bujhaya nahin hanooz.

Be hosh ho ke jald tujhe hosh aa gaya,
Main bad naseeb hosh mein aaya nahin hanooz.

Tu kaarobar-e-shauq mein tanha nahin raha,
Mera kisi ne haath bataaya nahin hanooz.

Gardan ko aaj bhi tiri baanhon ki yaad hai,
Yeh mannaton ka tauq barhaya nahin hanooz

Mar kar bhi aaegi yeh sada qabr-e-Josh se,
"Be dard main ne tujh ko bhulaya nahin hanooz"

جوشؔ ملیح آبادی

قدم انساں کا راہِ دہر میں تھرّا ہی جاتا ہے
چلے کتنا ہی کوئی بچ کے ٹھوکر کھا ہی جاتا ہے
نظر ہو خواہ کتنی ہی حقائق آشنا، پھر بھی
ہجومِ کشمکش میں آدمی گھبرا ہی جاتا ہے
خلافِ مصلحت میں بھی سمجھتا ہوں مگر ناصح!
وُہ آتے ہیں تو چہرے پہ تغیّر آ ہی جاتا ہے
ہوائیں زور کتنا ہی لگائیں آندھیاں بن کر
مگر جو گھِر کے آتا ہے وُہ بادل چھا ہی جاتا ہے
شکایت کیوں اسے کہتے ہو؟ یہ فطرت ہے انساں کی
مصیبت میں خیالِ عیشِ رفتہ آ ہی جاتا ہے
شگوفوں پر بھی آتی ہیں بلائیں یوں تو کہنے کو
مگر جو پھول بن جاتا ہے، وہ کملا ہی جاتا ہے
سمجھتی ہیں مآلِ گل، مگر کیا زورِ فطرت ہے!
سحر ہوتے ہی کلیوں کو تبسّم آ ہی جاتا ہے

Josh Malihabadi

Human feet cannot but stagger in the path of life,
We cannot help stumbling however hard we try.

Even if we possess a deep discerning eye,
We cannot but feel unnerved when the storms arrive.

I know 'tis not a wise thing, O counsellor wise,
My face cannot but change when he comes in sight.

Let the winds roar and rage, let the gales blow,
They cannot dissolve the cloud, once it gathers might.

This is human nature, call it not "complaint",
We remember happier days, when harsh times arrive.

The buds too are prone to blight, we don't deny,
But once a bud becomes a flower, it cannot but die.

Though they know the fate of flowers, yet by instinct force!
As the dawn breaks, the buds begin to smile.

Qadam insaan ka raahe-dahar mein tharra hi jaata hai,
Chale kitna hi koi bach ke thokar kha hi jaata hai.

Nazar ho khwah kitni hi haqiqat aashna, phir bhi,
Hajum-e-kash-ma-kash mein aadmi ghabra hi jaata hai.
Khilaaf-e-maslihit main bhi samajhta hun, magar naasih,
Woh aate hain tau chehre par taghaiur aa hi jaata hi.

Hawaain zor kitna hi lagaain aandhian ban kar,
Magar jo ghir ke aata hai, woh baadal chha hi jaata hai.

Shikaait kyon ise kahte ho? Yeh fitrat hai insaan ki,
Museebat mein khayaal-e-aish-e-rafta aa hi jaata hai.

Shagufon par bhi aati hain balaaein yun tau kahne ko,
Magar jo phool ban jaata hai, woh kumla hi jaata hai.

Samajhti hain ma-all-e-gul, magar kya zor-e-fitrat hai,
Sahr hote hi kalion ko tabassum aa hi jaata hai.

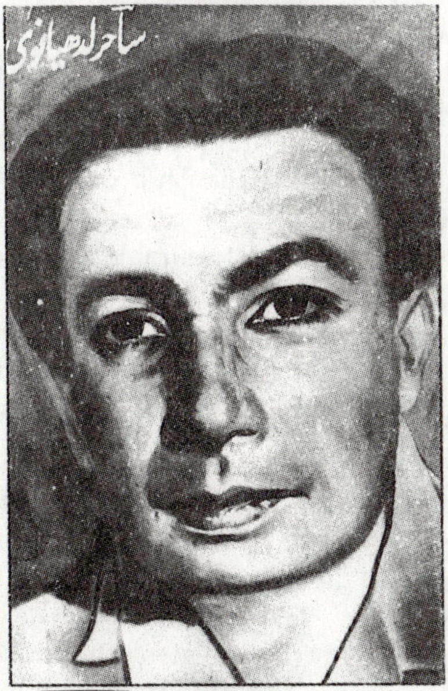

Abdul Haie Sahir Ludhianvi
(1922-1980)

ABDUL HAIE SAHIR LUDHIANVI
(1922 - 1980)

Sahir was the son of a rich landlord, known for his love of pleasure and luxury. He had married eleven times, but had only one male issue - Sahir - to inherit his estate and perpetuate his race. After he fell out with Sahir's mother, the landlord father went to the court to claim guardianship of his son. But Sahir preferred to stay with his mother, foregoing a life of luxury in favour of a more contented and honourable existence. Sahir had his education at Government College, Ludhiana, from where, however, he was externed, perhaps, for his non-conformist behaviour. But his native city is proud of his prodigal son as is proved by the re-naming of a street in Ludhiana as "Sahir Ludhianvi Road".

Though Sahir gave ample evidence of his poetic abilities right in his college days, he really shot into fame with the publication, in 1943, of his poetical collection: *Talkhian*. Two poems of this volume, *Taj Mahal*, and *Chakley*, became immediately popular. In the former, the poet elicits our sympathies for the artisans and labourers without whose skill and industry such a dream in marble could not have been concretised. In *Chakley*, the poet peeps behind the veil of boasted Eastern piety, and shows us the stinking brothels and their unfortunate inmates, for whose tragic fate the society alone is to blame.

Apart from the enlightened radical vision which informs his poetry, Sahir wins our admiration through his simple, unaffected style, which, without breaking with the tradition of rhyme, *radif*, and metre, seems fresh and forceful — unencumbered with far-fetched conceits, pseudo-mystical thought, or over-embellished diction. Whether he writes *nazms*, *ghazals*, or songs, he articulates his thoughts with sincerity, spontaneity, and directness.

Goaded by economic necessity, Sahir went to Bombay and started writing film songs. He made a signal contribution towards improving the quality of these songs, by enriching their content, and toning up their language. Cinema brought him fame and money, but it obstructed, one feels, the full growth of his poetic genius, so that the public had to wait in vain for another collection, as authentic and artistic as *Talkhian.* His film songs were published under the title: *Gata Jae Banjara.* But film songs, written to suit a particular mood and measure, are different from lyrical poetry, which springs as naturally as a mountain spring. His long poem, *Parchhaiaan,* is an impressive anti-war document. The insistent note of pain and pathos heard in his *nazms* and *ghazals,* is the result of both environmental and personal frustration, for, despite his romantic temperament, and despite the opportunities that came his way, Sahir was a lonely man, who remained unmarried all his life. He died in 1980 at the age of 58.

عبدالحیٔ ساحرؔ لدھیانوی

ہوس نصیب نظر کو کہیں قرار نہیں
میں منتظر ہوں مگر تیرا انتظار نہیں

ہمیں سے رنگِ گلستاں، ہمیں سے رنگِ بہار
ہمیں کو نظمِ گلستاں پہ اختیار نہیں

ابھی نہ چھیڑ محبّت کے گیت اے مطرب
ابھی حیات کا ماحول خوشگوار نہیں

تمہارے عہدِ وفا کو میں عہد کیا سمجھوں
مجھے خود اپنی محبّت پہ اعتبار نہیں

نہ جانے کتنے گِلے اس میں مضطرب ہیں ندیم
وہ ایک دِل جو کسی کا گِلہ گداز نہیں

گریز کا نہیں قایل حیات سے لیکن
جو سچ کہوں کہ مجھے موت ناگوار نہیں

یہ کِس مقام پہ پہنچا دیا زمانے نے
کہ اب حیات پہ تیرا بھی اختیار نہیں

Abdul Haie Sahir Ludhianvi

Nowhere can a lusting eye ever find content,
I'm all eyes, indeed, but not for you, my friend.

We make the spring bloom, we make the garden glow,
Yet we have no control in the garden's management.

Sing not, O, lutanist, songs of love, as yet,
Life doesn't these days a pleasant face present.

How can I trust your promises of faith,
When I can't vouch for my own deep intent.

Who knows how many plaints herein lie suppressed,
Albeit my heart is seemingly content.

Although I don't believe in running away from life,
To be frank, I won't mind if my life may end.

Lo, the world has brought me to such a sorry pass,
Where even you cannot resolve my predicament.

Hawas naseeb nazar ko kahin qaraar nahin,
Mein muntezir hun, magar tira intezaar nahin.

Hamin se rang-e-gulistaan, hamin se rang-e-bahaar,
Hamin ko nazm-e-gulistaan pe ikhtiaar nahin.

Abhi na chher mahabbat ke geet, ai mutrib,
Abhi hayaat ka maahaul khushgawaar nahin.

Tumhaare ahd-e-wafa ko main ahd kya samjhun,
Mujhe khud apni mahabbat pe aitbaar nahin.

Na jaane kitne gile is mein muztarib hain, nadeem,
Woh ek dil jo kisi ka gila-gudaaz nahin.
Gurez ka nahin qaayal hayaat se lekin,
Jo sach kahun ke mujhe maut naagwaar nahin.

Yeh kis maqaam pe pahuncha diya zamaane ne,
Ke ab hayaat pe tera bhi ikhtiaar nahin.

ساحر لدھیانوی

تنگ آچکے ہیں کشمکشِ زندگی سے ہم
ٹھکرا نہ دیں جہاں کو کہیں بے دلی سے ہم
مایوسیِ مآلِ محبت نہ پوچھیے!!
اپنوں سے پیش آئیں ہیں بیگانگی سے ہم
لو آج ہم نے توڑ دیا رشتۂ اُمید
لو اب کبھی گلہ نہ کریں گے کسی سے ہم
ابھریں گے ایک بار ابھی دِل کے ولولے
گو دب گئے ہیں بارِ غمِ زندگی سے ہم
گر زندگی میں مِل گئے ہم اتفاق سے
پوچھیں گے اپنا حال تری بے بسی سے ہم
اللہ رے فریبِ مشیت کہ آج تک
دُنیا کے ظلم سہتے رہے خامُشی سے ہم

Sahir Ludhianvi

I'm grown aweary of the fretful stir of life,
I'm afraid lest I may spurn the world outright.

Mark the deep despair caused by love belied,
We greet even our friends with suspicious eyes.

Lo, here we snap today the flimsy thread of hope,
Henceforth we will not raise even a plaintive cry.

Once again will surge and swell the passions now suppressed,
Though we are now subdued by the cares of life.

If by chance we meet again at some point of time,
I'll inquire about my state from your helpless plight.

My God! the deceptive might of fate ordained!
We have borne the worldly wrongs without asking 'why'

Tang aa chuke hain kashmkash-e-zindagi se hum,
Thukra na den jahaan ko kahin be dili se hum.

Maayusi-e-maal-e-mahabbat na puchhieye,
Apnon se pesh aae hain begaangi se hum.

Lo aaj hum ne tor diya rishta-e-umeed,
Lo ab kabhi gila na karenge kisi se hum.

Ubhrenge ek baar abhi dil ke walwale,
Go dab gaye hain baar-e-ghum-e-zindagi se hum.

Gar zindagi mein mil gaye phir ittafaaq se,
Puchhenge apna haal tiri be basi se hum.

Allah re fareb-e-mashiat, keh aaj tak,
Duniya ke zulm sahte rahe khamshi se hum.

ساحر لدھیانوی

جب کبھی ان کی توجہ میں کمی پائی گئی
از سرِ نو داستانِ شوق دُہرائی گئی

بِک گئے جب تیرے لب پھر تجھکو کیا شکوہ اگر
زندگانی بادہ و ساغر سے بہلائی گئی

اے غمِ دُنیا تجھے کیا علم تیرے واسطے
کن بہانوں سے طبیعت راہ پر لائی گئی

کیسے کیسے چشم و عارض گردِ غم سے بجھ گئے
کیسے کیسے پیکروں کی شانِ زیبائی گئی

دِل کی دھڑکن میں توازن آچلا ہے خیر ہو
میری نظریں بجھ گئیں یا تیری رعنائی گئی

اُن کا غم، اُن کا تصور، ان کے شکوے اب کہاں
اب تو یہ باتیں بھی اے دِل ہو گئیں آئی گئی

جراتِ انساں پہ گو تادیب کے پہرے رہے
فطرتِ انساں کو کب زنجیر پہنائی گئی

Sahir Ludhianvi

Whenever I find a cooling of his attitude,
I relate my tale of love, all over, anew.

When you have sold your lips, why do you complain?
If with the cup and flask I my life delude.

O, carking cares of life, what dost thou know?
With what strange excuses I temporised my mood.

What lustrous eyes and cheeks were buried in the dust of grief,
What exquisite beauties lost their radiant hue!

My heart beat is settling down, help me, O God!
Either you have lost your glow, or my light is fused.

His grief, his thought, his plaints — all's buried in the past,
These things are now become forgotten interludes.

Who can the human mind of its strength denude?
Though the human courage is by civilisation subdued.

Jab kabhi unki tawujjuh mein kami paai gai,
Az sar-e-nau daastaan-e-shauq duhraai gai.

Bik gaye jab tere lab phir tujhko kya shikwa agar,
Zindagaani baada-o-saaghir se bahlaai gai.

Ai ghum-e-duniya, tujhe kya ilm tere waaste,
Kin bahaanon se tabiat raah par laai gai.

Kaise kaise chashm-o-aaraz gard-e-ghum se bujh gae,
Kaise kaise paikron ki shaan-e-zebaai gai.

Dil ki dharkan mein tawaazan aa chala hai, khair ho,
Meri nazren bujh gaeen, yaa teri raanaai gai.

Unka ghum, unka tasawwur, unke shikwe ab kahan,
Ab tau baaten bhi ai dil ho gaeen aai gai.

Jurrat-e-insaan pe go taadeb ke pahre rahe,
Fitrat-e-insaan ko kab zanjeer pahnaai gai.

ساحر لدھیانوی

عقاید وہم ہیں، مذہب خیالِ خام ہے ساقی
ازل سے، ذہنِ انسان بستۂ اوہام ہے ساقی
حقیقت آشنائی اصل میں گُم کردہ راہی ہے
عروسِ آگہی پروردۂ ابہام ہے ساقی
مبارک ہو ضعیفی کو خِرد کی فلسفہ دانی
جوانی بے نیازِ عبرتِ انجام ہے ساقی
ابھی تک راستے کے پیچ و خم سے دِل دھڑکتا ہے
مِرا ذوقِ طلب شاید ابھی تک خام ہے ساقی
وہاں بھیجا گیا ہوں چاک کرنے پردۂ شب کو
جہاں ہر صبح کے دامن پہ عکسِ شام ہے ساقی
مرے ساغر میں مَے ہے اور ترے ہاتھوں میں بربط ہے
وطن کی سرزمیں میں بھوک سے کہرام ہے ساقی
زمانہ برسرِ پیکار ہے پُر ہَول شعلوں سے
ترے لب پر ابھی تک نغمۂ خیام ہے ساقی

Sahir Ludhianvi

Religion is an empty dream, o'r beliefs a sham,
Superstitious is human mind since the world began.

Questing the Reality misguides our steps,
Reason coronated confounds the sense of man.

Welcome are the aged folk to the philosophic mind,
Youth does not care the ultimate to scan.

The twists and turns of the path set my heart ashiver,
My questing zeal, mayhap, cannot firmly stand.

I am sent to such a place to lift the veil of night,
Where even the morning fears the night's encroaching hands.

I hold the brimful cup, you, saqi, the lute,
Famine stalks unchecked all over o'r land.

The world is all ablaze with the flames of war,
You, saqi, still remain Khayyam's ardent fan.

Aqaaid wahm hain, mazhab khayaal-e-khaam hai, saqi,
Azal se zehn-e-insaan basta-e-ohaam hai, saqi.

Haqiqat aashnaai asal mein gum karda raahi hai,
Aroos-e-aagahi parwurda-e-abhaam hai, saqi.

Mubaarik ho zaeefi ko khird ki falsafa daani,
Jawani be nayaaz-e-ibrat-e-anjaam hai saqi.

Abhi tak raaste ke pech-eo-khum se dil dharkta hai,
Mira zauq-e-talab shaaid abhi tak khaam hai, saqi.

Wahaan bheja gaya hun chaak karne parda-e-shab ko,
Jahaan har subah ke daaman pe aks-e-shaam hai, saqi

Mere saaghir mein mai hai aur tere haathon mein barbat hai,
Watan ki sar zameen mein bhuk se kuhraam hai, saqi.

Zamaana bar sar-e-paikaar hai pur haul sholon se,
Tire lab par abhi tak-naghma-e-Khayyam hai, saqi.

ساحرؔ لدھیانوی

خودداریوں کے خون کو ارزاں نہ کر سکے
ہم اپنے جوہروں کو نمایاں نہ کر سکے

ہو کر خراب مے ترے غم تو بھلا دیئے
لیکن غمِ حیات کا درماں نہ کر سکے

ٹوٹا طلسمِ عہدِ محبت کچھ اس طرح
پھر آرزو کی شمع فروزاں نہ کر سکے

ہر شے قریب آ کے کشش اپنی کھو گئی
وہ بھی علاجِ شوق گریزاں نہ کر سکے

کس درجہ دل شکن تھے محبت کے حادثے
ہم زندگی میں پھر کوئی ارماں نہ کر سکے

مایوسیوں نے چھین لیے دل کے ولولے
وہ بھی نشاطِ روح کا ساماں نہ کر سکے

Sahir Ludhianvi

We couldn't discard our self-respecting ways,
As such we couldn't our inner worth display.

Drowning ourselves in the cup, we could forget your grief,
But the woes of life could not be assuaged.

The magic of the plighted troth broke in such a way,
Never again the flame of love its head dared to raise.

Everything sheds its lustre when viewed too close,
Even he couldn't control my manic phase.

How depressing were indeed the accidents of love!
No desire dared survive in my heart dismayed.

Disappointments have robbed me of my verve and zeal,
Even my love couldn't my drooping spirits regale.

Khud-daarion ke khun ko arzaan na kar sake,
Hum apne jauharon ko numayaan na kar sake.

Ho kar kharaab-e-mai tire ghum tau bhula dieye,
Lekin ghum-e-hayaat ka darmaan na kar sake.

Toota talisam-e-ahd-e-mahabbat kuchh is tarah,
Phir aarzoo ki shama firozaan na kar sake.

Har shai qarib aa ke kashish apni kho gai,
Woh bhi ilaaj-e-shauq-e-gurezaan na kar sake.

Kis darja dil shikan the mahabbat ke haadse,
Hum zindagi mein phir koi armaan na kar sake.

Maayusion ne chheen lieye dil ke walwale,
Woh bhi nishaat-e-rooh ka saamaan na kar sake.

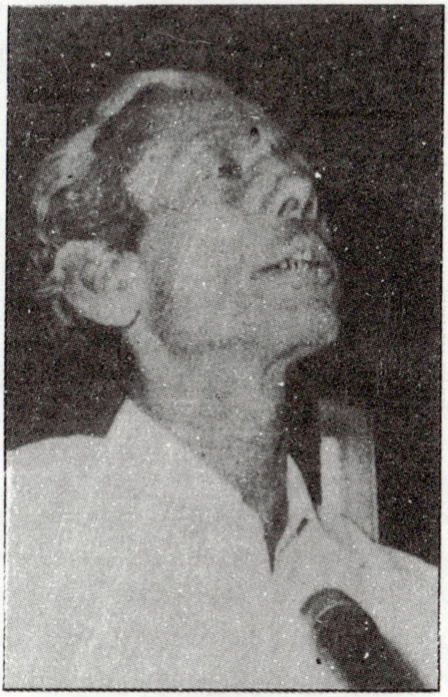

Nasir Kaazmi
(1925-1972)

NASIR KAAZMI
(1925 - 1972)

Nasir Kaazmi was born at Ambala in East Punjab, in 1925. After the creation of Pakistan in 1947 he moved to Lahore where he stayed till his death in 1972. It was at Lahore that he developed and displayed his poetic genius, and earned the reputation of being a front-ranking poet of the new Urdu *ghazal.* He also worked as an editor of the Urdu journals, *Auraq-e-Nau,* and *Hamayun,* and enjoyed a good position in the world of letters, not only in Pakistan, but also in India and abroad. He has left behind him three collection of *ghazals: Barg-e-Nai,* 1954, *Dewan,* 1957, and *Pehli Baarish,* which was published posthumously in 1975.

As a poet Nasir Kaazmi was influenced by Firaq Gorakhpuri among the moderns, and through him, by Mir Taqi Mir, the great master of the *ghazal.* He shows this influence in the simplicity and musicality of his language, in the choice of shorter measures for his *ghazals,* and in his controlled expression of melancholic thought and feeling. He has no fondness for heavy, stylised diction, nor for the stereotyped images and allusions. This, combined with the sincerity of sentiment, and spontaneity of expression, makes an instant appeal to an average reader. Consequently, he has become a great favourite with the *ghazal* singers in both parts of the Indian subcontinent. His *ghazals* give an effective expression to the twentieth century sense of world-weariness and disillusion. The world of his poetry is the world of subdued twilight, or of dark night with, occasionally, a star or two aglimmer in the firmament, or of dew-drenched grass. Both in his mood and mode of writing he is a lyricist *par excellence,* who can cast a spell on his readers by virtue of his sincerity, sweetness, and pathos. Apparently artless and simple, Nasir Kaazmi makes skilful and sophisticated use of paradox and ambiguity to interpret the contraries and contradictions of life.

ناصر کاظمی

اپنی دُھن میں رہتا ہُوں
میں بھی تیرے جیسا ہُوں

او پچھلی رُت کے ساتھی
اب کے برس میں تنہا ہُوں

تیری گلی میں سارا دِن
دُکھ کے کنکر چنتا ہُوں

مُجھ سے آنکھ ملائے کون
میں تیرا آئینہ ہُوں

تُو جیون کی بھَری گلی
میں جنگل کا رستہ ہُوں

آئی رُت مجھے روئے گی
جاتی رُت کا جھونکا ہُوں

اپنی لہر ہے اپنا روگ
دریا ہُوں اور پیاسا ہُوں

Nasir Kazmi

Ever centred in my thoughts,
I resemble you a lot.

O, partner of the yesteryear,
This year I'm alone, alas!

All day long in your lane,
I, the hurtful stones amass.

Who can look me in the face?
I'm but your looking glass.

You are the bustling street of life,
I, the lonesome jungle path.

The coming season shall weep for me,
I'm the season's dying draught.

In my wave lies my bane,
I'm a river, athirst withal.

Apni dhun mein rahta hun,
Main bhi tere jaisa hun.

O, pichhli rut ke saathi,
Ab ke baras main tanha hun.

Teri gali mein sara din,
Dukh ke kankar chunta hun.

Mujh se aankh milaaey kaun,
Main tera aaeena hun.

Tu jeevan ki bhari gali,
Main jungle ka rasta hun.

Aati rut mujhe roegi,
Jaati rut ka jhonka hun.

Apni lahar hai apna rog,
Darya hun aur payasa hun.

ناصر کاظمی

تو اسیرِ بزم ہے ہم سخن تجھے ذوقِ نالۂ نے نہیں
ترا دل گداز ہو کس طرح یہ ترے مزاج کی لے نہیں

ترا ہر کمال ہے ظاہری ترا ہر خیال ہے سرسری
کوئی دل کی بات کروں تو کیا ترے دل میں آگ تو ہے نہیں

جسے سُن کے روح مہک اُٹھے جسے پی کے درد چہک اُٹھے
ترے ساز میں وہ صدا نہیں ترے میکدے میں وہ مے نہیں

کہاں اب وہ موسمِ رنگ و بُو کہ رگوں میں بول اُٹھے لہو
یُوں ہی ناگوار چبھن سی ہے کہ جو شاملِ رگ و پے نہیں

ترا دل ہو درد سے آشنا تو یہ نالہ غور سے سُن ذرا
بڑا جاں گسل ہے یہ واقعہ یہ فسانۂ جم و کے نہیں

میں ہُوں ایک شاعرِ بے نوا مجھے کون چاہے مرے سوا
میں امیرِ شام و عجم نہیں میں کبیرِ کوفہ و رے نہیں

یہی شعر ہیں مری سلطنت اسی فن میں ہے مجھے عافیت
مرے کاسۂ شب و روز میں ترے کام کی کوئی شے نہیں

Nasir Kaazmi

A captive of convention, friend, you cannot relish sad strains,
Such music cannot melt your heart, this is not your favourite vein.

Superficial is all your skill, casual every thought,
What should I talk about the heart? Your heart lacks the flame.

Hearing which the soul may bloom, drinking which the pain may laugh,
Your lute doesn't produce that tune, your tavern doesn't that wine contain.

Gone the season of hues and scents, which made the heart pulsate,
A little unpleasant prick is left, which doesn't stir the roots and veins.

If you have a compassionate heart, hark this wail with care,
It's a stark fact of life, not a tale of kings and queens.

I'm not an Arabian chief, nor a reverend sage,
I'm a poor voiceless poet, by everyone disdained.

This my verse is all my wealth, source of solace deep,
Nothing for your taste or use doth my bowl contain.

Tu aseer-e-bazm hai hum sakhun, tujhe zauq-e-naala-e-nai nahin,
Tira dil gudaaz ho kis tarah, yeh tire mizaj ki lai nahin.

Tira har kamaal hai zaahiri, tira har khayaal hai sarsari,
Koi dil ki baat karun tau kya, tire dil mein aag tau hai nahin.

Jise sun ke rooh mahak uthe, jise pi ke dard chahk uthe,
Tire saaz mein woh sada nahin, tire maikade mein woh mai nahin.

Kahan ab woh mausim-e-rang-o-boo, ke ragon mein bol uthe lahu,
Yunhi naagawaar chubhan si hai, ke jo shaamil-e-rug-o-pai nahin.

Tira dil ho dard se aashna, tau yeh nala ghaur se sun zara,
Bara jaan gasal hai yeh waqia, yeh fasana-e-jam-o-kai nahin.

Main hun ek shair-e-be nawa, mujhe kaun chahe mere siwa,
Main amir-e-Sham-o-Ajam nahin, main kabir-e-Kufa-o-Rai nahin.

Yehi shair hain miri saltanat, isi fun mein hai mujhe aafeeat,
Mire kasa-e-shab-o-roz mein, tire kaam ki koi shai nahin.

ناصر کاظمی

اِس دُنیا میں اپنا کیا ہے
کہنے کو سب کچھ اپنا ہے

یُوں تو شبنم بھی ہے دریا!
یُوں تو دریا بھی پیاسا ہے

یُوں تو ہیرا بھی ہے کنکر
یُوں تو مٹی بھی سونا ہے

مُنہ دیکھے کی باتیں ہیں سب
کِس نے کِس کو یاد کیا ہے

تیرے ساتھ گئی وہ رونق!
اب اس شہر میں کیا رکھا ہے

بات نہ کر صورت تو دِکھا دے
تیرا اِس میں کیا جاتا ہے

دھیان کے آتشدان میں ناصرؔ
بُجھے دِنوں کا ڈھیر پڑا ہے

Nasir Kaazmi

What's it that we own at all?
Though we talk of owning all.

Yes, the dew is river at heart,
The river is thirsty on its part.

For that matter diamond is stone,
And dust is gold, so they call.

All is hollow talk on face,
Who remembers whom at all?

Gone with you the joys of yore,
Now this place attracts me not.

Do not speak, but show your face,
You've nothing to lose at all.

Nasir, in the hearth of mind,
Lie the ashes of the past.

Is duniya mein apna kya hai?
Kahne ko sab kuchh apna hai.

Yun tau shabnam bhi hai darya,
Yun tau darya bhi payasa hai.

Yun tau hira bhi hai kankar,
Yun tau mitti bhi sona hai.

Munh dekhe ki baaten hain sab,
Kis ne kis ko yaad kiya hai?

Tere saath gai woh raunaq,
Ab is shahr mein rakhha kya hai!

Baat na kar, surat tau dikha de,
Tera is mein kya jaata hai.

Dhyaan ke aatishdaan mein, Nasir,
Bujhe dinon ka dher para hai.

ناصر کاظمی

کچھ یادگارِ شہرِ ستمگر ہی لے چلیں
آئے ہیں اِس گلی میں تو پتھر ہی لے چلیں

یُوں کس طرح کٹے گا کڑی دھوپ کا سفر
سر پر خیالِ یار کی چادر ہی لے چلیں

رنجِ سفر کی کوئی نشانی تو پاس ہو
تھوڑی سی خاکِ کوچۂ دلبر ہی لے چلیں

یہ کہہ کے چھیڑتی ہے ہمیں دِل گرفتگی
گھبرا گئے ہیں آپ تو باہر ہی لے چلیں

اِس شہرِ بے چراغ میں جائے گی تُو کہاں
آ اے شبِ فراق تجھے گھر ہی لے چلیں!

Nasir Kaazmi

Some souvenir from the tyrant town we should carry home,
Let's at least from this street gather a few stones.

Let's wrap our friend's memory like a sheet round our head,
How else in this burning sun shall we journey all alone?

Some relic of the rigours of travel we must retain,
A little dust, if nothing else, from this street be taken home.

This is how it teases me, my sorrow-shrivelled heart:
If aweary, take me out, let us wildly roam.

Where will you find refuge in this lightless town?
Come along, O night of severance, we'll take you home.

Kuchh yaadgaar-e-shahr-e-sitamgar hi le chalen,
Aae hain is gali mein tau pathhar hi le chalen.

Yun kis tarah katega kari dhoop ka safar,
Sar par khayaal-e-yaar ki chaadar hi le chalen.

Ranj-e-safar ki koi nishani tau pass ho,
Thori si khaak-e-kucha-e-dilbar hi le chalen.

Yeh kah ke chherti hai hamen dil-gariftgi,
Ghabra gaey hain aap tau baahar hi le chalen.

Is shahr-e-be-chiragh mein jaaegi tu kahan,
Aa ai shab-e-firaq tujhe ghar hi le chalen.

ناصر کاظمی

زباں سُخن کو سُخن بانکپن کو ترسے گا
سخن کدہ مری طرزِ سُخن کو ترسے گا

نئے پیالے سہی تیرے دور میں ساقی
یہ دور میری شرابِ کہن کو ترسے گا

مجھے تو خیر وطن چھوڑ کر اماں نہ ملی
وطن بھی مجھ سے غریب الوطن کو ترسے گا

انھی کے دم سے روشن ہیں بستیوں کے چراغ
زمانہ صحبتِ اربابِ فن کو ترسے گا

بدل سکو تو بدل دو یہ باغباں ورنہ
یہ باغ سایۂ سرو و سمن کو ترسے گا

ہوائے ظلم یہی ہے تو دیکھنا اِک دن
زمین پانی کو، سورج کرن کو ترسے گا

Nasir Kaazmi

Tongue will yearn for gift of speech, speech for turn of phrase,
Poetic meets will stand bereaved of my style and grace.

New goblets wheel around, doubtless, in your town,
My old wine will sure be missed, saqi, in your age.

I, of course, did restless toss ever since I left my home,
My homeland too must have missed this exile unfortunate.

To them we owe the lamps of love burning bright in every heart,
The world will yearn for the men of art who once did fill the stage.

Change the gardener if you can, otherwise in vain,
You'll look for the rose and cypress, and their cooling shade.

If the cruel wind of times continues to sway,
Earth will lie drained of water, sun deceived of rays.

Zabaan sakhun ko, sakhun baankpan ko tarsega,
Sakhun kadah miri tarz-e-sakhun ko tarsega.

Naye payaale sahi tere daur mein, saqi,
Yeh daur meri sharab-e-kuhan ko tarsega.

Mujhe tau khair watan chhor kar amaan na mili,
Watan bhi mujh se gharib-ul-watan ko tarsega.

Inhi ke dam se firozaan hain millaton ke chiragh,
Zamana suhbat-e-arbab-e-fan ko tarsega.

Badal sako tau badal do yeh baghbaan, warna,
Yeh baagh saaya-e-sarv-o-saman ko tarsega.

Hawa-e-zulm yehi hai tau dekhna ik din,
Zamin paani ko, suraj kiran ko tarsega.

Rajinder Manchanda Bani
(1932-1981)

RAJINDER MANCHANDA BANI
(1932 - 1981)

Rajinder Manchanda Bani was born at Multan (Pakistan), in November 1932. After the partition of India in 1947, he migrated to Delhi, where he completed his education, and obtained a Master's degree in Economics from Panjab University. He worked as a teacher in a private school, pursuing, at the same time, his poetic interest with determined zeal and dedication. He also participated in the literary and cultural life of Delhi, and soon distinguished himself as a distinctly original poet, both in his thought and style. Apparently endowed with a stout physique, Bani suffered from serious physical ailments, including rheumatism and renal disease, which became the cause of his early death. Apart from the problem of failing health, he had to contend with the straitened financial condition, indifference of his friends and relations, and inadequate literary appreciation. But he endured these hardships with courage, and found in poetry his chief strength and solace. He died in 1981 at the age of 49.

Bani is a poet of the neo-classical *ghazal.* Though he adheres to the tradition of rhyme and *radif,* he almost dispenses with the use of conventional imagery, of rose and nightingale, candle and moth, of wine and saqi, nor does he lean upon classical allusions, to express his thought and feeling. He draws his imagery from the observation of nature and the universe. One of his famous metaphors, "shafaq-shajar", shows his constant concern with "the kindred points of heaven and home." The metaphor of "quest", "travel", or "flight", is another recurring metaphor of his poetry. Apart from connotating man's search for identity, purpose, or Truth, this metaphor too shows the poet's interest in the two worlds of matter and spirit, the finite and the infinite. Bani has a refreshingly original style commensurate with the content of his poetry. In one of his couplets he says that for him poetry implies a lifelong struggle with words, an attempt to extend the strength and scope of language. Like Firaq Gorakhpuri, Bani makes an effective use of Hindi diction, so as to bring his language close to the language of common, but cultured, speech. Bani is a thoughtful poet, thoughtful, and thought-provoking, and his *ghazals* compel the reader to think and reflect. He makes frequent use of paradox and ambiguity to convey the complexity of thought and feeling. His poetic works are available in three collections: *Harf-e-Moetbar*, (1972), *Hisab-e-Rang*, 1976, and *Shafaq-Shajar*, published posthumously in 1983.

راجیندر منچندا بانی

ہری سُنہری خاک اُڑانے والائیں
شفق شجر تصویر بنانے والائیں
خلا کے سارے رنگ سمیٹنے والی شام
شب کی مژہ پر خواب سجانے والائیں
فضا کا پہلا پھول کھِلانے والی صبح
ہوا کے سُر میں گیت ملانے والائیں
باہر بھیتر فصل اُگانے والا تو
تِرے خزانے سدا لٹانے والائیں
چھتوں پہ بارش، دور پہاڑی، ہلکی دھوپ
بھیگنے والا، پنکھ سکھانے والائیں
چار دِشائیں جب آپس میں گھل مِل جائیں
سنّاٹے کو دُعا بنانے والائیں
گھنے بنوں میں، شنکھ بجانے والائیں
تِری طرف گھر چھوڑ کے آنے والائیں

Rajinder Manchanda Bani

I'm the scatterer of dust, golden-hued and green,
I'm the painter of trees, and of twilight scenes.

Evening swallows all the colours suspended in the space,
I deck the lashes of night with the glimmering dreams.

Morning wakes the virgin buds, sets them all abloom,
I merge my music with flowing winds and beams.

You produce the wealth of crops, within and without,
I squander away your stores, sweep them all clean.

Rain on roof, hills at distance, mildly shining sun,
I drench myself in rain, bask my wings in beams.

When the four directions all together blend,
I build a solemn prayer from the silent scene.

You blow the conch shell in the forests deep,
I renounce my home, run to catch the gleam.

Hari sunehri khaak uraane wala main,
Shafq-shajar tasvir banane wala main.

Khila ke saare rang sametne wali sham,
Shab ki mizha par khwaab sajaane wala main.

Faza ka pahla phool khilane wali subah,
Hawa ke sur mein geet milane wala main.

Bahar bhitar fasal ugaane wala tu,
Tire khazane sada lutane wala main.

Chhaton pe baarish, dur pahari, halki dhoop,
Bhigne wala, pankh sukhane wala main.
Chaar dishaaen jab aapas mein ghul mil jaaen,
Sannate ko dua banane wala main.

Ghane banon mein shankh bajane wala tu,
Tiri tarf ghar chhor ke aane wala main.

باقیؔ

دوستو کیا ہے تکلّف مجھے سر دینے میں
سب سے آگے ہوں میں کچھ اپنی خبر دینے میں

پھینک دیتا ہے اِدھر پھول وہ گاہے گاہے
جانے کیا دیر ہے دامن مرا بھر دینے میں

شاعری کیا ہے کہ اِک عمر گنوائی ہم نے
چند الفاظ کو امکان و اثر دینے میں

بات اِک آئی ہے دِل میں نہ بتاؤں اُس کو
عیب کیا ہے مگر اظہار ہی کر دینے میں

اسے معلوم تھا اِک موج مرے سر میں ہے
وہ جھجکتا تھا مجھے حکمِ سفر دینے میں

میں ندی پار کروں سوچ رہا ہوں باقیؔ
موج مصروف ہے پانی کو بھنور دینے میں

Rajinder Bani

What problem can I have in laying down my head, O friends,
I'm the first to announce myself, first to give consent.

He does bestow a flower on me every now and then,
Who knows when he'll fill my lap with bounty without end!

What's poetry? To spend your life struggling with the words,
To tap their potential, their strength and scope extend.

I have something to say, better I desist,
But what is wrong if I reveal my intent?

He knew that a secret wave surged within my brain,
So he was cautious about ordering my banishment.

I should now ford the stream, thus I cogitate,
The wave is weaving whirlpools from end to end.

Dosto, kya takalluf hai mujhe sar dene mein,
Sab se aage hun main kuchh apni khabar dene mein.

Phaink deta hai idhar phool woh gahe gahe,
Jaane kya der hai daaman mira bhar dene mein.

Shairi kya hai, ke ik umr ganwaai hum ne,
Chand ilfaaz ko imkaan-o-asar dene mein.

Baat ik aai hai dil mein, na bataaun us ko,
Aib kya hai magar izhaar hi kar dene mein.

Use maalum tha ik mauj mire sar mein hai,
Woh jhijakta tha mujhe hukam-e-safar dene mein.

Main nadi paar karun, soch raha hun Bani,
Mauj masruf hai paani ko bhanwar dene mein.

باغی

مرے بدن میں پگھلتا ہوا سا کچھ تو ہے
اِک اور ذات میں ڈھلتا ہوا سا کچھ تو ہے
مِری صدا نہ سہی، ہاں مرا لہو نہ سہی
یہ موج موج اچھلتا ہوا سا کچھ تو ہے
جو میرے واسطے کل زہر بن کے نکلے گا
تِرے لبوں پہ سنبھلتا ہوا سا کچھ تو ہے
بدن کو توڑ کے باہر نکلنا چاہتا ہے
یہ کچھ تو ہے، یہ مچلتا ہوا سا کچھ تو ہے
یہ میں نہیں .... نہ سہی، اپنے سرد بستر پر
یہ کروٹیں سی بدلتا ہوا سا کچھ تو ہے
مرے وجود سے جو کٹ رہا ہے گام بہ گام
یہ اپنی راہ بدلتا ہوا سا کچھ تو ہے
جو چاٹتا چلا جاتا ہے مجھ کو اے باغیؔ
یہ آستین میں پلتا ہوا سا کچھ تو ہے

Rajinder Bani

There must be something in my body, which gives a melting feel,
Ever-changing and reshaping, something deep concealed.

It may not be my voice, nor even my blood,
That which leaps and bounds within, something doth reveal.

That which will burst like venom from your lips for me,
Something lies on your lips, balanced tremulously.

Something forcing itself out, from my body's cage,
This restless something, hidden inside, is something indeed.

It is not myself, agreed, but on this bed so cold,
Something must be there, tossing, ill-at-ease.

Something pairing off from life, minute by minute, step by step,
Something changing, shifting, suggests a presence deep.

Something licking away my being, Bani, unperceived,
Something sure is there growing inside my sleeve.

Mire badan mein pighalta hua sa kuchh tau hai,
Ik aur zaat mein dhalta hua sa kuchh tau hai.

Miri sada na sahi, haan mira lahu na sahi,
Yeh mauj mauj uchhalta hua sa kuchh tau hai.

Jo mere waste kal zahar ban ke niklega,
Tire labon pa sambhalta hua sa kuchh tau hai.

Badan ko tor ke bahar nikalna chahta hai,
Yeh kuchh tau hai, yeh machalta hua sa kuchh tau hai.

Yeh main nahin, na sahi, apne sard bistar par,
Yeh karwaten si badalta hua sa kuchh tau hai.

Mire wajud se jo kat raha hai gaam ba-gaam,
Yeh apni raah badalta hua sa kuchh tau hai.

Jo chaat-ta chala jaata hai mujhko, ai Bani,
Yeh aasteen mein palta hua sa kuchh tau hai.

باقیؔ

دمک رہا تھا بہت یُوں تو پیرہن اُس کا
ذرا سے لمس نے روشن کیا بدن اُس کا

وہ خاک اُڑانے پہ آئے تو سارے دشت اُس کے
چلے گداز قدم تو چمن چمن اُس کا

وہ جھوٹ سچ سے پرے، رات کچھ سُناتا تھا
دلوں میں راست اُتر گیا سُخن اُس کا

عجیب آب و ہوا کا وہ رہنے والا ہے
مِلے گا خواب و خلا میں کہیں وطن اُس کا

وہ روز، شام سے شمعیں دُھواں دُھواں اُسکی
وُہ روز، صبح اُجالا کِرن کِرن اُس کا

مری نظر میں ہے محفوظ آج بھی باقیؔ
بدن کَسا ہوا، ملبوسِ بے شکن اُس کا

Rajinder Bani

His robe was glimmering bright, already, of course,
Enough was a soft caress to set his body aglow.

When possessed by wanderlust he spares no wilds,
When with gentle grace he steps, gardens to him bow.

Something beyond fact or fiction did he say at night,
His words sank into the heart like a sharp arrow.

He dwells aloof somewhere in a strange clime,
In the land of dreams, mayhap, he may be explored.

Every evening come alive His tapers smoke-enveloped,
With His rays, row on row, every morning glows.

Even today my eyes retain his image, sharp and clear,
His body taut and trim, ship-shape his robes.

Damak raha tha bahut yun tau parahan uska,
Zara se lamas ne roshan kiya badan uska.

Woh khak uraane pe aae tau saare dasht uske,
Chale gudaaz qadam tau chaman chaman uska.

Woh jhoot such se pare raat kuchh sunaata tha,
Dilon mein raast utar gaya sakhun uska.

Ajib aab-o-hawa ka woh rahne wala hai,
Milega khwaab-o-khila mein kahin watan uska.

Woh roz sham se shamen dhuan dhuan uski,
Woh roz subah ujala kiran kiran uska.

Miri nazar mein hai mehfooz aaj bhi Bani,
Badan kasa hua, malboos-e-be-shikan uska.

باقیؔ

جانے وہ کون تھا اور کس کو صدا دیتا تھا
اُس سے بچھڑا ہے کوئی ، اتنا پتہ دیتا تھا

اُس کی آواز کہ بے داغ سا آئینہ تھی
تلخ جملہ بھی وہ کہتا تو مزہ دیتا تھا

دن بھر ایک ایک سے وہ لڑتا جھگڑتا بھی بہت
رات کے پچھلے پہر سب کو دُعا دیتا تھا

وہ کسی کا بھی کوئی نشہ نہ بجھنے دیتا
دیکھ لیتا کہیں اِمکاں تو ہوا دیتا تھا

اِک ہُنر تھا کہ جسے پا کے وہ پھر کھو نہ سکا
ایک اِک بات کا احساس نیا دیتا تھا

جانے بستی کا وہ اِک موڑ تھا کیا اُس کے لیے
شام ڈھلتے ہی وہاں شمع جلا دیتا تھا

ایک بھی شخص بہت تھا کہ خبر رکھتا تھا
ایک تارا بھی بہت تھا کہ ضیا دیتا تھا

رُخ ہوا کا کوئی جب پُوچھتا اُس سے باقیؔ
مٹھی بھر خاک ، خلا میں اُڑا دیتا تھا

Rajinder Bani

Who he was, we didn't know, nor to whom he called,
One could only make out that he had someone lost.

Honest, clear was his voice like the polished mirror,
Even a harsh word from him gave delight to all.

He would quarrel with everyone right from morn till night,
At early dawn he would rise, and pray for one and all.

He wouldn't let the people's zeal fade away or flunk,
He would rather fan the flame slumbering in their hearts.

He had learnt a special knack, which he never lost:
To shed uncommon light on things of common sort.

At a particular bend in town he would light a lamp at eve,
What that bend to him implied none knew at all.

Enough was that one good man, concerned about each and all,
A single star in the sky, a single ray dispelling dark.

Whenever, Bani, someone asked him how the wind did blow,
He would take a pinch of dust, and let it blow and fall.

Jaane woh kaun tha aur kisko sada deta tha,
Us se bichhra hai koi itna pata deta tha.

Us ki aawaz ke be-dagh sa aaeena thi,
Talakh jumla bhi woh kahta tau maza deta tha.

Din bhar ek ek se woh larta jhagarta bhi bahut,
Raat ke pichhle pahr sab ko dua deta tha.

Woh kisi ka bhi koi nasha na bujhne deta,
Dekh leta kahin imkaan tau hawa deta tha.

Ik hunar tha ke jise paa ke woh phir kho na saka
Ek ik baat ka ahsaas naya deta tha.

Jaane basti ka woh ik mor tha kya us ke lieye,
Sham dhalte hi wahaan shama jala deta tha.

Ek bhi shakhs bahut tha ke khabar rakhta tha,
Ek tara bhi bahut tha ke zaya deta tha.

Rukh hawa ka koi jab puchhta us se, Bani,
Muthhi bhar khaak khila mein ura deta tha.

Glossary of Literary Terms Used in the "Introduction"

Nazm : In a broader sense the term is used to describe all "kinds" of poetry, as distinguished from prose. However, in its literary sense, a *nazm* is a well-organised, logically evolving poem (unlike the *ghazal*), where each individual verse subserves the need of the central, controlling thought or theme. Though the *nazm* is traditionally written in rhymed verse, there are many examples of *nazms* in unrhymed verse, or even in free verse.

Masnavi : Generally a long narrative poem—much longer than the *ghazal*—embodying religious, romantic, or didactic stories. It is written in rhyming couplets, with each couplet having a different rhyme and *radif.*

Marsia : An elegy written to mourn the death of a great man or a dearly loved person. In its stricter sense, traditionally accepted in Urdu, a *marsia* is an elegy written, specifically, in honour of the martyrdom of Hazrat Amam Hussain or his comrades of the Karbla fame.

Qasida : A panegyric, or a poem written in praise of a king or a nobleman, or a benefactor. As in a *ghazal* the opening couplet of a *qasida,* is a rhyming couplet, and its rhyme is repeated in the second line of each succeeding verse. The opening part of the *qasida,* where the poet may talk in general about love or beauty, man or nature, life or death, is called *tashbib* or *tamheed.*

Rubai : A self-sufficient quatrain, rhyming a,a,b,a, and dealing, generally, with a single idea, which it is customary to introduce and develop with the aid of similes in the first three lines, and conclude, with concentrated effect, in the fourth line. Romantic, philosophic or didactic themes are the favourite subjects of the *rubai.*

Index of First Lines

(The name of the poet is mentioned at the end of the line)